SINOLOGY IN POST-COMMUNIST STATES

Sinology in Post-Communist States

Views from the Czech Republic, Mongolia, Poland, and Russia

Edited by Chih-yu Shih

The Chinese University Press

Sinology in Post-Communist States:
Views from the Czech Republic, Mongolia, Poland, and Russia
Edited by Chih-yu Shih

Published in cooperation with the Institute for Advanced Studies in
Humanities and Social Sciences, National Taiwan University

Grateful acknowledgement is made to *Mongolian Journal of International Affairs*
for permission to reproduce previously published articles in the Introduction and in
Chapters 2, 8, 9, 10, 11 and 12.

ISBN: 978-962-996-694-2

The Chinese University Press
The Chinese University of Hong Kong
Sha Tin, N.T., Hong Kong
Fax: +852 2603 7355
E-mail: cup@cuhk.edu.hk
Website: www.chineseupress.com

Printed in Hong Kong

Contents

Part II Being Sinologists in Post-Communist Societies

List of Contributors

Enkhchimeg Baatarkhuyag received her doctoral degree in national development from National Taiwan University in fall 2014. She is a research fellow affiliated with the Institute of History of the Mongolian Academy of Sciences. Her areas of expertise include Mongolian modern history, Chinese modern history, and Mongolian international relations.

Ter-Hsing Cheng (also known as James Cheng) received his Ph.D. in Sociology from Charles University, Czech Republic in 2009. He is currently an assistant professor in the Department of Sociology, Soochow University, Taiwan. His main research fields include political sociology, historical sociology, international migration, and area studies of Central and Eastern Europe. His research interests include collective memory, civil society, and Chinese immigrants in Central and Eastern Europe.

Sergey Dmitriev (Ph.D.) is a senior researcher of the Department of China at the Institute of Oriental Studies, Russian Academy of Sciences, and a faculty member of the Department of Chinese History in the Institute of Asian and African Studies at Moscow State University. His research interests include the Tangut and the Uighurs, Eurasian Nomads, the history of Central Asia, Mongolian Studies, Silk Road Studies, and Sino-Tibetan Linguistics.

Valentin C. Golovachev (Ph.D.) is a senior research fellow at the Institute of Orientology, Russian Academy of Science. His research interests include the ethnic history of China and Taiwan, Russian-Chinese relations, the history of Russian sinology, and international China studies. Since 2008, he has been serving as the director of the Russian component of "The Epistemology of China Studies: Oral History Project" initiated by National Taiwan University.

Bogdan J. Góralczyk is a professor at the Centre for Europe, University of Warsaw. He was the former Ambassador of Poland to Thailand, the Philippines and Republic of the Union of Myanmar (Burma; 2003–2008) and the Chief of the Cabinet of the Polish Foreign Minister (2001–2003). As a prolific author who has published widely in Polish, English and Hungarian, his research interests include China, Asia-Pacific, global order, post-Communist transformation, and European integration. He published the first biography of Dr Sun Yat-sen in Polish in 2013 and edited *Poland-China: Yesterday, Today, Tomorrow* (Toruń, 2014). He is currently editing a new volume, *European Union on the Global Scene: United or Irrelevant?*

Marina Kuznetsova-Fetisova (Ph.D.) is a junior research fellow at the Institute of Oriental Studies, Russian Academy of Sciences. Her research interests include ancient Chinese history, the archaeology of Bronze Age China, the site of Yinxu representing the ancient city of Yin, ancient crafts, early writing systems, and oracle bones inscriptions.

Melissa Shih-hui Lin received her Ph.D. in General Linguistics from Charles University in Prague in 2002. From 2003 to 2011, she taught at the Department of Indigenous Languages and Communication at Donghwa University. Currently she is an associate professor of Slavic languages and literature department at National Chengchi University. Her research interests are sociolinguistics, Czech and Taiwan indigenous languages.

Olga Lomová is professor of Chinese literature at Charles University in Prague. Her research interests include poetry, traditional historiography, and the ideology of modernization in the twentieth century.

Alexander Pisarev graduated from the Institute of Asian and African Studies of Moscow State University (IAAS) in 1974. He taught at the IAAS from 1974 to 1996. He is now professor in the Graduate Institute of European Studies at Tamkang University, Taiwan.

Anna Rudakowska is an assistant professor in the Department of Global Political Economy, Tamkang University, and Senior Associate Researcher at the Institute of European Studies (IES) and the Department of Political Science (POLI) at Vrije Universiteit Brussel (VUB). She welcomes e-mails at anna_taiwan@hotmail.com.

Chih-yu Shih teaches China studies, civilizational politics, and the anthropology of knowledge in the Department of Political Science of National Taiwan University. He is editor-in-chief of the journal *Asian Ethnicity*. His areas of research include comparative epistemology of China studies and international relations theory.

Alexei D. Voskressenski is Dean of the School of Political Affairs and Professor of Comparative Politics and Asian Studies, MGIMO-University (Moscow). He received his M.A. (summa cum laude) in Chinese Studies from Moscow State University, holds a Ph.D. in Government Studies from the University of Manchester, and a Ph.D. in Asian History from the Institute of Far Eastern Studies (Moscow). He also edits the Russian journal *Sravnitel'naya Politika* (Comparative Politics).

Anna Zádrapová graduated from the Sinology and Czech Literature Departments at Charles University. She is currently a Ph.D. candidate working on Czechoslovak sinology and Jaroslav Průšek.

Introduction: An Anthropology of Knowledge in Post-Communist Sinology

Chih-yu Shih

This book discusses how socialist and Communist legacies had an impact on the evolution of the intellectual history of China and on Chinese studies in four former Communist party-states—the Czech Republic, Mongolia, Poland, and Russia. After the end of the Cold War, the research agenda in these four countries has not evolved with any apparent shared orientation, nor have these countries been in close cooperation in accordance with a top-down imposed division of labor. It is thus difficult to detect a direct influence of the sinology of the Communist period on current research today. However, this book argues that a much stronger legacy than what is observable superficially exists in each of these research communities. One of these strong influences involves pedagogical and family lineages. Pedagogically, sinological training that stresses language and the classics did not disappear during the interlude of the Communist period. To varying degrees, it also continues to exist today. In addition, many contemporary China scholars in these societies have inherited an interest in China from their families, particularly from their fathers. There has also been a revival of a certain self-understanding embedded in the civilizational imagination, which reconnects the contemporary generation to the older generations.

Even in those societies that on the surface appear to be anti-Communist, for example, the Czech Republic and Poland, a rediscovery of humanist China in the past or a distaste for the rise of Communist China in the twenty-first century can be traced to an aversion to their own Communist pasts after the breakup of the Soviet bloc. This aversion is informed by the pro-Western approach in China studies. Together with the return of the humanities, they merge into a familiar image of China divided by a repressive regime and a repressed population. The liberal tradition in Czech intellectual history as well as a Catholic anti-Communist component in Poland, which say more about the home societies of these sinologists than they say about China, have been part of this lingering aversion to the Communist party-state structure in China. In other words, the seeming rupture in the research agenda after the fall of communism actually reflects a contradictory and indirect impact of the Communist period that seeks a departure from communism. In this formulation of China, the self-understanding of post-Communist sinologists looms critical in determining their orientations. Nevertheless, such sinologists are more engrossed in an agenda dealing with the Chinese humanities than in an agenda dealing with their social science or policy think-tank counterparts.

Academically, neither the deductive method supported by a universal theoretical framework nor the quantitative method has prevailed in these post-Communist societies. The ability to read and interpret Chinese documents, official or popular, contemporary or classical, continues to occupy the concerns of sinologists in the four societies. These skills primarily rely on the self-confidence among the sinologists to understand Chinese culture and Chinese people. They have acquired this self-confidence from their training in the reading of the classics, which reveal those cultural and political sensibilities that are usually inaccessible from the vantage point of social science pedagogy. Finally, despite the decline in the Sino-Soviet alliance, the past socialist brotherhood between the former Soviet Union and China has left a positive impression in Russia toward their Chinese comrades in certain sectors of the sinological community.

Given the curious discovery of post-Communist sinology, the conclusions in this volume have major implications for the evolution of intellectual history and its analysis. There has been an emerging interest in the genealogy of contemporary ideas as a way to expose the constructed nature of knowledge. Alongside the long tradition of the sociology of knowledge, which is more about the structural forces undergirding the production of knowledge, genealogical research attends to the coincidental, circumstantial, and ruptured characteristics of a seemingly consensual base of knowledge. Nonetheless, they both look to the macro-level conditions for explanations about the establishment of a given piece of knowledge. In contrast, research on post-Communist sinology emphasizes the importance of individualized agency to practice sinology, rendering sinology not only a statement of identity, but also a strategy to survive politics during tumultuous times. The following discussion elaborates on the broader epistemological implications of these features for the study of intellectual history.

1. Encounters and Choices between Civilizations and Ethnicities

Studying China in the global age involves interactions between two sets of identities—those of the observers and those of China. Each set comprises choices at three levels: civilizational, national, and (sub) ethnic. Take, for instance, Mongolia.[1] Mongolia is representative of a nomadic and prairie civilization, as opposed to a maritime, agricultural, or industrial civilization. It is a sovereign nation in quest of a potential alliance with Japan or the United States in order to balance its two powerful neighbors, namely, China and Russia. Furthermore, Mongolia denotes an ethnic group in the Chinese autonomous region of Inner Mongolia. Needless to say, references to China evoke similar images of civilizations, nations, and (sub)ethnic groups. When a Mongolian scholar engaged in research on China, or, conversely, when a Chinese scholar engages in research on Mongolia, the scholar (subject) should be aware of which identity he or she is coming from. Accordingly, the intellectual choice of identity becomes intrinsic to scholarship on China, the Chinese, or China studies.[2] Any choice or change in choice designates an institutional identity that has a bearing on the distribution of public as well as private rights and duties. In addition, such a choice affects the balance in social relationships. Thus, scholarship dealing with these choices is by necessity multi-sited, political, and global, and, accordingly, it is inevitably anthropological.

Due to widespread perceptions that China is on the rise, designation of China's identity has become essentially a political matter. This may be a consolidated decision that reinforces a specific identity and relationship with China. Or, alternatively, this may be a transformational decision that ushers in a new and different identity for China. Nevertheless, scholars rarely unilaterally determine the meaning of such decisions or choices, nor are such choices invariable over time. The possibility of the significance of each choice constitutes a discursive site of constant contestation. Such contestation centers on whether China should be viewed as a threat and if indeed it is a threat, against whom is this threat posed. Moreover, the contestation implies how one should treat agents that willingly or reluctantly carry the identity of China. This is why studying China is a political as well as a personal engagement, especially in light of studies of the Chinese classics as well as the Chinese government's call for a harmonious society during the past decade. This political engagement speaks to both China's identity and the researcher's self-identity and therefore it may be highly controversial and volatile over time.

Civilizational history and individualized intellectual possibilities lie at two extremes of the identity dimension, with endless sites between the two extremes. The political nature of identity implies the impossibility of a stable identity. Identity is always about strategic choice. The fluidity of identity over time and place may be instantaneous and strong under globalization. However, even though fluidity of this sort often generates a wish for a permanent solution, the unavailability of any stable solution frequently leads to frustrations that require and produce mechanisms of projection onto a scapegoat. Traveling to multiple sites, each of which are either suffering or enjoying its own identity matrix, resembles an anthropological moment that provides opportunities to appreciate the politics of possibilities and to broaden one's thinking. The quest for an anthropology of knowledge seeks to open up and share. Traveling physically to different communities, in combination with traveling intellectually to different discursive constructions, at the same time is the practice of self-criticism. Colleagues from all over the world who have generously supported this epistemological exercise with their own self-criticisms have contributed to and have provoked thinking and changes in thinking, such as those that have come together in the reflections on civilizations, nations, and (sub)ethnic groups in this volume.

For contemporary social scientists outside of North America or Western Europe, pretending that an objective China exists may be a departure from imperialist history, its associated civilizing burden, and its unwarranted sense of superiority. A social scientist presumably no longer must be obsessed with the backward identity of China or feel responsible for remedying it. However, the seemingly natural and normal objectivism in European and North American social science is neither natural nor neutral once the nascent Asian intellectual reflections on the politics of knowledge, especially knowledge regarding China studies as a component of area studies, is put into perspective.[3] The civilizational embedding of scientism actually inspires American and Western European elites to take an objective approach, rendering their own civilizational past ostensibly irrelevant. This explains why a return to civilizational consciousness becomes an epistemological prescription for the obsessive-compulsive drive for objectivism that, incidentally, exposes the political nature of social science.

2. Sinology as a Substitute for an Objective China

China's many colonized neighbors can no longer appreciate the discourse of the objectivists. Their otherwise insignificant choices, meaningless to the mainstream research literature, nevertheless compose a variety of creative possibilities for worlding or re-worlding. Based on their quest for subjectivities from within the sinic world order, what used to define the sinic world order—for example, the tribute system, Daoist philosophy, ethnic kinship, political territorial sovereignty, and so on— no longer holds true or is no longer practical. However, this finding does not mean that these neighbors coordinate in these deconstructive exercises or that deconstruction is incompatible with the nascent sinicization. For the majority of Korean thinkers, for example, a Korean historical trajectory exists outside of the sinic world order, bearing the burden of the tribute system through its various vicissitudes. In turn, for the majority of Mongolian thinkers, a Mongolian historical trajectory exists independently over a vast territory, which the Yuan dynasty turned into a sub-empire, foreshadowing the eventual reunification of the great Mongolian nationality. In contrast, a small group of Vietnamese sinological veterans tightly hold to their sinic identity to support a distinctive national position, whereas deterritorialized Southeast Asian Chinese scholars greatly undermine any attempts at a centered arbitration of Chineseness.[4]

Multi-sited reinterpretations of the sinic order challenge the singular text of "China's rise" as well as that of the "China threat" and point to a different intellectual history and, ultimately, a different view of global international relations. China's rise has already generated multi-sited understandings both inside and outside of China's territorial borders. Chongqing, the leading municipal region in Central China that was once (before the purge of its leader) consciously developing a China model in contrast to the Western model parallels, in a manner of speaking, Guangdong, which deliberately combines liberalization and one-party rule. Both were led by capable leaders who possessed both confidence and a vision and who kept an eye on each other. One need not mention the age-old competition between Shanghai and Beijing, or any other smaller, allegedly "unique" sites, attempting to approach socialist reform in their own ways. Further challenges come from other sites, such as Tibet, Xinjiang, Hong Kong, and Taiwan, where Chinese borders are increasingly obscured not only territorially, but also socially and politically. A transition from one Chinese territorial site to another usually requires a distinctive understanding of what China is. How China is continuously becoming another China is therefore contingent upon how each site, as low as the individual household and as high as the national regime, acts upon its own historical trajectory. Neighboring nations certainly join in this constant process of becoming part of "China's rise" and, as a result, China also becomes part of its own becoming. Borders and sites multiplying in this complicated manner almost certainly undermine high politics in the imagery produced by the conventional international relations literature. Among possible sites, however, are the long-ignored socialist sites and their pre-socialist trajectories.

Sites are where the identity strategies emerge. The multiple sinic orders arising from the various sites, which appear to belong to an over-riding sinic order, reflect different identity strategies that meet through their interactions. These strategies, derived from different historical trajectories, construct their own China through the mechanisms of encounters and choice. Through such encounters, each site is constrained by the physical and discursive contexts from which its strategies emerge; through choice, each site combines and recombines cultural resources to give them meaning. This is how no one site can monopolize the meaning of the sinic order. All sites are able to come up with new or recycled meanings. Ironically, the sinic order survives in name or in imagination, if not in substance, as all strategies interact and continuously adapt.

Sinicization has enhanced the vitality and resonance of the intellectual history of sinology. It has facilitated the spread of American capitalist market practices within the Chinese economy, the nationalist and rights rhetoric within Chinese politics, the idea of the "balance of power" within China's foreign policy, and the multi-culturalism within

China's global diasporic communities. Conceptual and institutional adaptations of sinicization and the different forms of resistance, re-appropriation, and feedback they engender have rendered sinicization all the more important. The responses, requiring knowledge of both the Euro-American and the Chinese forms of civilization, motivate agents to be cognizant of the positions they occupy between the different civilizations. Sinicization, as well as sinology, often implies not only China as a nation-state, but also the Chinese residing in Indochina and Taiwan who mediate between the Chinese and their own various forms of identity. They act as both producers and consumers of civilization who maneuver among collective, familial, and individual centers of allegiance.[5]

3. Sinologists as Anthropologists of Knowledge

Self-knowledge is the foundation of sinology. Becoming a sinologist involves multi-sited processes that deconstruct the stereotypical notions of China's rise in the twenty-first century. The pre- and post-socialist sinologists in this volume have actively participated in this sort of sinicization. Their strategic choices have been shaped by their specific historical contexts, thus there are wide variations in their adaptations. Because they are positioned at different sites, they do not respond to China's rise in similar ways.

Methodologically, the authors in the book rely on the aforementioned anthropology of knowledge, which stresses the relevance of encounters and choices that mirror and reproduce those responsible for the survival of human groups in the process of knowledge production. Specifically, the volume includes interviews with senior sinologists as well as literature reviews. The authors pay particular attention to the choices of sinologists facing the constraints of their social and professional encounters. Between the pre-socialist traditions and the post-socialist globalism, there were unlimited cultural as well as epistemological sites where one could acquire perspectives through learning, practicing, or simulating particular identity strategies that made sense to the sites at specific points in time. Each site in itself is home to many possible alternative identities, so not only may the choice of an identity at a particular site be unstable over time, but the choice of a site itself may be unstable as well. This reduces the choice of identity to no more than the act of taking on a particular role, except that it usually requires a conscious, context-specific, and immediate decision.

Globalization obscures the distinction of identity due to its increasingly destabilizing effects on self-other relations. Intellectual paths that are influenced by the transformation, overthrow, lingering-on, disappearance, reproduction, fading, or backfiring of the party-state in the post-socialist states as well as their foreign relations are destined to encounter such dislocations in self-other relations, generating frustration, hope, emptiness, fear, opportunity, and other types of anxiety. Accordingly, sites are as much intellectual and psychological as they are social and physical.

Underpinning this intellectual history project is a conviction that individual professional trajectories necessarily reflect choices, both conscious and subconscious, about epistemological possibilities permitted by the social conditions about which individuals have no immediate choice. The two mechanisms that facilitate intellectual growth are, first, encounters with existing epistemological perspectives beyond one's own volition and, second, choices that strategically select, recombine, and renovate perceived (im)possibilities. The mechanism of encountering constrains the range of intellectual puzzles;[6] the mechanism of choice reflects the strength of volition.[7] Whereas encountering is largely socially prepared and yet unavoidably mediated by coincidence, choice is indicated by the existence of alternatives that are either preserved or are created by the differing decisions and narratives of others. Between one's choice and encounters, which are beyond one's own choice, there is the second-ordered mechanism of travel. All of these can be conceived of in terms of physical movement and career paths. Travel always involves choices that facilitate the ensuing encounters, hence, it is a second-ordered mechanism that breeds individual intellectual growth.

A methodological note on travel is useful here. Reflections on one's choice of a site about which one has written different things about China could more easily begin by recalling one's travel experiences—as an immigrant, a student abroad, a conference participant, a visiting scholar, a field researcher, a tourist, or other such experiences, whether mentioned or not on one's curriculum vitae—whereby encounters that necessitate constant decision making are essential. Similar pressures to make different choices also take place when hosting, willingly or not, visiting travelers in various forms—when surrendering to their governing bloc, enlisting their services, reading their writings, subscribing to their ideology, consuming their products, marrying their members, and so on. Travel intrinsically is a method of China studies and also a methodology of re- or de-Sinicization.

4. The Intellectual History of Sinology as Sinicization

The present book invites reflections on various trajectories of intellectual history specifically pertaining to how China is accessed through knowledge about China in different communities and life biographies. Given the multiple identities in the world, one's own self-understanding is essential to an understanding of China. Decisions made regarding ever-evolving individual biographies challenge the objectivity of knowledge.[8] Knowledge of China and the practices associated with China complement one another in China as well as elsewhere.[9] The evolution of China knowledge proceeds along trajectories of intellectual growth, each of which is embedded in its own social practices. This is particularly relevant in the age of globalization and amidst the arguably "age of rising China." As symbols of China fill in one's life practices, the China scholar's approach to the study of China increasingly interferes with his or her own self-understanding.

The study of individualized intellectual history regarding China is therefore at the same time an anthropological study of knowledge. China involves a process of self-becoming among its scholars and their communities, and is thus intrinsically composed of a phenomenon of human evolution. Historical bearings of one's social and cultural backgrounds comprise the epistemological foundation for one's writings on China. They incorporate various biographies that have given rise to unusually rich but often mutually incompatible intellectual resources and inspirations, including, at the very least, the collective memory of all those groups with which one has sequentially identified oneself throughout one's life. In my own past, for example, these historical bearings refer to political and social movements and wars fought in the name of, or targeted at, China and the associated political upheavals that caused social cleavages, political turmoil, ideological confusion, and, at times, anti-foreign, anti-colonial, or anti-Chinese nationalism.

China scholarship in Taiwan, for example, involves choices by scholars with respect to encountered and constantly reinterpreted imaginations of how Chinese names, identities, and images have occurred.

Due to its colonial history, the Civil and Cold War legacies, and internal cleavages, political turmoil, ideological confusion, and, at times, anti-foreign, anti-colonial, or anti-Chinese nationalism. China scholarship in Taiwan consists of strategic shifts among the Japanese, American, and Chinese approaches to the subject as well as their combinations and recombinations. The mechanisms of choice, including the travel that can orient, reorient, or disorient existing views of China, produce conjunctive scholarship. The rich repertoire of views on China, together with the politics of identity, challenge the objective stance of the social sciences to the extent that no view of China can be exempt from political implications and politicized social scrutiny.[10] Concerns about exigent propriety in a social setting are internal to knowledge production. Therefore, understanding the process by which all the historically derived approaches inform China scholarship in Taiwan through the mechanism of encountering reveals both the uncertain nature of knowledge in general and the uncertain worldwide meanings associated with China in particular.

The academics in this volume illustrate a variety of geographical, linguistic, and temporal possibilities in their lives. They were born in different national communities, they lived and worked in different countries, and their occasional reliance on languages other than their professional languages all suggest that sinicization does not have to proceed in either Chinese or English. Rather, the use of third languages can be a statement about one's being, where one is from, and where one is heading. In brief, sinicization reveals in one individual the existence of multiple cultural-geographical selves. Later in their careers, many of these academics experienced a growing concern about their home countries, often reflected in a shift, occurring consciously and rationally, in their academic and political agendas and in the frequency of their visits. This fact is a healthy antidote to the common preconception that structures are all-determining. As revealed by these individual lives, nothing can be farther from the truth.

Even far-reaching views that seek to associate China with very specific images, such as "China's rise," "all under heaven," or "Chinese characteristics," represent choices, not inevitabilities; the lives and works of these academics contradict any such notions. If one insists on the nation-state as the only viable civilizational actor in world politics, Huntingtonian clashes of civilizations may have some plausibility.

Academics living and working in transnational careers, however, have been free to choose practices unrelated, or even resistant, to the constraints and opportunities imposed or provided by nation-states. The promotion or denial of Chinese distinctiveness always involves choices. Thus, no view of China can be politically neutral. Sinicization is unavoidably shaped and impacted by conceptions of identity and political practice.

This does not mean that actors have full control over their scholarly work on China or over their self-identifications that implicitly or explicitly inform their perspectives. No academic can control either the larger forces that prompt their civilizational encounters or the liminal positions they hold. Their choice of language, for example, does not go unnoticed by one community or the other. Home and host countries pose structural constraints simply because they differ from one another. Any narrative strategy about China cannot help but activate these differences. Yet meaningful choices persist, including both the choice of sides and the avoidance of the choice of sides. Structural determinacy thus fails to remove the capacity for strategic indeterminacy. Adaptation, and even self-revocation, is the norm of biography.

5. Framework of the Book

This book introduces reflections based upon personal encounters in Russia, the Czech Republic, Poland, and Mongolia. These various sites have been home to long traditions of sinology and Oriental studies. Before the socialist period, their philological traditions were based largely on the legacy of French sinology. Thereafter, they all experienced an interlude during Communist Party rule and accordingly, to some extent, these sites became politically and ideologically connected to one another. Starting from the 1990s and continuing for the past two decades we have witnessed a transformation—a fading, overthrow, or lingering on—of the Communist rein over scholarship on ancient as well as modern China studies. To what extent this will involve a reconnection with or a revival of past scholarship and to what extent the party-state's legacy has or will be sustained, backfire, re-emerge, or disappear are among the questions discussed in the volume.

In the first part of the book—"Doing Sinology in Post-Communist States"—Olga Lomová and Anna Zádrapová discuss those factors that contributed to the development of an academic environment that made possible the Prague School (as identified by Leo Ou-fan Lee) and its achievements. Melissa Shih-hui Lin, based on interviews collected by Olga Lomová and Anna Zádrapová from 2010 to 2011, relies on critical discourse analysis (CDA) to disclose the relationship between the different choices of "China" as a lexical or textual device in the discourse of Czech sinologists and how they tried to re-construct the identity of "China." Both chapters attest to the significance of language and identity in the development of local diversity in Czech sinology. They show the relevance of the political situations in both Czechoslovakia and China during the 1940s and 1950s to the rise and continuation of Czech sinology.

Enkhchimeg Baatarkhuyag and Chih-yu Shih examine interviews with veteran sinologists in Mongolia and trace the evolution of Mongolian studies on modern Chinese history. In this process, they specifically concentrate on the importance of language in Mongolian scholarship, but also on Sino-Mongolian relations, controversial issues, and changing attitudes. Next, Anna Rudakowska, taking the epistemological debate on the study of China as a point of reference, looks at the evolution in the understanding of sinology as an academic discipline in Polish academia. Although these debates have significantly influenced sinological training at the University of Warsaw, other sinological centers in Poland have not been affected. Based on interviews, Rudakowska provides insights into the discourse of scholars and their various epistemological debates.

Three Russian papers, examining the cycles in various epistemic communities, focus on different issues related to academic identity. Based on extensive interviews, Valentin C. Golovachev looks at the transnational connections between the socialist countries during the Soviet period (1917–1991), a period when Russian sinologists were greatly restricted in their personal and professional exchanges with colleagues and people in China as well as in other countries. Golovachev's analysis is based on extensive interviews. Alexander Pisarev tackles the theoretical foundation of Soviet studies on social relations in traditional and semi-traditional China. With reference to the recent literature, he demonstrates the choice of partisans of the "Asiatic mode of production" to retrieve the framework of "Chinese traditional society." Finally, Alexei D. Voskressenski examines how problems in

Soviet, and later Russian, sinology have been related to the uneven development of the discipline because of ideological barriers and decreasing material and human resources. These problems have affected the integrity of research and have constrained China studies in post-Soviet Russia.

In the second part of the book—"Being Sinologists in Post-Communist Societies"—Bogdan J. Góralczyk provides an initial attempt to describe Polish sinology and the individual choices, both vocational and social and political, of Polish sinologists. He proposes individual systematization, which fragments this history into many chapters, collective as well as individual, from the "real socialist" era (1950–1989) until after the democratic breakthrough of 1989. He adopts the proposition of a constantly increasing diversification of this initially small circle of highly specialized individuals, which of late has been growing ever more rapidly.

In the Czech Republic, Olga Lomová and Anna Zádrapová discover the motivation for the study of Chinese—Chinese poetry in translation by Bohumil Mathesius (1888–1952)—by Průšek and his Prague School scholars. At that time, being a sinologist also meant being an enthusiast for classical Chinese poetry as presented by a non-specialist. Lomová and Zádrapová demonstrate the existence of a certain ideological network that combined traditional topoi about the Orient with genuine and serious study of Chinese civilization and they question to what extent the creation of sinology in postwar Czechoslovakia was part of a romantic enchantment and an unreflected search for "The Other." Along the same lines, Ter-Hsing Cheng finds that socialist China in the 1950s offered two possibilities for the development of sinology; first, friendly relations among the socialist countries, including overseas students and, second, studies of contemporary Chinese literature. The social framework of the collective memory of Czech sinologists should be understood as falling somewhere in the region of the mutual penetration of sinology and socialist China. Cheng discusses the links between New China and other socialist countries as well as relations between Průšek and socialist China. He also analyzes Czech sinological experiences in the 1950s based on Halbwachs's theory of collective memory.

Next, Sergey Dmitriev suggests that the dramatic history of Tangut studies may be viewed as a real *quinta essentia* of the fate of Oriental studies in Russia. A very rich collection of various Tangut books was discovered in a mausoleum in the dead city of Khara-Khoto in 1908; almost all of these texts in the Tangut language were thereafter collected in Saint-Petersburg. As a result, Russian Tangutology rapidly assumed great importance, and Russian specialists, especially Aleksej Ivanov, took the initial steps to understand the Tangut language and history that had remained hidden for so long. In contrast, the academic establishment provides a different picture of Russian sinology. In her research notes based on thirty-three interviews, Marina Kuznetsova-Fetisova summarizes the various reasons that led veteran sinologists to embark on China studies. For over half of the sinologists, the choice was not the result of strong personal interest. Instead, their decisions were closely related to the politics of the USSR at the time. In the late 1940s and the early 1950s, the USSR had decided to prepare a large number of sinologists to contribute to the Chinese modernization process.

6. A Note on the Original Project

This book is actually part of much larger transnational project entitled Comparative Epistemology of China Studies (at http://politics.ntu.edu. tw/RAEC), which began early in this century. Co-sponsored primarily by the Ministry of Education and the Ministry of Sciences and Technologies (previously called the National Science Council) of Taiwan, the project includes both an oral history component and a curriculum component that can be used for the writing of M.A. and Ph.D. dissertations. Theoretically, it encompasses the study of intellectual history embedded in civilizational and international politics. The hosts of the project are the Research and Educational Center for China Studies and Cross-Taiwan Strait Relations in the Department of Political Science at National Taiwan University. Initially funded with a grant from the Chiang Ching-kuo Foundation in 2002–5, it grew out of a pilot project in Japan under the leadership of Professor Hirano Ken'ichirō, with the support of his colleagues Nakamura Yūjirō and Tsuchida Akio. Subsequently funded by the National Science Council of Taiwan, the College of Social Sciences at National Taiwan University, and the Graduate Institute of Political Science at National Sun Yatsen University, along with a number of smaller grants, the project has continued through 2015 and will be extended thereafter.

The project has generated over 200 interviews with institutional and individual participants from all over the world (including, by nationality for the sake of convenience, American, Australian, Bangladeshi, Belgian, Burmese, Czech, German, Hong Kong/Macau, Indian, Italian, Japanese, Kazakhstani, Korean, Malaysian, Mongolian, Nepali, Pakistani, Russian, Singaporean, Sri Lankan, Taiwanese, Turkish, and Vietnamese scholars), producing over sixty monographs, and a number of journal articles. In addition to the interviews conducted by members of the Japanese pilot project, individual coordinators in Australia, China, Germany, Hong Kong, Korea, Mongolia, Taiwan, and Singapore as well as Chinese scholars, and interviews on the intellectual history of national and international sinology are also being jointly conducted via partnerships with the Association for Asia Scholars in New Delhi, the Institute of China Studies at the Vietnamese Academy of Sciences, the Department of Chinese Studies of Hanoi University, the Asian Research Center of Chulalongkorn University, the Institute of Chinese Studies of the University of Malay, the Department of Chinese Studies of City University of Hong Kong, Ho Chi-minh City University of Social Sciences and Humanities, the Department of Sinology of Ghent University, the Institute of Oriental Studies of Sapienza University of Rome, the Institutes of Oriental Studies and Far Eastern Studies at the Russian Academy of Sciences, the Center of East Asian Studies at Charles University, and the Department of Chinese Studies at Warsaw University. Throughout, the Center for Foreign China Studies at the Chinese Academy of Social Sciences has provided a wide range of technical support.

We should also express here the grief we felt over the loss of the following participants during the project's first fifteen years: Buu Cam and Nguyen Ton Nhan from Vietnam, Wei Weixian from Singapore, Liao Kwang-sheng and Rui Ho-cheng from Taiwan, Mizoguchi Yūzō and Ishikawa Shigeru from Japan, Danny Van Den Bulcke from Belgium, Lidia Ivanovna Golovatcheva, Irena Slawinska, Nadezhda Vinogradova, Yury M. Garushyantz, and Oleg Borisovich Rakhmanin from Russia, Milena Doleželová-Velingerová from the Czech Republic, and Mira Sinha Bhattacharjea and Vidya Praksh Dutt from India, all interviewees, and Vladimir Ganshin from Moscow, a coordinator and interviewer of the Russian project.

Notes

1. Dulam Bumochir and Chih-yu Shih, eds., "Special Issue: Mongolia: Civilization Nationality, and Ethnicity," *Asian Ethnicity*, Vol.15, No. 4 (2014), pp. 417–585.

2. Chow Bing Ngeow, Tek Soon Ling, and Pik She Fan, "Pursuing Chinese Studies Amidst Identity Politics in Malaysia," *East Asia*, Vol. 31, No. 2 (2014), pp. 103–122.

3. Amitav Acharya and Barry Buzan, "Why is There No Non-Western International Relations Theory?" *International Relations of the Asia-Pacific*, Vol. 7, No. 3 (2007), pp. 287–312; Wu Guoguang, "Politics Against Science: Reflections on the Study of Chinese Politics in Contemporary China," *Journal of Chinese Political Science*, Vol. 16, No. 3 (2011), pp. 279–297.

4. William A. Callahan, *Contingent States: Greater China and Transnational Relations* (Minneapolis: University of Minnesota Press, 2004); Takeshi Hamashita and Heita Kawakatsu, eds., *Umi to shihonshugi* (Ocean and Capitalism) (Tokyo: Toyokeizaishinposha, 2003); Peter J. Katzenstein, ed., *Sinicization and the Rise of China: Civilizational Processes Beyond East and West* (New York: Routledge, 2012); Brantly Womack, *China Among Unequals: Asymmetric Foreign Relations in Asia* (Singapore: World Scientific Press, 2010).

5. Chih-yu Shih, "Special Issue: Chineseness and Chinese Studies in Southeast Asia; Introduction: The Beauty of Being Accurate," *Asian Ethnicity*, Vol. 16, No. 2 (2015), pp. 1–7.

6. Sandra G. Harding, *Is Science Multicultural? Postcolonialisms, Feminisms, and Epistemologies* (Bloomington: Indiana University Press, 1998); Paul Diesing, *Science and Ideology in the Policy Sciences* (New Brunswick, NJ: Transaction Books, 2005); Nico Stehr and Volker Meja, eds., *Society and Knowledge: Contemporary Perspectives in the Sociology of Knowledge and Science* (New Brunswick, NJ: Transaction Books, 1987).

7. Gary D. Phye, ed., *Handbook of Academic Learning: Construction of Knowledge* (San Diego: Academic Press, 1997), pp. 52, 110; Jason Stanley, *Knowledge and Practical Interests* (Oxford: Oxford University Press, 2005); Robert C. Stalnaker, *Our Knowledge of the Internal World* (Oxford: Oxford University Press, 2008).

8. Paul Diesing, *How Does Social Science Work? Reflections on Practice* (Pittsburgh: University of Pittsburgh Press, 1991); Michael E. Latham, *Modernization as Ideology: American Social Science and "Nation Building" in the Kennedy Era* (Chapel Hill: University of North Carolina Press, 2000).

9. Baogang He, "The Dilemmas of China's Political Science in the Context of the Rise of China," *Journal of Chinese Political Science*, Vol. 16, No. 3

(2011), pp. 257–277; Sujian Guo, ed., *Political Science and Chinese Political Studies: The State of the Field* (Dordrecht: Springer, 2013); Wu, "Politics Against Science," pp. 279–297.

10. Chih-yu Shih, "China, China Scholarship, and China Scholars in Postcolonial Taiwan," *China: An International Journal*, Vol. 12, No. 1 (2014), pp. 1–21.

Part I

**Doing Sinology from
Post-Communist Perspectives**

Chapter 1

*Beyond Academia and Politics:
Understanding China and Doing Sinology in
Czechoslovakia after World War II*

Olga Lomová and Anna Zádrapová

1. Introduction

After World War II, Czechoslovakia,[1] though a small country in Central Europe without any previous sustained tradition of Chinese studies,[2] developed, within a very short time, a vigorous academic discipline of sinology centered at Charles University in Prague.[3] During the 1960s, Czechoslovak sinology represented by Professor Jaroslav Průšek (1906–80) and the first generation of his students became prominent internationally, especially in modern Chinese literature studies. Czechoslovak scholars embraced this little-studied orientation bringing into focus new material on modern Chinese literature, but also traditional popular culture, such as theater, storytelling, and so forth, using new perspectives and methodologies (mainly structuralism, semiotics, and Marxist theory) and primarily comparative approaches. As a result, Průšek and his students formulated new progressive ideas about Chinese literature and culture, which had a considerable impact on further explorations in similar directions outside of Czechoslovakia. In the early 1970s Czechoslovak sinology began to be acknowledged as a specific "Prague School."[4] Through direct collaborations and personal exchanges Czechoslovak sinology also had an immediate and decisive impact on the establishment of new China studies in the German Democratic Republic and, to some extent, in Poland as well.[5]

One of the most important methodological innovations of the Prague School was the way the relationship between modern and traditional Chinese culture was explored. Jaroslav Průšek insisted that modernity, as it found expression in the efforts of the May Fourth Movement, despite its antitraditionalism and program of Westernization, could not be properly understood without a closer look at premodern Chinese literature and society. His view, at the time still very rare in academic circles and popular awareness alike, saw modernity in Chinese literature (and potentially also in other spheres of human life in China) being nourished not only by the West, but also rooted in its own domestic traditions. Thus in order to understand modern China, indigenous developments toward modernity needed to be taken into account.[6] In his efforts to better understand the process of emerging modernity in China Jaroslav Průšek, both as a professor at Charles University and, after 1952, also as director of the Oriental Institute of the Czechoslovak Academy of Sciences, initiated collaborative projects simultaneously exploring issues in both traditional and modern China. These ideas developed into a large project, organized by his students, on comparative studies of similar processes in various Asian literatures.[7]

Jaroslav Průšek was not only the first professor of Chinese and Japanese language and literature at Charles University, he was a true *"spiritus movens et agens"* in early Czech sinology.[8] As memoirs by his former students reveal, he was a leading initiator on many levels: he succeeded in attracting students to the subject, he inspired students with his original ideas and innovative research methodology, and he supported his students in both academic and personal issues.[9] Průšek is also remembered as a person of great personal charm, able to arouse in his students his own enthusiasm and emotional attachment to China.

A closer look at Czechoslovak sinology as it evolved through the 1950s reveals that high academic aspirations notwithstanding, doing sinology at that time also meant close involvement in popularization, including translations of Chinese literature for Czech readers and other forms of regular interactions with the general public. This is well captured in an interview with Augustin Palát:

> "We all had to act as the propagators of China; we translated, gave lectures, opened exhibitions, and so forth. Although it was fairly annoying sometimes, and sometimes even at the expense of our own work, our sinologists had close contacts with the audience and informed the general public about

Chinese events and production. This made us different from our Western colleagues. As opposed to the Western world at that time, we translated a huge number of Chinese books."[10]

Palát is referring to the situation in the early 1950s, i.e., after the Communist takeover both in Czechoslovakia (1948) and in China (1949). The nonacademic dimension of early Czechoslovak sinology can be partly explained by a shared Communist ideology with its emphasis on "service to the people" and it was positively informed by political affinities. But in fact the situation was more complex, as reaching beyond academia had been a remarkable characteristic of the work of Czechoslovak sinologists even before 1948 (or 1949). It was the result of the overall historical situation, and it resonated with a broader interest in Chinese culture that went back to the war years, if not earlier.

2. The War Period

Before Jaroslav Průšek succeeded in creating the first sinology chair at Charles University in 1945, he was employed at the Oriental Institute— an independent institution established in 1922 with the aim of collecting and spreading knowledge about (mostly contemporary) Asia. Its primary tasks were to support general knowledge about Asia and to bolster Czechoslovak trade with "the countries of the Orient," including China. The institute received partial financial support from the Czechoslovak government.[11] During World War II, when Czechoslovakia fell apart and was occupied by Nazi Germany (the Sudetenland was annexed by Germany, the eastern part became "independent" Slovakia, and Bohemia and Moravia became a German protectorate in March 1939), Czech universities were closed. Unlike the universities, the Oriental Institute remained open to the public and it organized evening language courses and public lectures on various aspects of Asian traditions. These courses attracted brilliant young people who were denied a university education. Memoirs from that period reveal that for young students the courses at the Oriental Institute were a form of spiritual resistance against the Nazi occupation. The general atmosphere and the dedication of the students are vividly illustrated in excerpts from an interview with Professor Augustin Palát, a former student at the Oriental Institute and later Jaroslav Průšek's closest collaborator:

"I was interested in various courses: I studied English twice a week, Russian once a week, Spanish, Chinese once a week. … I lived in Žižkov at that time and it took me two hours to get from the Avia factory (where I worked during the Nazi Total Einsatz) and back home. One went to the Vysočany terminals, then to Krocínka in Prosek by foot, and there was a factory bus already waiting to take us to Avia. One had to climb three hundred and fifty stairs before getting from Vysočany to Prosek. I had to plan properly: I came back from the factory before seven pm, popped off to the Automat for quick supper, and from 7 p.m. until nine attended the language course."[12]

Průšek was already respected as a scholar in Chinese studies during the war, even though he did not hold any formal academic positions. Two times during the war he was offered a professorship in Germany: by Professor Ramming in Berlin and by Professor Hänisch in Leipzig. But in both cases he declined as he did not want to be in the service of German institutions.[13] Instead, apart from teaching in the evening classes at the Oriental Institute, Průšek became active as a translator of Chinese philosophy and literature and as an author of articles on these topics addressing a wider non-specialist audience. In his popular writings, Průšek presented a sympathetic vision of Chinese culture, both exotic and ancient but at the same time relevant to the contemporary world in general and to people in Czechoslovakia in particular. Among his writings from the war period, there are translations of *Lunyu* (論語) (1940), a collection of Tang poetry prepared in collaboration with Bohumil Mathesius (1942),[14] a popular article on Li Bai (李白) (1942) reinforcing the earlier established image of a wine-drinking and freedom-loving genius, several medieval vernacular stories, and also a translation of personal memoirs by a late-Qing literatus Shen Fu (沈復), *Fusheng liu ji* (浮生六記) (1944).

In his translations published during the war, Průšek develops a romantic vision of Chinese traditional culture. (Each translation was always preceded by an extensive introductory essay.) Of course, this vision has to be read against the background of the Nazi occupation of Czechoslovakia and the war raging throughout Europe.[15] Thus for the first generation of Czech sinologists, the encounter with China was conditioned by a search for hope during the dark days of war and discovery of an alternative in Chinese culture to provide a remedy to the crisis in Europe.

Průšek was an excellent translator and writer, and his books were widely read during the war years. However, the most popular among

Průšek's war publications was his personal memoir of his pre-war visit to China that was first published in 1940 under the emotive title *Sestra moje Čína* (*My Sister China*).[16] This book was not only popular among general readers, it was also crucial in arousing interest in China among an entire generation of future sinologists. Most of Průšek's students mention this book as an important factor in their decision to study Chinese, including those students who started to study Chinese after the war, such as Milena Doleželová-Velingerová:

"When reading it [*My Sister China*] today I no longer understand what was so fascinating about it because it contains huge mistakes. All in all, it was Průšek's style and his personal enthusiasm for China that had nothing in common with the political situation. He recorded his memories and experiences, as well as his own interpretation of China. I think that was what attracted us the most. And his literary style was amazing too! When I read this book at the age of eighteen, I still didn't know what to do with my life. I was a student in the final year at gymnasium and I had always been interested in languages, especially the northern languages of Scandinavia. I wanted to do something different from the others. This was a pretty strong incentive for me from the beginning. And as I read the book, I said to myself, this is it!"[17]

In addition to being a travelogue and personal memoir from Průšek's visit to China in 1932–34, *My Sister China* is an introduction to Chinese history and culture, both ancient and modern, including literature, some of which is presented in translation, including two May Fourth poets—Bing Xin (冰心) and Xu Zhimo (徐志摩), thus providing the readers with authentic voices by China's poets. During his stay in China, Průšek passionately absorbed everything he encountered about Chinese culture, and he did his best to encounter as much as possible. We read here about the Chinese mentality shaped by ancient Chinese philosophy as well as about the interest of modern Chinese intellectuals in the ideas of the Western world, and also, for example, about Průšek's fascination with traditional theater and street artists and about professional female singers and courtesans. Even opium smoking is mentioned (which is not presented in a negative way!). In *My Sister China*, Průšek is unfolding his dreamlike vision of the timeless, harmonious, and peace-loving Chinese culture, but he is also paying attention to the dim realities that surrounded him at the time. Additionally, he presents informative passages on Chinese history.

The book reveals Průšek's sympathetic spirit as well as his considerable skills as a writer. Enchanted by what he sees with his own eyes, he creates a vivid picture of the large, ancient, and colorful Chinese world undergoing transformation, yet maintaining its own distinctiveness. Most of the chapters have a typical structure: first we are introduced to some real situation that the writer experienced in China. This is followed by an informative commentary on relevant issues in Chinese history or culture. Thus, while depicting his own experiences, he also constructs the world of China as living history, consisting of an intermingling of the trivial and the noble with the past and the present:

> "The picture show is not much better. Hung inside sheds as well as on the walls outside are long scrolls, thousands of sheets of paper and silk, selling at anywhere between two and fifteen dollars apiece. ... In the old days, Chinese ... would never have pasted over all the walls of their homes with pictures. Rather, they kept them rolled up and boxed, and depending on their mood at a particular moment—the most important factor in the process of absorbing art—they would sometimes take out a winter landscape ... and on another occasion, say, a portrait of a beautiful woman."[18]

There are two other striking features in *My Sister China* about the way in which Průšek presents aspects of Chinese culture to the Czech audience: the strong aesthetic appeal of the traditional sophisticated literati culture and the wisdom of Chinese philosophers as understood by Průšek, i.e., a humanistic philosophy expressing opposition to violence and enhancing the values of peaceful coexistence, the importance of education, and a general respect for cultural values. In some respects, Průšek's vision of Chinese tradition can be perceived as a continuation of the sinophilia rooted in the European Enlightenment. It also resonates with the image presented by Lin Yutang (林語堂) in his *My Country and My People*. Lin's book was translated into Czech shortly before the war and published with a preface by Pearl S. Buck, another author whose novels set in China were well-known to Czech readers. Yet the publications by Průšek and his students and colleagues after 1945 vehemently rejected the past old ideas of an exotic Orient (not only China). This approach is reflected in the title of a new journal of the Oriental Institute, *Nový Orient* (New Orient), which began publication in the fall of 1945.

3. Aspects of Domestic and International Politics

Sinology as an independent academic discipline began at Charles University shortly after the war. In late 1945 the Department of Far Eastern Philology and History, as it was called at that time, was established after successful lobbying by Jaroslav Průšek with the Ministry of Education. In 1947 Průšek became the first full professor in the department, and in the same year a program in sinology at Charles University was approved by the Ministry of Education.

In the late 1940s some of Průšek's former war time students from the Oriental Institute finalized their sinological education abroad. Berta Krebsová studied in France (1946–47) and Věna Stunová-Hrdličková and Zdeněk Hrdlička studied at Harvard University (1946–48). Upon their return, they became, together with Průšek, the first teachers of Chinese language and history. Other early teachers of sinology included Augustin Palát (born in 1926), Jarmila Kalousková (1908–89), Danuše Kalvodová (1928–2003), Danuška Heroldová-Šťovíčková (1929–76), and Daniela Šejnohová (1929–2011).

Without a doubt, sinology in post-war Czechoslovakia was part of the broader domestic political situation and of the relations between Czechoslovakia and China, first the Republic of China (ROC), and later the People's Republic of China (PRC). The link to politics was evident from the very beginning in terms of the support provided by the Czechoslovak Ministry of Foreign Affairs to "Orientalist" societies (i.e., civic societies, such as the Czechoslovak-China Society) with the goal of promoting knowledge about Asia among the general public and cultivating mutual understanding. This was coupled by the presence of representatives of the Chinese embassy at important meetings of the Czechoslovak-China Society (see below). From the very beginning, Czechoslovak institutions cultivating China-related studies and spreading knowledge about Chinese culture were in close and friendly contact with representatives of the ROC embassy in Prague. The embassy must have informed the Chinese government about the creation of the Czechoslovak-China Society, since two months after its inauguration Chiang Kai-shek (蔣介石 Jiang Jieshi) sent a congratulatory telegram. This telegram, dated 22 February 1946 from Chongqing, was translated and published in *Nový Orient*.[19]

A crucial person in the contacts between Czechoslovakia and the Chinese government after World War II but before 1949 was Lone

Liang (梁龍 Liang Long),[20] the ambassador of the ROC to Prague beginning from 18 December 1946. In fact, this was his second mission to Prague (the first was 1936–39). During the war he was in charge of the European Section in the Chinese Ministry of Foreign Affairs in Chongqing, and in this position he cultivated close contacts with Czech diplomats. During his second mission to Prague Lone Liang provided financial support for China-related projects at the Oriental Institute, including support for the library and for the Czechoslovak-China Society.[21] Ambassador Liang was also involved in two exhibitions of Chinese art in Prague. Both exhibitions were acclaimed in the Czech media as extraordinary events testifying to the greatness and vitality of Chinese traditions.[22]

After the Communist takeover of Czechoslovakia in February 1948, friendly relations with the ROC initially remained unchanged. But at the same time the Czechoslovak government welcomed unofficial representatives of the Chinese Communists to establish a European branch of the Xinhua News Agency (新華社) in Prague. It was registered in the autumn of 1948.[23] The proclaimed aims of the Prague Xinhua office were to publish a bulletin of news from Yan'an in English and to distribute it to India as well as to some countries in Europe, North America, and Africa.[24] Additionally, it was charged with collecting information on Western reporting on China. The office was also entitled to establish contacts with government representatives in foreign countries.[25] Chinese employees in the Prague Xinhua office soon also established informal contacts with Czech people, including young sinologists. We know from our interviewees that there were lively contacts between the Xinhua reporters and the students of sinology (personal communication with Věna Hrdličková and Augustin Palát). This was one of the few ways to meet Chinese people in Czechoslovakia and know more about China at that time.

Another important political event, which brought Czechoslovak sinologists and Communist China closer together before the establishment of the PRC, occurred on the occasion of the World Congress of Advocates of Peace held in April 1949 in Paris. When the French authorities refused visas to many delegates, including those from China, then largely controlled by the Communists, the Congress was held simultaneously in Prague, which was already under Communist rule. The Chinese delegation to Prague consisted of about 40 members,

including writers and historians, for example Guo Moruo (郭沫若) and
Zheng Zhenduo (鄭振鐸), the painter Xu Beihong (徐悲鴻), and other
personalities later to become important figures in the PRC. Jaroslav
Průšek already personally knew some of them from his pre-war sojourn
in China.[26] Czech students eagerly interpreted for them, as it was a rare
opportunity to meet Chinese people in Prague, a city without any
Chinese minority.

Upon the establishment of the PRC on 1 October 1949, Czechoslovakia, along with the USSR and Poland, was among the first countries
to recognize the new government of China. This occurred on 4 October
1949, and the next day Czechoslovakia ceased its relations with the
ROC. The political alliance was almost immediately followed by
cultural exchanges, including support for sinology both at Charles
University and at the Oriental Institute. This support meant a radical improve-
ment in the material background for teaching and research. Prof. Palát
remembers:

> "When Průšek tried to enforce something for the existence of the discipline
> in 1947 or 1948, he got always the same stereotypical answer: 'We are in the
> middle of building the Two-year Plan; we have no time now.' After the PRC
> was established, this changed overnight. The authorities wanted crowds of
> people who would be able to speak Chinese in the shortest possible time."[27]

The political friendship between Czechoslovakia and China started
to deteriorate after the Sino-Soviet split became open in 1960. This also
meant that personal contacts were much more difficult, including first
limiting and later eliminating the student and academic exchanges.
Given the particular situation in Czechoslovakia at the same time as
Stalinism was being rejected and the country was undergoing a process
of political liberalization, eventually culminating in the Prague Spring
of 1968, the worsening of political relations with China did not directly
negatively impact on academic activities. Sinology as an already well-
established discipline in Czechoslovak academia continued without
interruption, despite the worsening political relations with PRC. In fact,
it began to yield its best fruit during the atmosphere of liberalization in
the 1960s. In addition, general interest in Chinese culture based on
positive views about China and its traditions continued uninterrupted as
well. Political events did have a strong negative impact on Czechoslovak
sinology only after 1968, but this is outside of the scope of the present
chapter.

4. Emerging Sinology and Stalinist Ideology

Despite the support provided by the new Czechoslovak government to the study of China, students who entered university in about 1950 remember that the main difficulty they encountered was the lack of dictionaries and books about China. They used all sorts of sources in different European languages, many of which were from the pre-war period. Interestingly, despite the close political partnership between Czechoslovakia with the Soviet Union, students from that period recall that they rarely used any Soviet literature.

Recollections by Průšek's former students about their studies during the period of Stalinism in the early 1950s are almost identical in one respect—they all deny any political pressure on the content of their studies under Jaroslav Průšek, neither in his lectures, nor in the topics assigned to them for their papers and graduation theses. Such statements seem surprising today, with our retrospective understanding of what was occurring at that time in Czechoslovakia. Of course, we can speculate to what degree they reflect the subjectivity of the speakers, or to what extent they may be projections of today's strongly critical perspective on the Communist past. Nevertheless, it is true that Průšek and his students managed to maintain high research standards and to generally avoid simplifications along the lines of the official ideology. To a large extent, the Stalinist ideology, if present at all in Czech sinological literature during that time, was projected into the interest of popular culture (the culture of the "oppressed masses"); the political rhetoric was largely found in formal introductions and here and there on the surface, as well as in some of the vocabulary used. Stalinist flavor is apparent in Průšek's book-length study of Yan'an literature, but even here there are discussions of genuine research questions and use of previously unknown valuable sources rather than simple acquiescence to the official ideology.[28]

Průšek's unique personality must also be taken into consideration when discussing the compliance of early Czechoslovak sinology to contemporary politics. Průšek was a respected scholar and he was unwilling to compromise on scholarly principles in his work. At the same time, he was initially sympathetic to communism, working in a field that was regarded by the authorities as most important. As a result, he could and did "cover up" activities that might not have necessarily been in tune with the propaganda of the time (as is revealed in the interviews) and he even successfully defended students who had political difficulties.

With respect to the atmosphere at that time we cannot avoid the substantial comments by Professor Zbigniew Słupski in his interview about the deeply inherent self-censuring that was a necessity of the times.

> "One could not start talking carelessly and show disgust for the regime, and we had to join the May Day parade. I had grown up in the atmosphere of Hitler's Germany in the 1940s, when one had to be careful not to speak Polish,[29] not to say anything about the Third Reich. ... I was well-educated. I knew how to behave, always on the side, not to talk much, not to believe people, especially people who were unknown. ... I can remember the following kind of situation: In cases when someone started a conversation on a delicate topic or tried to ask sensitive questions, Průšek would talk him out of it. Not by some pressure methods, but he would say: 'Well, go away from this, you can't discover anything, you can't even write about it ... you know.' One could not work on some topics, it was self-evident. But take this: In case you want to work on something, you should do it properly. If a topic existed that was impossible to treat properly, one opted not to deal with it."[30]

The interesting topic of the positioning of early Czechoslovak sinology within the political and ideological pressures of the time still awaits further study. Rich archival material exists for such research in the thus far little explored archives of Charles University, the Ministry of Information, the Oriental Institute, and other relevant institutions.

5. Between an Academic Discipline and Popular Enlightenment

Apart from holding the first chair in Chinese studies at Charles University, after the war Průšek also continued his activities at the Oriental Institute, which until 1952 remained an independent institution primarily addressing a non-specialized audience. Popularization was among its foremost tasks, as well as support for international cultural exchanges. In these efforts, the Oriental Institute collaborated with the Czechoslovak Ministry of Foreign Affairs and with the embassies of the Asian countries in Prague.

In 1945, on the initiative of the Oriental Institute, the Society for Cultural Contacts with the Orient was established, publishing the monthly journal *Nový Orient* (New Orient). Important figures in the creation of the journal were Zdeněk Hrdlička (1919–99), former student of Jaroslav Průšek from the war years, and of course Průšek himself, as well as other Czechoslovak scholars. The journal was dedicated to spreading knowledge among wider audiences about Asian and African countries, with special emphasis on culture, including translations of Asian literature, ethnographic photographs, and reproductions of ancient and modern art. Considering the fact that the first number of *Nový Orient* was issued on 15 October 1945, i.e., less than five months after the end of the war, the creation of the new journal was a remarkable achievement.[31]

In the opening address of the new journal the editors distanced themselves from the "colonial notion of the Orient," speaking in a manner that Edward Said would appreciate, and emphasized their understanding of the "Orient" as a purely geographical designation. It was emphasized that the "Eastern" cultures to be explored represented important contributions to mankind, and they should be viewed as part of universal human culture expressing "the same humanity—painful and humiliated, but also hopeful, believing, and victorious."[32]

Soon after the establishment of the Society for Cultural Contacts with the Orient, Průšek initiated the Czechoslovak-China Society. On 19 December 1945, during the inaugural meeting of the society, in the presence of the chargé d'affaires of the ROC, Průšek, as the newly elected president of the society,[33] did his lecture entitled "Hodnoty čínské kultury" (The Values of Chinese Culture). In his speech he deliberated on the question of what Chinese culture meant to Europe and he presented what he called the "Chinese humanistic tradition" as very close and dear to contemporary Europe, especially to the recent Czech experience. He also speculated about the close analogies between certain features in Chinese culture and Czech culture during the national revival movement of the nineteenth century, a political and social project emphasizing cultural and moral efforts to build up an independent and progressive nation. Průšek claimed that the Confucian idea of moral government was particularly close to the sensibilities and historical experience of the Czech nation. He concluded his speech with praise of Chinese art for upholding its distinct feature of the "notion of eternity in which the timeless law of nature is more important than self-expression of an individual."[34]

This speech as well as other articles by Průšek published in *Nový Orient* during 1945–48 reveal a continuing enthusiasm and admiration for Chinese culture as a source of inspiration for Europe, which had been shattered by the war. This is reflected on the pages of *Nový Orient* in articles also by other authors. The first volumes (1945–49) of the journal reveal a sustained interest in Chinese traditional art and literature. Of course, the journal published materials about all Asian countries, but since its beginning China was prominently featured on its pages. As far as the arts were concerned, popularization focused on traditional China. The close relationship between specialists in China studies and non-specialist aficionados is revealed by the presence of Czech painters or poets who had been interested in China already during the pre-war period. Thus we find original articles about Chinese painting by well-known artists and collectors of art (L. Kuba and E. Filla),[35] Chinese music by a musician and musicologist (V. P. Mlejnek), Chinese architecture by an avant-garde architect (P. Smetana), and also reports about art exhibitions and reproductions. Translations from Chinese literature published in *Nový Orient* initially were almost entirely from traditional Chinese literature, in particular the poets Li Bai, Wang Anshi (王安石), and Su Dongpo (蘇東坡), prepared mostly by B. Mathesius in collaboration with Jaroslav Průšek.

From its establishment in 1945, ten issues of *Nový Orient* have been published every year. In 1952, following the Soviet example, the Oriental Institute was incorporated into the newly established Czechoslovak Academy of Sciences. The main task of the institute was changed to become primarily a research institution. Nevertheless, scholars working at the institute still continued their popularizing efforts, and *Nový Orient* continued to be published more or less in the same format. Popularization of knowledge about Asia was undertaken in close connection with the research work; articles on various aspects of culture and translations were often high quality by-products of the new research.

Some brief statistics reveal that even after the political changes of 1948 (and 1949), China continued to be regarded as a country of remarkable artistic tradition and great poetry. During the first ten years after the establishment of the PRC, *Nový Orient* published on classical Chinese poetry 39 times and on modern poetry, mostly represented by authors from the pre-Liberation period, 33 times. Among the modern poets, Ai Qing, who was a personal friend with Palát, figured prominently, and his early modernist writings appeared indiscriminately side by side with later political poetry, in both cases translated into Czech in a good poetic idiom. With respect to PRC poetry, there was also interest in amateur poets, including poetry from the Great Leap Forward.[36] Symptomatic of Czechoslovak admiration for the Chinese poetic tradition, the ideological aspects are not prominent in its presentation. Instead, poetry by peasants was polished in translation by Czech poets and presented as another example of the living tradition going back to the Tang masters. The same is the case with poems by Mao Zedong (毛澤東), published occasionally in *Nový Orient* and later also collected in book form, together with illustrations in the style of Chinese ink painting by a Czech painter.[37]

Modern fiction was discussed and presented in translation 37 times. Lu Xun (魯迅) received the most attention; his work appeared 14 times. Interestingly, four of the articles dedicated to Lu Xun are translations of his poetry. Other authors appearing repeatedly on the pages of *Nový Orient* are Guo Moruo (introduced as a poet and as a writer of historical fiction and drama) and Ding Ling (丁玲).[38] In the first decade of the journal, theatre and the art of storytelling appear in extensive articles and translations 11 times and articles on Chinese painting appear 10 times.

The conscientious effort to build public knowledge about China led the publishers of *Nový Orient* to report also on Czech books about China, including translations of Chinese literature as well as selective foreign publications on contemporary China (for example, *Chungking Diary* by Robert Payne and *The Battle for Asia* by Edgar Snow). The reviews are not totally apologetic; they praise the selected titles, but they also point out their shortcomings, thus revealing the high standards of the reviewers, Průšek among them.

Most obvious is the increase in the number of Chinese topics between 1949 and 1950 (the fifth year of *Nový Orient*), starting with the autumn special double issue. A huge amount of informative political materials about the newly established People's Republic of China including biographies of Mao Zedong, Zhu De (朱德), and Zhou Enlai (周恩來), were published side by side articles on Mao Zedong's views about agricultural problems. However, the overtly political message is accompanied by translations of the Tang masters Du Fu (杜甫) and Li Bai in the idiom of Bohumil Mathesius, thus again confirming how the

Czechoslovak public at that time made little distinction between Communist and traditional China.

Simultaneously with articles on the ethical and aesthetic values of Chinese tradition and their relevance for contemporary Europe, Průšek also occasionally published articles on current issues in Chinese politics. He apparently took this task very seriously, as already in the first three issues of *Nový Orient* (1945–46) he serialised an article entitled "Structural Changes in the Far East." This extensive essay was divided into three parts: "Political Changes," "Economic and Social Changes," and "Cultural Changes," providing rather detailed information about basic issues in twentieth-century Chinese politics and culture.[39]

In 1945 *Nový Orient* published an article entitled "The Life of Modern Chinese Women" based on a successful public lecture given by Mme. Tseng, the wife of the chargé d'affaires of the ROC embassy in Prague;[40] a sequel was published four months later.[41] We are informed in a short editorial that her speech, organized on the premises of the Oriental Institute, attracted such great interest that there was insufficient seating for the public.

Interestingly, Průšek's reporting on post-war China between 1945 and 1948 was not partial, either to the Kuomintang or to the Communists. Rather, his presentations of the current situation in China give the impression that he believed that the two parties could coexist and govern the country together. Such a view was not rare at that time; it was also promoted by others, particularly some American journalists and activists, whose writings Průšek frequently cites.

At the beginning of 1948 an extensive interview with Anne Louise Strong,[42] conducted and translated by Průšek, was included in his article "What is New in Red China, Republican, and Red?" Here Strong stresses the positive impacts of the economic reforms in "Red China," seeing them not as the basis for a future communism but as a way to build a healthy capitalist system. At the same time, Strong also echoes her belief in the moral values of the Chinese people which should be regarded as examples for the West, much in the same way Průšek earlier extolled the Chinese tradition: "The world needs high moral pathos so characteristic of the New China. In Europe we too often look only for immediate effect and result, and we easily overlook that without much moral effort and integrity no enterprise can be lasting."[43]

From Průšek's writings in *Nový Orient* on contemporary politics before 1949, an interesting picture of contemporary China emerges, in which the Communists and the Kuomintang are not represented as antagonistic forces. This is also well-illustrated by photographs of Chiang Kai-shek and Mao Zedong, placed side by side in the first issue of *Nový Orient*. Such misconceptions of what was occurring in China can be partly explained by a lack of information; however, the main reason seems to be the simple fact that from the distance of post-war Czechoslovakia both Chiang Kai-shek with the Nationalist government and Mao Zedong with the Communists were perceived as members of the same anti-fascist alliance. Above all, for Průšek, as well as for his students and many other people in Czechoslovakia, they both were representatives of the admirable Chinese culture.

6. Presenting Chinese Literature and Art

The popularization work by early Czech sinologists found its most powerful expression in translations of Chinese literature, ancient and modern, and in popular articles about literature and art. Some have already been mentioned in relation to *Nový Orient,* but the most important platform for such activities was published books.[44] In this regard, again it was Jaroslav Průšek who set the example. Shortly after the war Průšek published his masterly translation of the late Qing classic *Laocan youji* (老殘遊記) (1947; second printing in 1960) with an extensive study of its author, Liu E (劉鶚) (1857–1901), and of the Chinese novel at the beginning of the twentieth century. In Průšek's selection of titles for translation there is no visible adaptation to any political demands. His other book-length translations published in the 1940s and 1950s, represented an enlarged selection of medieval colloquial stories (1947, second printing in 1954, third printing in 1964, and fourth printing, posthumously in 1991), selections from the *Liaozhai zhiyi* (聊齋誌異) stories by Pu Songling (蒲松齡) (1955, second printing in 1963 and new edition, posthumously in 2004), and a new edition of Shen Fu's *Fusheng liu ji* (1956). With the exception of Dana Kalvodová (1928–2003), who published selected plays by Guan Hanqing (關漢卿) in 1955, Průšek's students only began to work on larger projects of translations from classical literature in the 1960s.

In addition to traditional literature, Průšek also introduced to Czech readers modern classics of the May Fourth generation. His first publication of Chinese literature in Czech translation dates back to 1938 when he prepared a selection of eight stories by Lu Xun. In 1951 he published another Czech translation of selected works by Lu Xun, this time prepared together with Berta Krebsová, his former student at the Oriental Institute and later his wife. The selection reflects Průšek's literary taste of the period and his romantic interest in poetry in relation to China. In addition to the standard first collection of Lu Xun's writings, *Nahan* (呐喊), the same volume contains a collection of Lu Xun's symbolic prose poems, *Yecao* (野草). Also the overall visual effect of the book is definitely more poetic than representative of social criticism or revolution.

Other translations represented different genres and authors, including poetry by Bai Juyi (白居易) (1958), Lin Yutang's *Moment in Beijing* (1948), and stories by Zhao Shuli (趙樹理) from the Yan'an period (1951). Průšek also wrote informative essays contextualizing the translated work in the history of Chinese literature as well as in contemporary political events, if relevant. A Czech translation of a collection of Zhao Shuli's short stories (originally published as 李有才 板話 *Li Youcai banhua*) merits special attention. It was prepared by students who had read the stories in Průšek's seminar; the status of the book as student reading material is confirmed by the number of copies in the university library.

The number of book-length translations from Chinese prepared by young sinologists, some of them still students, rose dramatically after 1950. According to incomplete data in the register of the Czech National Library, between 1951 and 1953 six or seven books of translation from the Chinese appeared annually. Later, the number dropped to three or four titles, but after 1960 it once again increased. At the same time, popular books were published by young Czech sinologists about Chinese literature, film, and especially visual art (including several informative exhibition catalogues).[45]

The translations of Chinese literature were always accompanied by informative prefaces or postscripts. Another feature of these books, symptomatic of the image of China in Czechoslovakia at that time, was their careful visual presentations. Artistic illustrations often accompanied the texts, either using original Chinese works or works by Czech artists, who often borrowed inspiration from Chinese art; a carefully designed book cover in "Chinese style" was the rule. There was also strong interest in traditional ink painting and folk woodblock prints. In contrast, new Chinese art inspired by Soviet socialist realism was rarely present, even in translations of Chinese socialist realism literature.

As already noted, interest in traditional Chinese art in Czechoslovakia went far beyond sinological circles. Admiration among Czechoslovak artists for Chinese art also underscores a book-length reportage by Czech avant-garde cartoonist and writer Adolf Hoffmeister (1902–73) who traveled to China in 1953 and spent three months visiting different places of historical importance and meeting colleagues in artistic circles.[46] Hoffmeister included in his book numerous reproductions of Chinese art, the majority of which were well-known masterpieces of traditional painting, as well as portraits of Chinese people whom he had met in person, done in his "Chinese" style. Hoffmeister's book contains detailed information about the history of the visual arts in China (without indicating his sources), introducing primarily literati painting, and traditional woodblock prints. It also discusses efforts dating back to the 1920s and the 1930s to adapt the traditional techniques and genres to modern artistic sensibilities. Accompanying this historical information, there is contemporary folk art, including photographs of the artefacts. The Chinese Communist policy of using art as propaganda is extensively presented as well, but the author seems not to see any contradiction between emphasizing the strong aesthetic appeal of Chinese works of art and the dictates of politics.

This creates a mixture of old and new, literati and peasant, and individualistic and collectivistic visions of art, which from today's perspective seem totally incompatible. For Hoffmeister, as for the Czech sinologists of the time, the embodiment of a belief in the creative continuity of traditional art in the PRC was the painter Qi Baishi (齊白石) (1864–1957), who was an idol of many art lovers in Czechoslovakia. Hoffmeister describes his art in terms of "realism" and "people's art." At the same time, in between the lines of Hoffmeister's book one can perceive a considerable distance from Soviet-style socialist realism. This leads one to question whether admiration for Chinese "people's" and "realistic" art imbued with the "national spirit" was not also a form of resistance against the Soviet cultural dogma imported to Czechoslovakia in the early 1950s.

7. Conclusion

In 1948, before the Communist takeover in China, Jaroslav Průšek and Augustin Palát translated a book-length reportage, *Journey to Red China* (English 1947; Czech 1948) by Robert Payne, an American correspondent in China. Payne had visited Yan'an in 1946 and had provided a sympathetic picture of the "liberated areas." The book must have been particularly interesting for Průšek as it combined idealized information about Communist politics with observations on literature in Yan'an, including translations of revolutionary poetry. The book, like many other books dealing with Chinese culture or presenting translations of Chinese literature published earlier in Czechoslovakia, was carefully edited and printed, using a graphic design with Chinese motifs. Poetry quoted by Payne in his book was polished by one of the best Czech poets of the time, František Halas (1901–49). Průšek provided the Czech translation of Payne's volume with a short concluding essay, commenting on recent developments in China and on the moral authority of the Chinese Communists, presenting them as practitioners of values "important in Chinese ethics throughout millennia." These values, according to Průšek, include humility, tolerance, and a sort of primordial democracy epitomized in "an old folk saying *bu qi min* [不欺民], not to cheat the people." In this essay, Průšek also writes: "In this high moral authority I see the great contribution of China to the spiritual treasure of humankind. We again have to listen to good and wise voices and, by elevating the people, bring it to goodness and true humanity."[47]

Průšek largely shared with his students the same admiration and hope that the Communist revolution in China was the ultimate realization of the ancient domestic tradition understood in terms of humanism. Such a belief made it natural for a sinologist in Czechoslovakia to welcome the Communist victory in China in 1949. Thus, after Czechoslovakia and China became close political allies in the socialist "camp" and Czechoslovakia formed an originally unexpected coalition with Stalinist ideology, the old dream of the "light coming from the East" was once more rehearsed. Among Czechoslovak intellectuals, this strange marriage of ideas and imaginations was supplemented by a modernist aesthetic sensibility inherited from members of pre-war avant-garde circles, many of whom expressed admiration for Chinese ink painting, calligraphy, or Beijing opera.[48]

This improbable mixture of ideas and aesthetic attachments is particularly well documented in the special issue of *Nový Orient* published shortly after the establishment of the PRC in 1949. Here a long apologetic article by Jaroslav Průšek on revolutions in Chinese history eventually culminating in the "victory of the Chinese people led by Mao Zedong" is accompanied without further commentary by numerous translations of Tang poetry, mostly by Du Fu and Li Bai. The Tang poetry translations are interspersed with several revolutionary poems by authors who today are largely forgotten, translated in a manner not very different from the Czech versions of the Tang masters. The translator, Bohumil Mathesius, transformed all of these works without distinction into good Czech poetry with a modernist touch.

Both the political situation and the continuing admiration for the romantic vision of Chinese culture were favorable for the shaping of the academic field of sinology actively reaching a wider public. Literary translation became a respected discipline among Czechoslovak sinologists and it has never been regarded as less important than academic research. Quite to the contrary, translation and popularization usually went hand in hand with research, mutually enriching one another.

Notes

1. In 1993 Czechoslovakia was divided into two countries—the Czech Republic and the Slovak Republic. Today, both Czech and Slovak sinologists acknowledge the Czechoslovak heritage. See the interview with Dr. Marian Gálik from Bratislava. See http://politics.ntu.edu.tw/RAEC/comm2/InterviewCZ03.pdf.

2. Prague University has a history of traditional "Oriental Studies" going back to the nineteenth century. Serious research on China-related topics began with Rudolf Dvořák (1860–1920) in the 1880s. See Olga Lomová, "Rudolf Dvořák: první český orientalista a překladatel Tao-te-ťingu" (Rudolf Dvořák: First Czech Orientalist and Translator of *Daodejing*), *Hluboká tajemnost Tao* (Deep Mystery of Dao) (Prague: CCK-ISC, 2008), pp. 7–27, and Olga Lomová, "Tao-te-ťing v proměnách času (1878–1971)" (*Daodejing* in Historical Perspective, 1878–1971), *Fragmenta Ioannea Collecta Supplementum*, No. 3 (2010), pp. 203–216. However Rudolf Dvořák did not have any direct students and the university did not recruit any scholars to teach about China after Dvořák's sudden demise.

3. Unlike the general distinction of sinology (a more classical philologically-oriented discipline) and Chinese studies (related to area studies and the

social sciences in its manner of research and teaching on China that began in the United States after World War II), in Czechoslovakia such a distinction did not exist. The discipline of sinology has always consisted of text-oriented research, but the textual interpretations and analyses could be informed, to various degrees, by structuralist or Marxist theories. Terminologically, the distinction between "sinology," and "Chinese studies" does not exist in the Czech Republic until now.

4. On the Prague School, see Leo Ou-fan Lee, ed., *The Lyrical and the Epic: Studies of Modern Chinese Literature* (Bloomington: Indiana University Press, 1980), p. 7. There has been a recent new wave of interest in the Prague School, particularly in the Chinese-speaking world. In Taiwan it is related mainly to discussions about the "Chinese lyrical tradition," similar to some ideas on Chinese lyricism expressed by Jaroslav Průšek half a century ago.

5. On Czechoslovakia's impact on the GDR, see Eva Müller, "In Commemoration of the Work of Professor Jaroslav Průšek in Berlin and Leipzig," *Acta Universiatis Carolinae, Orientalia Pragensia*, Vol. 16, No. 3 (2009), pp. 11–24. On Poland, see the interview with Professor Zbigniew Słupski on 8 March 2011. Available at http://politics.ntu.edu.tw/RAEC/comm2/InterviewCZ08.pdf (accessed 8 September 2014).

6. Průšek's essays on this issue are generally accessible in the collection by Leo Ou-fan Lee. See Leo Ou-fan Lee, "Introduction," in *The Lyrical and the Epic*; Merle Goldman, ed., *Modern Chinese Literature in the May Fourth Era* (Cambridge: Harvard University Press, 1977).

7. The result of the large collaborative project was published as Zlata Černá, et al., *Setkání a proměny: vznik moderní literatury v Asii* (Encounters and Changes: The Formation of Modern Literature in Asia) (Prague: Odeon, 1976). Zlata Černá was also one of Průšek's students in the 1950s. See the interview, available at http://politics.ntu.edu.tw/RAEC/comm2/InterviewCZ10.pdf (accessed 8 September 2014). An earlier version of the research articles collected in this book was also published in English. See Oldřich Král, *Contributions to the Study of the Rise and Development of Modern Literatures in Asia* (Prague: Oriental Institute, 1965).

8. Augustin Palát, "Jaroslav Průšek Sexagenerian," *Archiv Orientální*, No. 34 (1966), pp. 481–493.

9. See the interview with Věna Hrdličková, 29 June and 18 July 2010. Available at http://politics.ntu.edu.tw/RAEC/comm2/InterviewCZ06.pdf (accessed 8 September 2014).

10. Interview with Augustin Palát, 8, 15, and 22 June 2010. Available at http://politics.ntu.edu.tw/RAEC/comm2/InterviewCZ02.pdf (accessed 8 September 2014).

11. On the history of the Oriental Institute, see *Asian and African Studies in*

Czechoslovakia (Moscow: Nauka Publishing House, 1967). For Czechoslovak trade and diplomatic exchanges with China during the first half of the twentieth century, see Ivana Bakešová, *Legionáři v roli diplomatů: československo-čínské vztahy 1918–1949* (Legionaries as Diplomats: Czechoslovak-Chinese Relations, 1918–1949) (Prague: Filozofická fakulta UK, 2013). Interest in Czechoslovak business circles in China before World War II is attested to also by the fact that Průšek's first visit to China in the early 1930s was partly sponsored by the famous Czech shoemaking company, Bata, for which Průšek wrote the first Czech textbook on modern Chinese language (published 1938).

12. Interview with Augustin Palát, 8, 15, and 22 June 2010. Available at http://politics.ntu.edu.tw/RAEC/comm2/InterviewCZ02.pdf (accessed 8 September 2014).

13. Vlasta Mádlová and Augustin Palát, *Jaroslav Průšek: Prameny k životu a dílu zakladatele pražské sinologické školy* (Jaroslav Průšek: Sources on the Life and Work of the Founder of the Prague School of Sinology) (Prague: Masarykův ústav a Archiv AV ČR, 2011), p.14.

14. Bohumil Mathesius (1888–1952) was a Czech poet, literary critic, and translator of poetry from several European languages. He became famous for his translations of Chinese poetry, originally based on German, French, Russian, and even Latin sources. Later he began to collaborate with Jaroslav Průšek, who provided him with direct translations from the Chinese that Mathesius changed into his poetic idiom. Fascination with Chinese poetry in Czechoslovakia since the 1920s is dealt with in detail in Chapter 9 of this book.

15. It should be emphasized here that in presenting his aesthetically and ethically appealing picture of ancient China Průšek was not inventing anything totally new. He was following and further developing an earlier cultural imagination of the Czech people (and in fact of all of Central Europe, if not wider) going back at least to the late nineteenth century, when the wisdom of Confucius was first introduced to Czech audiences by Rudolf Dvořák, and again to 1920s, when the wisdom of China was represented by Laozi. See Lomová, "Tao-te-ťing v proměnách času (1878–1971)."

16. The title was inspired by a book of a Soviet poet, later to become a Nobel prize winner, Boris Pasternak, *Sestra moya, zhizn* (Life—My Sister). Thus the title also reveals Průšek's admiration for leftist avant-garde literature. The second edition was published in 1947 and an English translation, published in Prague by Karolinum in 2003, was initiated by Professor Li Yih-yuan, a noted anthropologist at the Academia Sinica and the first president of the Chiang Ching-Kuo Foundation. References in the article are to the English edition. The Chinese translation is *Zhongguo: Wo de jiemei* (中國 : 我的姊妹) (Beijing: Waiyu jiaoxue yu yanjiu chubanshe, 2005).

17. Interview with Milena Doleželová-Velingerová, 4 and 18 October 2010. Available at http://politics.ntu.edu.tw/RAEC/comm2/InterviewCZ04.pdf (accessed 8 September 2014).

18. Jaroslav Průšek, *My Sister China* (Prague: Charles University, 2003), p. 362.

19. *Nový Orient*, No. 4 (1945–46), p. 1.

20. His son Liang Hsi-huey, who became a historian after World War II, has published his memoirs, including his childhood stay in Prague (*Berlin Before the Wall: A Foreign Student's Diary with Sketches*, New York: Routledge, 1990). The book contains interesting observations on his father's life in Prague after the war and the Communist takeover, but there are also numerous inaccuracies.

21. Bakešová, *Legionáři v roli diplomatů*, 2013, p. 161.

22. Interest in Chinese art in Czechoslovakia dates back to exhibitions organized by Vojtěch Chytil in 1923. On Vojtěch Chytil (1896–1936), see Michaela Pejčochová (貝米沙), "Yige Jiekeren zai Zhongguo: Qi Dier yu Bulage guoli meishuguan de Zhongguo huihua shoucang" (A Czech in China: Vojtěch Chytil and the Collection of Chinese Painting in the National Gallery in Prague), *Yishu shoucang + sheji* (Art Collection + Design), Vol. 4, No. 55 (2012), pp. 136–141.

23. Bakešová, *Legionáři v roli diplomatů*, p. 157.

24. On the Xinhua office in Prague, see ibid.

25. In charge of the Prague branch was Wu Wentao (吳文濤); among its employees was Wu Xueqian (吳學謙), later minister of foreign affairs in the PRC.

26. In his interview, Professor Palát also remembers Chinese members of the delegation of the International Students League in Prague with whom he was already in contact before 1949.

27. Interview with Augustin Palát, 8, 15, and 22 June 2010. Available at http://politics.ntu.edu.tw/RAEC/comm2/InterviewCZ02.pdf (accessed 8 September 2014).

28. In this book Průšek expresses strong support for Mao's ideas about literature in the service of politics. Yet, at the same time, sometimes rather confusingly, he refers to aesthetic value as an important aspect of the new literature and he searches for modernity in traditional forms. He pays special attention to the relationship between the new literature written in "national forms" and medieval vernacular literature, confirming his idea of a living Chinese tradition and its continuity under communism. See his *Literatura osvobozené Číny a její lidové tradice* (Literature of Liberated China and its Popular Origins) (Prague: Nakl. ČSAV, 1953). The book was translated into German in 1955.

29. Professor Słupski is a Polish minority born in Czechoslovakia.

　　　　　　　　　　　　　　　　　　　Olga Lomová and Anna Zádrapová

30. Interview with Zbigniew Słupski. Available at http://politics.ntu.edu.tw/ RAEC/comm2/InterviewCZ08.pdf (accessed 8 September 2014).

31. The editor-in-chief of *Nový Orient* was Vincenc Lesný, a Sanskrit and Bengali scholar famous in Czechoslovakia from the pre-war years, a personal friend of Rabindranath Tagore, and also a mentor and collaborator with Průšek during the war (Průšek's translation of the *Lunyu* by Confucius was published in 1940 under his name together with that of Průšek). Practical matters were in the hands of Zdeněk Hrdlička, one of Průšek's war time students. His wife, V. Hrdličková, remembers how much effort he put into the project, managing every detail, including taking care of the paper and quality of the print—not easy tasks shortly after the war. Later, in 1960, an international version, *New Orient Bimonthly*, was published in English. The purpose of the English journal was different, it aimed at providing information about the new results of research on Asia and Africa, both in Czechoslovakia and abroad.

32. Editorial, "Našim čtenářům" (To Our Readers), *Nový Orient*, No. 1 (1945–46), p. 1.

33. Poet and translator Bohumil Mathesius was its vice president.

34. Jaroslav Průšek, "Hodnoty čínské kultury" (The Values of Chinese Culture), *Nový Orient*, No. 5–6 (1945–46), pp. 14–16.

35. Ludvík Kuba (1863–1956) published his own book about Chinese art in 1946. See Ludvík Kuba, *Moje Čína* (My China) (Prague: private print, 1946). Emil Filla (1882–1953), who in his last years created a number of paintings in "Chinese" style, experimenting with techniques and composition studied from Chinese paintings, wrote a book on landscape painting in which he also discusses extensively the Chinese tradition (published posthumously in the book *Jan van Goyen, úvahy o krajinářství* (Jan van Goyen: Reflections on Landscape Painting) (Prague: SNKLHU, 1959).

36. A book-size anthology of Great Leap Forward poetry was published in 1960, already after the split with the USSR, without critical reflection on the political context. *Na zemi vyšlo plno lamp* (Many Lamps Raising from the Earth), Prague: SNKLHU, 1960. Translated by a sinologist (Marta Ryšavá) in collaboration with a poet (Ladislav Fikar), with a preface by Chinese "peasant poet" Wang Laojiu 王老九, as well as an essay on Chinese poetry by Jaroslav Průšek.

37. Mao Ce-tung, *Osmnáct básní na staré nápěvy* (Eighteen Poems to Ancient Tunes) (Prague: Československý spisovatel, 1958).

38. *Shafei nüshi de riji* (沙菲女士的日記), translated by Dana Kalvodová, was published in book form in 1955.

39. Jaroslav Průšek, "Strukturální přesuny na Dálném východě" (Structural Changes in the Far East), *Nový Orient*, Nos. 1–3 (1945–46).

40. Mme. Tseng, "Život dnešní čínské ženy" (The Life of Modern Chinese Women), *Nový Orient*, No. 4 (1945–46), p. 1.

41. Mme. Tseng, "Poválečné problémy čínské ženy" (Problems for Chinese Women after the War), *Nový Orient*, Nos. 8–9 (1945–46), p. 1. We are not able to identify the speaker.

42. Anna Louise Strong (1885–1970) was an American journalist and social activist. In the 1920s and 1930s she wrote sympathetically about the Soviet Union where she had lived for some time before 1936. She visited China several times after the 1920s, eventually settling there in 1958 as one of China's prominent "foreign friends." After 1949 she published extensively in support of Communist China.

43. Jaroslav Průšek, "Co nového v Číně vládní i rudé? Rozhovor s Anne Louise Strongovou" (What is new in China, Republican, and Red? Interview with Anne Louise Strong), *Nový Orient*, Nos. 4–5 (1947–48), p. 109.

44. Other translations could also be occasionally found on the pages of Czechoslovak literary journals of the period. For example, in celebration of the tenth anniversary of the PRC, *Světová literatura* (World Literature) published a special issue dedicated to modern Chinese literature.

45. Another source of information for the wider public consisted of travel memoirs by members of Czechoslovak delegations, political as well as cultural that toured China from 1952 to 1953. These usually also contained excursions into Chinese history and traditional culture based on information provided by or in consultation with Czech sinologists. In 1951–54 thirteen such books were published, as well as several similar titles translated from German and Russian.

46. Adolf Hoffmeister, *Kuo-chua: Cestopisná reportáž o čínském malířství* (*Guohua*: A Traveler's Report about Chinese Painting) (Prague: SNKLHU, 1954).

47. Jaroslav Průšek, "Na okraj Payneho Cesty do Rudé Číny" (Some Remarks on Payne's *Journey to Red China*), in Robert Payne, *Cesta do Rudé Číny* (Journey to Red China), translated by Jaroslav Průšek and Augustin Palát (Prague: Družstevní práce, 1948), pp. 207, 208.

48. Also at this time a unique collection of twentieth-century Chinese art was built up in the National Gallery. For details, see Michaela Pejčochová, "The Formation of the Collection of 20th-Century Chinese Painting in the National Gallery in Prague: Friendly Relations with Faraway China in the 1950s and Early 1960s," *Arts Asiatiques*, No. 67 (2012), pp. 98–106, and by the same author, *Masters of the 20th-Century Chinese Ink Painting from the Collections of the National Gallery in Prague* (Prague: National Gallery in Prague, 2008).

Chapter 2

Linguistic Choices for the Identity of "China" in the Discourse of Czech Sinologists

Melissa Shih-hui Lin

1. Introduction

Language plays an important role in the creation and maintenance of social and political ideologies, and ideological positions are reflected in discourse through such linguistic choices.[1] This chapter, based on linguistic choices in nine interviews with Czech sinologists, investigates the process of the creation of ideology and especially the formation of the identity of "China."

For the most part, these nine Czech sinologists began their sinological studies in the 1950s. At that time, sinology in Czechoslovakia was beginning to flourish under the leadership of Professor Jaroslav Průšek (1906–1980). However, Průšek was not the first Czech interested in China. In the nineteenth century, Rudolf Dvořák (1860–1920), professor of Oriental Languages at Charles University in Prague, was the first Czech scholar to become involved in studies about China. He was a translator of many languages. Chinese was only one of his many interests, and therefore he did not specialize too deeply in the field of sinology.[2] Nevertheless, his popular works about China were widely recognized by the general public. But after Průšek, there was no one to continue his studies. At the beginning of the 1920s, Bohumil Mathesius (1888–1952) began to translate Chinese poetry, but only via third languages. At that time, his translations did have some influence on those interested in China. However, true systematic research about China did not begin in Czechoslovakia until after World War II. During the 1950s, Průšek at Charles University in Prague, and later at the Oriental Institute of the Academy of Sciences of the Czech Republic, participated in the emergence of the Prague School of Sinology. There are still some important sinologists who are very active today who began their work at the Prague School. In 2010 and 2011, Olga Lomová and her student Anna Zádrapová from Charles University in Prague interviewed nine first-generation Czech sinologists.

This chapter will examine the language of the respective interviewees. This investigation of the intellectual history of China studies in Czechoslovakia is based on how the mutual constitution of sinology, sinologists, and their sinic world proceeded through individual career paths.[3] It is interesting, and also important, to discuss the content of the interviews as well as what the term "China" meant to each individual interviewee. The results of the interviews will be used to construct the image of "China" in the field of sinology in this post-socialist community.

2. Background

In 1937, Průšek returned to Czechoslovakia from travels in China and Japan and began to teach about China. Even during the Nazi occupation (1939–1945), he continued to offer evening classes, which served as a source of spiritual fulfillment for his followers during the difficult war years. In 1947, Průšek was appointed head of the Department of Far Eastern Studies at Charles University. The teaching staff consisted mainly of students who had taken his courses during the wartime years, including Augustin Palát, Věnceslava Hrdličková, and Berta Krebsová, as well as more recent graduates, such as Oldřich Král. For this chapter, both Palát and Hrdličková were interviewed. The other interviewees, including Zlata Černá, Milena Velingerová, Marián Gálik, Zdenka Heřmanová, and Josef Kolmaš, were students of Průšek after the war and after the Communist takeover in 1948.

In April 1949, even before the PRC was established, a Chinese delegation led by Guo Moruo visited Prague. Xu Beihong was also a member of this delegation. Their original destination was Paris where a peace congress was taking place, but because they were not given visas, they ended up staying in Prague for two or three weeks. Their stay unintentionally encouraged students in Prague who were involved in China studies at that time. Thereafter, in the 1950s, this first generation of followers of Průšek played key roles in China studies in Czechoslovakia, especially in the field of modern Chinese literary studies, and they later came to be recognized as members of the "Prague School of Sinology."

According to Lomová and Zádrapová,[4] the basic contributions of the Prague School of Sinology can be summarized as collecting and presenting rarely studied primary sources, such as those on modern Chinese literature, popular theatre, storytelling, and philosophy during the Han dynasty, and combining these presentations with innovative methodological approaches, including structuralism, semiotics, and Marxist theory.

However, in the 1960s, the interactions and cooperation between Czechoslovakia and China, including academic and student exchanges, were interrupted due to the changed political environment. In Czechoslovakia, there was a period of liberalization, but, at the same time, China was suffering from the turmoil of the Cultural Revolution. Beginning in the mid-1970s, some reforms were launched in China, but the initial normalization movement actually began in Czechoslovakia. Consequently, the 1950s was a period when Czechoslovakia and China had the most frequent contacts, and it was also a period when our interviewees began their China studies. In 1968, the attack by the Soviet army, i.e., the Prague Spring, adversely affected Sino-Czech relations and had a negative influence on sinological studies in Czechoslovakia. Over the course of the following twenty years, Czech sinology became increasingly isolated from the outside world. During that period, most sinologists were forced to give up their jobs, and some of them stopped conducting research in their fields of interest. For example, at that time Heřmanová was forced to write reports about China for the Czech government and had to translate Chinese daily newspapers and the Constitution of the People's Republic of China, tasks that were irrelevant to her true interest in Chinese literature. However, sinologists at that time still tried their best to continue their own research in private. For example, Heřmanová and Danuška Heroldová completed nine volumes of Czech-Chinese dictionaries on a very limited budget between 1974 and 1984.

After the Velvet Revolution in 1989, there was a dramatic change in the Czech social and political systems. At the same time, the global position of China was rising. Interactions between Czech and China became more active, leading to growing progress in the field of Czech sinology. Although the interviewees for this chapter, having graduated in the 1950s, were by this time growing old and in some cases had already died, their influence on Czech sinology was still very strong. Some of the interviewees believe that Průšek had intended to establish the various basic disciplines of sinology via each of his students. This implies that Průšek chose his students based on their disciplines. Although not all of the interviewees agree with this conclusion, Průšek's former students together have responsibility today for different areas of Chinese culture. The current state Czech sinological studies appear to be a systematic network created by Průšek's students and his followers.

In this chapter, the nine Czech sinologists interviewed by Olga Lomová and her student Anna Zádrapová from 2010 to 2011 answered the following question: "How did you start to study sinology?" Based on their answers, we found that the Czech sinologists interpreted the term "China" in many different ways. The main focus of the chapter is a presentation of the lexical or textual devices employed by the interviewees. An investigation into the meaning of "China" in the minds of these sinologists provides some new insights about the Prague School of Sinology.

3. Methodology

This chapter is based on interviews with nine Czech sinologists who began their China studies during the 1950s. The interviews were conducted by current Czech sinologists. Since the materials that are analyzed in this chapter were not collected by the author, we examine the interviews as a whole because the interviewer-interviewees were involved in somewhat different social activities during their respective interviews. The interviewer and interviewees shared many situated meanings and cultural models. An interview is akin to a collaborative discussion, in which the two parties enact their mutual affiliation through language.[5]

An interview is one form of larger meaningful units for discourse analysis, dealing with how the choice of articles, pronouns, and tenses affects the structure of the discourse, the relationship between utterances in the discourse, and the moves made by the speakers to introduce a new topic, change the topic, or assert a greater role in the relationship with the other participants.[6] Analysts have suggested that discourse analysis is an interpretive activity because its purpose is to help the receivers of the message understand the meaning of the text and the producers of the message. However, in this chapter the author will follow the argument based on Halliday and Hasan's functional discourse analysis:[7] the purpose of discourse analysis is explanation not interpretation; its purpose is to explain why the discourse expresses the meaning. In other words, the purpose of "interpretation" is to understand the meaning of the discourse, but the purpose of "explanation" is to clarify how the discourse expresses its meaning. That is to say, the purpose of functional discourse analysis is to evaluate the discourse. Before an evaluation, discourse analysis must first study the discourse from the perspective of "what is the meaning of the discourse?", "how does the discourse express the meaning?", "why does the discourse express the meaning?" and so on. In all, functional discourse analysis is an explanatory activity to evaluate the discourse.

In this chapter, the author will examine the interview materials within the scope of critical discourse analysis. The goal of the analysis is not only to explain and evaluate the discourse in the interviews, but also to focus on the relationship between some specific language units and the process of ideology formation. Discourse reproduces existing social relations and structure, and aspects of the discourse have ideological significance.[8] In past decades, critical linguistics and critical discourse analysis have made significant contributions to illuminating the relationship between language and ideology.[9] In critical discourse analysis, Fairclough follows systematic linguistics[10] to assume that language in a text simultaneously functions ideationally in the representation of experience and the world, interpersonally in constituting social interactions among the participants in the discourse, and textually by tying together parts of a text into a coherent whole and tying the texts to situational contexts.[11] In this chapter, the critical discourse analysis will focus on how sinologists talk about and evaluate "China" to disclose the relationship between lexical or textual devices in the choice of the term "China" and how they try to construct the ideology of "China" in their discourse.

On the one hand, discourse about "China" connects intimate details of the personal experience to broader social relations, and, on the other hand, it provides useful social insights into social processes and events based on what these sinologists have to say about their personal experiences. The larger social context of what people have to say is also important to analyze the social discourse and the politics that are included in an interpretation of ideological construction.[12]

4. Analysis and Discussion

According to Shih,[13] an analysis of choice is important because it may reconstitute our knowledge to incorporate both scientific and judgmental components. Moreover, it may reveal an emotionally embedded history of knowledge. In this chapter, the linguistic choice of the term "China" in the discourse of Czech sinologists reveals their ideas about "China"; an analysis of these linguistic choices will help reconstitute our own knowledge about "China." In the following, we will investigate these linguistic choices.

An investigation of the linguistic choices for the term "China" is based on "cohesion." Cohesion is represented by the grammatical and lexical links within a text or a sentence that holds the text together and gives it meaning.[14] Linguistically, there are two main types of cohesion: grammatical, referring to the structural content, and lexical, referring to the language content of the piece. Due to the grammatical or lexical cohesion, the choice of words for one specific term can be interpreted as a whole. It provides clues for interpreting events or experiences. That is to say, lexical items not only construct particular ideological representations of experiences or events but also have expressive value that imply the producer's positive or negative evaluations of actions, participants, or events.[15]

Based on lexical or grammatical cohesion, this chapter will present some examples of how Czech sinologists choose certain terms when they refer to China. The choices of linguistic forms in the interviews reflect the ideological positions of "their China." Some linguistic devices are employed to emphasize either a positive value or a negative value. The analysis in this chapter will focus on nouns, noun phrases, and verbal phrases/clauses.

Nouns and noun phrases:

(1) China was *the last thing for me.*[16]
(2) China is *a country with a great future.*[17]
(3) When we read Mathesius, we asked ourselves: what is this Chinese language like, *such beautiful poetry.*[18]
(4) What do I want to do with Chinese. ... I said I wanted to *do something special.*[19]

In these examples, the noun phrases *"the last thing for me," "a country with a great future," "such beautiful poetry,"* and *"something special"* are all positive expressions for the term "China." These linguistic items not only construct particular ideological representations of the experience or events but also have expressive value to imply the producer's positive evaluation. In example (1), Gálik is recalling when he first began to study Chinese, and in examples (2) and (3), Hrdličková is referring to her and her husband's first impressions of China. In example (4) Velingerová is describing the reason she intended to study Chinese.

There is yet another example that conveys a very positive evaluation of "China."

In the following example: Heřmanová explains her motivation for working on Chinese translation:

(5) People seemed to be hungry for *exotic things*, China was *admired.*[20]

In example (5), the connotation of the noun phrase *"exotic things"* does not necessarily imply something absolutely positive or absolutely negative; however, due to the addition of the term *"admired,"* it is understood that the term, *"exotic things"* definitely is meant to convey a positive evaluation. Example (6) below provides an additional example:

(6) As I said, the study of China is *a matter for enthusiasts*; at that time, they were eager to know all about China, *a country that was so different.*[21]

In example (6), Palát is describing the Chinese studies situation in the 1960s. He refers to the lack of attention to China studies at that time.

For example, those interested in the romance languages studied them in high school and learned about the related histories, cultures, and literature. Study of the romance languages was required so there was no choice but to study them. This was especially the case in Austria, Germany, and England. In contrast, at the time there was only one page devoted to China in high school textbooks. So, in example (6), Palát emphasizes the study of China was "*a matter for enthusiasts,*" people who were eager to learn about a "*country so different.*" The evaluation of these noun phrases referring to the term "China" is quite positive. Only such a positive evaluation would motivate people to devote themselves to such a "*different*" subject.

There are also examples revealing a neutral evaluation based on an unclear expression. In example (7), Slupski expresses his opinion about teaching sinology:

> (7) Palát told me sinology ought to follow Průšek's studies: history, philosophy, and literature—those three main subjects. My personal opinion is slightly different: I would add the comparative aspect to both sinology and its teaching. People felt China was *an original, peculiar civilization.* But if you talked about Chinese culture, you needed a comparative background to make the difference obvious. People couldn't discover it, they didn't care, and they didn't think about it. Students had to be directed to look for the differences.[22]

In example (7), although the connotation of the term "*peculiar*" is more negative, it becomes neutral because of the adjective "*original.*" In this example, the evaluation of "China" is neutral and somewhat unclear.

There are also examples in the interviews that reveal a negative evaluation about "China." For example, when Dřínek mentions his impression of China in example (8), he notes:

> (8) Many *contradictions, backwardness,* but, on the other hand, *educated intelligence.*[23]

In example (8), nouns with negative expressions such as "*contradictions*" and "backwardness" are employed, but at the same time "*educated intelligence*"—a positive expression—is also employed, which conveys a neutral connotation, but with some contradictions, as Dřínek himself notes in the example. This "contradiction" also appears in other examples, as revealed in the following examples.

Verbal phrases/clauses

In the interviews there are also some verbal phrases/clauses used to describe the term "China." In example (9), Velingerová was asked about her first impression of China and her later impression after she became more involved in China studies.

> (9) Initially I was under the influence of Professor Průšek—*My Sister China.* For me China *was an idealized country, an absolutely fantastic country that I had to visit.* The second phase came after I saw China—*I discovered it wasn't so simple.*[24]

In the above example, Velingerová first uses *"an idealized country for me, an absolutely fantastic country that I had to visit"* to describe her first impression of China. But later she refers to her puzzlement, noting her uncertainty about her first impression: *"I discovered it wasn't so simple."* Although there is no "contradiction" in this example, still there is a sense of hesitancy and a lack of clarity in her later impression.

In examples (10) and (11), interviewee Gálik mentions his first and later impressions of China. His attitude went from being negative to becoming more positive. In example (10), Gálik was asked about his strongest impression of China. He replied by referring to his first arrival at Beijing airport in the late 1950s.

> (10) When I was in the aircraft above Beijing, I saw *corn and sorghum fields everywhere, quite different from what one sees today,* and after I entered the university, I was surprised that *nothing had been prepared, even though they had been informed of our arrival. …* I was surprised by the tiny airport. *The sole bellboy was sitting in a corner. I saw two or three buildings but that was all. I didn't get anything to eat on that first day.* Later, I had some snacks. When I walked outside the university gates, there was nothing but open space. Today the area between Beijing University and Qinghua University is all built up. At

that time, all I could see were the naked bottoms of the young Chinese. I was also surprised by their buggies. The weather was nice at that time, but later I found out they were naked in the winter as well. I couldn't really understand it.[25]

Gálik's description of his first arrival in China is not very positive: "*nothing was prepared even though they were informed of our arrival,*" "*I didn't get anything to eat on that the first day,*" and so on. In example (11), Gálik continues to describe his different images of "China" when he was 11 and 16 years old.

> (11) When I was 11, *the picture of China in my mind was that of opium smokers. The image was so terrible. I can still visualize it.* I had read various things in books: *Chinese are stingy and arrogant; they offer you something and they expect you to refuse it. So the image of China that I had in my mind wasn't very nice at all.* I can recall Tiananmen in 1949. *It was very interesting for me; what a change!* However, *I had received a Catholic education, so Mao Zedong was not my idol. But when I had the chance to study Chinese and saw that the perspective of China was good in this subject, I accepted it.*[26]

In example (11), Gálik uses the phrases "*the picture ... was one of opium smokers,*" "*The image was so terrible*" and "*Chinese are stingy and arrogant; they offer you something and they expect you to refuse it*" to describe his first negative impression of China when he was 11 years old. He says "*It was very interesting for me; what a change!*" to describe the positive change in his image of China when he was 16 years old, that is, after he had begun his China studies. At the same time, he notes that he did not agree with everything in China, he states: "*However, I had received a Catholic education, so Mao Zedong was not my idol.*" But his choice to study Chinese was based on a rational consideration: "*When I had the chance to study Chinese and saw that the perspective of China was good in this subject, I accepted it.*" From examples (10) and (11), it seems that Gálik's first impression of China was quite negative, but his attitude later became much more positive.

Another interviewee, Kolmaš, who studied Chinese as well as Tibetan in the 1950s, describes his impression of China as follows in example (12):

(12) China was *THAT* country, *you know*.[27]

In example (12), "*THAT*" is used as an intensive word and "*you know*" can be considered a discourse marker to emphasize the truth of the preceding clause. Kolmaš mentions this when he was referring to his translation work. In the interview, like Švarný, he does not employ any concrete lexical items to describe the term China. Example (12) reveals Kolmaš's complicated feelings and ambivalent evaluation of China.

The following example (13) explains the reason why several of the interviewees had ambiguous evaluations of "China."

(13) You know, the situation in the 1960s was very special. On the one hand, there was political pressure with respect to the negative information about China, but, on the other hand, *the attitudes of sinologists toward events in China were negative* as well. Our political positions were consistent with the political forces. But even so, *no one wanted to write negative things about China, even though we all knew there was nothing positive to say about the Chinese revolution. … People held back, they didn't want to become involved.*[28]

In example (13), Slupski attempts to describe the contradictions in the 1960s. He notes that although "*the attitudes of sinologists toward events in China were negative,*" "*no one wanted to write negative things about China.*" He concludes, "*People held back, they didn't want to become involved.*" He notes that the main reason was "*political pressure.*" It can be assumed that the ambivalent evaluations of the term "China" in example (12) are also related to the political situation at the time. The change in the evaluation may also reflect the political changes. The following table attempts to clearly explain these assumptions.

The above examples are arranged in Table 1 based on the interviewees' expressions of the term "China" (with the exception of Švarný because he does not describe the term "China" in his interview). In the table, "P" is positive, "N" is negative, and "?" indicates an ambiguous or ambivalent evaluation or a contradiction. "P→?" refers to a change in the evaluation from positive to unclear or neutral, and "N→P" indicates an initial negative evaluation that then changes to positive. These evaluations are based on extracts from the nine interviews and are not targeted at any particular individual.

Table 1: Responses of Interviewees

Interviewees / Examples	Gálik	Hrdličková	Velingerová	Heřmanová	Palát	Slupski	Dřínek	Kolmaš	Švarný
(1)	P								
(2)		P							
(3)		P							
(4)			P						
(5)				P					
(6)					P				
(7)						?			
(8)							?		
(9)			P→?						
(10)	N								
(11)	N→P								
(12)								?	
(13)						?			

Table 1 shows that Hrdličková, Palát, and Heřmanová chose linguistic items to indicate their positive evaluations of the term "China." In the interviews with Gálik and Velingerová, the evaluation of the term "China" changes over time. Slupski, Dřínek, and Kolmaš chose linguistic items to convey an ambiguous or contradictory evaluation. In the first group, Hrdličková and Palát were students of Průšek during the war in the 1940s and they began their studies of China much earlier than the others; Heřmanová was also a student of Průšek but this was after the war, i.e., after the Communist takeover in 1948. She was in China from 1953 to 1958, which was earlier than the others. Based on the nine interviews, the sinologists who had earlier contacts with China studies expressed more positive evaluations of the term "China." This may be due to the influence of the Communist regime at the time. Students who were more influenced by the Communist regime were more likely to make linguistic choices to express ambiguous or contradictory terms to refer to China.

It should also be noted that the interviewees repeatedly referred to Jaroslav Průšek. Palát mentions Průšek 97 times, Gálik 77 times, Kolmaš 59 times, Slupski 47 times, Velingerová 43 times, Hrdličková 31 times, Švarný 13 times, and Heřmanová 11 times. This may be indicative of the importance of Průšek in their sinological career paths. As Lomová and Zádrapová noted in 2012, "We all acknowledged that Průšek's publications and personal example were a decisive factor for studying Chinese language and sinology."

5. Conclusion

This chapter investigates how ideological positions regarding "China" are reflected through the choice of lexical or textual devices by Czech sinologists who studied during the 1950s. The discussion provides clues for interpreting events and experiences during the period of the emergence of the Prague School of Sinology.

According to the analysis and discussion in this chapter, some linguistic devices regarding the term "China" are employed to emphasize a positive attitude, and some are employed to demonstrate an ambiguous, or even contradictory, evaluation of China. It can be concluded that the differing evaluations are dependent on when the interviewees began their studies of China. Most importantly, the evaluations were influenced by the political climate at the time. Nevertheless, additional in-depth interviews and more relevant reference materials are necessary to support these conclusions.

Notes

1. R. Fowler and B. Hodge, "Critical Linguistics," in *Language and Control*, edited by R. Fowler et al. (London: Routledge and Kegan Paul, 1979), pp. 185–213.
2. European Association of Chinese Studies, *Survey, No.5: Czech, Hungarian, Slovakian, Slovenian Sinology* (1996).
3. Chih-yu Shih, "Comparative Intellectual History of Chinese Studies: Micro Identity and Macro Civilization," *Asian Research Trend New Series*, No. 7 (Tokyo, 2012).
4. Olga Lomová and Anna Zádrapová, "'The Songs of Ancient China': Myth of 'The Other' Appropriated by an Emerging Sinology." Paper presented at the International Conference on New Perspectives in East Asian Studies, Taipei, 2012.
5. James Paul Gee, *An Introduction to Discourse Analysis: Theory and Method* (London: Routledge, 1999).
6. M.A.K. Halliday and Hasan Ruqaiya, *Language, Context and Text: A Social Semiotic Perspective* (Geelong, Vic.: Deakin University Press, 1985).
7. M.A.K. Halliday and Hasan Ruqaiya, *Cohesion in English* (London: Longman, 1976).
8. Robert Hodge and Gunther Kress, *Language as Ideology* (2nd ed.; London: Routledge, 1993).
9. Norman Fairclough, *Critical Discourse Analysis: The Critical Study of Language* (London: Longman, 1995); Roger Fowler, *Language in the*

News: Discourse and Ideology in the Press (London: Routledge, 1991); Teun A. van Dijk, *News as Discourse* (Hillside, NJ: Erlbaum Associates, 1988); Teun A. van Dijk, *Racism and the Press* (London: Routledge, 1991).

10. M.A.K. Halliday, *Language as Social Semiotic: The Social Interpretation of Language and Meaning* (Baltimore: University Park Press, 1978).

11. Fairclough, *Critical Discourse Analysis.*

12. Janine L. Wiles, Mark W. Rosenberg, and Robin A. Kearns, "Narrative Analysis as a Strategy for Understanding Interview Talk," *Area*, Vol. 37, No. 1 (2005), pp. 89–99.

13. Shih, "Comparative Intellectual History of Chinese Studies."

14. Halliday and Ruqaiya, *Cohesion in English.*

15. Sai-hua Kuo, "Is There Only One China? Analyzing the Rhetoric of Chinese Nationalism in a Newspaper Article," *Journal of Asian Pacific Communication*, Vol. 11, No. 2 (2002), pp. 287–303.

16. Marián Gálik, interviewed by Olga Lomová and Anna Zádrapová, 2011.

17. Věnceslava Hrdličková, interviewed by Olga Lomová and Anna Zádrapová, 2010.

18. Ibid.

19. Milena Velingerová, interviewed by Olga Lomová and Anna Zádrapová, 2010.

20. Zdenka Heřmanová, interviewed by Olga Lomová and Anna Zádrapová, 2010.

21. Augustin Palát, interviewed by Olga Lomová and Anna Zádrapová, 2010.

22. Zbygniew Slupski, interviewed by Olga Lomová and Anna Zádrapová, 2011.

23. Vladislav Dřínek, interviewed by Olga Lomová and Anna Zádrapová, 2011.

24. Milena Velingerová, interviewed by Olga Lomová and Anna Zádrapová, 2010.

25. Marián Gálik, interviewed by Olga Lomová and Anna Zádrapová, 2011.

26. Ibid.

27. Josef Kolmaš, interviewed by Olga Lomová and Anna Zádrapová, 2011.

28. Zbygniew Slupski, interviewed by Olga Lomová and Anna Zádrapová, 2011.

Chapter 3

Surging between China and Russia: Legacies, Politics, and Turns of Sinology in Contemporary Mongolia

Enkhchimeg Baatarkhuyag and Chih-yu Shih

1. Sinology as Humanities and National Historiography

Sinology in Mongolia has a long tradition. Embedded in the exotic image of an agricultural civilization, it began as early as the thirteenth century with fascination about the legends and stories in the Chinese classics. This explains why literary studies and its foundation in language skills have been essential to Mongolian sinology. Added to this civilizational curiosity toward different ways of life is the quest for an exclusively Mongolian historiography in modern times. Contemporary Mongolian historians rely on various transnational sources, among which Chinese-language documents are primary, to construct a recorded national past. The significance of language skills looms even larger under these modern conditions.

As in all other socialist countries, however, the Soviet Union once exerted a great influence on Mongolian studies of China in terms of both methodology and subject for at least three decades. Post-socialist sinology has continued under the academic leadership of those trained during the Soviet period. Nevertheless, the reconnection with Chinese-language training in both China and Taiwan that has revived research on Chinese literature and historiography is more than apparent. The reconnection also explains the extension of the familiar style of research embedded in historical documents and records in contemporary social and political research.

Language-oriented sinology separates Mongolian scholarship from the North American preoccupation with scientific theorization. It parallels the humanistic sensibilities of the continental tradition. In the latter tradition, translation is the key to sinology. However, secular interests in Chinese novels and literature distinguish Mongolian sinology from the religious and philosophical interests that originated in the Church tradition. Furthermore, European scholars do not need to excavate historical accounts in the Chinese documents to cross-check or verify their own national path. Both features—civilizational exotics and national historiography—to a large extent explain why the impacts of the Soviet transformation quickly faded after the end of its political control. Although a political legacy of distrust or a dislike of China may remain among practitioners, the humanistic shift in sinology carried out by the current generation incorporates the legacy of those scholars trained in China in the 1950s.

The following discussion records this long tradition of Mongolian sinology, attending in particular to its historical periodization since the establishment of the Mongolian Republic in 1911 through the establishment of the People's Republic of China in 1949, the Sino-Soviet rift in the 1960s, the Cultural Revolution and the end of the Soviet bloc in 1990, and the recombination of earlier legacies in contemporary scholarship after democratization in the early 1990s. It argues that the current return to sinology has reconnected the current curriculum to a stress on the humanities and the past language training. The latter has arisen on a much greater scale. It affects the leading institutes and their evolution, the political and academic activities in sinology, and the individualized intellectual histories of several selected scholars.

2. A Brief Note on the Intellectual History of Sinology

The Mongolian tradition of sinology is largely unnoticed among contemporary Chinese academics. An emerging Sino-centric impression, well-represented by Chinese journalist Huo Wen, points to the alleged fears in the minds of contemporary Mongolian people of the possibility that China will someday reclaim sovereignty over Mongolia after reunification with Taiwan.[1] According to this view, the historical experiences of

Mongols as part of Chinese pre-modern history during both the Yuan and Qing dynasties make them ambivalent toward China. Moreover, the same view is underscored in the dramatic reversal in the economic rankings of Mongolia and China in the new century, also causing uneasiness among Mongolian people.

Apart from the Sino-centrism, however, a typical Mongolian historiography whose scope includes the entirety of the Eurasian continent cannot conceptualize China's (regional) rise as an intellectual threat to the nomadic, transcontinental identity of Mongolia. Displeasure about Chinese historiography that habitually treats the Mongolian past as part of Chinese civilization seems to be prevalent among Mongolian scholars. However, this is by no means based on fear. On the contrary, civilizational curiosity toward Chinese literature is intrinsically based on an estranged position, rendering the conspired absorption of Mongolia by China a bizarre claim that likely only fits the contemporary self-image of a rising China. The nascent revival of a greater Mongolian identity in Chinese Inner Mongolia is a noteworthy phenomenon. Anxiety toward the loss of identity, incurred by the enhanced contacts with a rising China, is much less true of Mongolia than it is of China's East and Southeast Asian neighbors.

Although contacts between the nomads and the Chinese during the Qin dynasty might not have yielded much empirical research, the breeding of Mongolian sinologists can be documented at least as far back as 1261 when Kublai Khan (1215–94) established the Yuan dynasty. Kublai Khan established the Hanlin Academy of National History to recruit 453 Mongolian scholars to translate the Chinese classics. The Imperial Academy began to train the children of the nobility in Chinese language and the Confucian classics. Their readings contained sophisticated historiographical accounts, such as *Zizhi tongjian* (The Comprehensive Mirror in Aid of Governing).[2] Additionally, translated literature in other languages, such as Arabic, Uygur, and Sanskrit, were likewise read during the same period. According to Chapters 26 and 137 of *Yuanshi* (The History of the Yuan), Tsagaan, Alintumur, Chuluundash, and Boldtumur were scholars assigned to translate the classics.

Contemporary sinologists are able to retrieve Boldtumur Chinsan's well-known 1307 work, *Achlalt nom*, which translated Confucius' words of wisdom. The original copy is currently held in the Palace Museum of

Beijing.[3] According to Ya Ganbaatar, who specializes in the ancient Mongolian style of Chinese translation, ancient translations into Mongolian were carried out via the Phags-pa phonetic alphabet developed by national adviser Phags-pa so the Yuan Mongols could understand Chinese words.[4] The Phags-pa phonetic alphabet likewise played an important role in introducing Buddhism to the Mongolian population because it borrowed much from the Tibetan. However, the phonetic system eventually disappeared due to difficulties in mastering it and its failure to spread. Nevertheless, interest in translation continued despite the overthrow of the Yuan dynasty.

During the seventeenth and eighteenth centuries, for example, sinologists satisfied Mongolian readers with a series of well-known Chinese classic novels, in addition to the important official histories. These included *Water Margin, Dream of the Red Chamber, Romance of the Three Kingdoms, Journey to the West, The Plum in the Golden Vase*, and *Spectacles in Ancient and Modern Times*. The chanting prose of the Tang dynasty was also translated. Philosophy attracted sinologists of all generations as well. During the same period, for example, the Confucian Four Books and Five Classics were again translated, this time from Chinese directly without the Phags-pa medium. Many narratives have more than one version since South and North Buryatia each has its own version, indicating the popularity of Chinese novels. During the early twentieth century, Dandaa (initially Ch. Demchigdorj, 1863–1932) spent six years completing the translation of *Yuanshi* in 1923. The Mongolian version of his translation consists of a total of 210 volumes. There are two Mongolian-language copies in the National Museum of Mongolia.[5]

Translation has been the spirit of Mongolian sinology throughout history. This is why literature is particularly germane to contemporary Mongolian understandings of China. Ya Ganbaatar summarizes three routes by which Chinese literature has been able to spread extensively in Mongolia.[6] Translation is the first route. Dramaturgy is the second route. The third route is narration. Accordingly, sinology exists in three discursive texts. These include the Confucian texts, classic novels, and dictionaries. According to Ya Ganbaatar's collection, there are at least 80 Chinese classic novels and 233 other works of literature currently available in Mongolian. There are Mongolian professional narrators who recite translated Chinese classical literature for the general public. As early as 1922, Khuree (Ulaanbaatar today) hosted the play *Journey to the West*.[7]

3. Political Intervention after 1949: The Sino-Soviet Conflict and the Cultural Revolution

Politics helped to boost the study of Chinese in Mongolia during the early days of the People's Republic of China. Ulaanbaatar offered diplomatic recognition to the PRC five days after its establishment on 1 October 1949. In 1952, the two sides signed an Economic and Cultural Cooperation Agreement, thereafter sending the first group of three Mongolian students, Chuluun Dalai, Gurbazar, and Bandikhuu, to Beijing for study. A second group of another three students, Dashpuntsag, Agvaansuren, and Rentsentsoo. Nyamaasuren was dispatched to Peking Univiersity in the following year. In 1956, a third group of four students, Luvsanvandan Manlajav, Choi Luvsanjav, G. Amiili, and M. Gombosuren, went to China. Later, the level of study reached the doctoral degree. The first cohort included Lhamsuren. Jamsran, Gunj. Sukhbaatar, Nyambuu Ishjamts, Elchinbuu Chimedtseren, and Jugdernamjil, all of whom became leading sinological scholars in either history or language in their subsequent careers. In 1957 Mongolian National University admitted fourteen students and began to offer Chinese. U. Gursed, together with the Chinese teachers recruited from China, taught the beginning classes. Simultaneously, U. Gursed published *Chinese-Mongolian Conversation and a Chinese-Mongolian Dictionary*. Younger teachers who had returned from China joined the faculty in 1958 to offer further courses in translation, literature, and history. Before it ceased operations in 1964 due to political reasons, 45 students had already completed the entire curriculum.

The flow of students to China ended due to the rising confrontation between Beijing and Moscow in the 1960s. Soviet troops were posted in Mongolia to prepare for a possible confrontation with China and exchanges with China were prohibited. The Chinese teachers in Mongolia were forced to return home. Out of necessity, the government arranged new positions for Mongolian teachers of Chinese. For example, L. Manlajav was shifted to the Mongolian Academy of Sciences. Ch. Dalai and R. Nyamaasuren were dispatched to the Mongolian embassy in China. Although Choi. Luvsanjav was allowed to remain on campus, he could only conduct research on Mongolian linguistics rather than research on Chinese linguistics. Bazarragchaa recalled his reassignment from the Chinese newspaper *Gongren zhi lu* (The Workers' Road) to the Chinese Department of Mongolian Radio. According to his recollections, the only exchanges between Mongolia and China over the air was about the weather. The train to Beijing carried no one else other than the crew. Students went to the USSR to study Chinese.[8]

The Cultural Revolution in China further complicated the conditions for sinology in Mongolia because the Red Guards had attacked the official Mongolian historiography. Their maps of China included Mongolia as part of Chinese territory. L. Manlajav vividly recalled "the map war." Exclusively Mongolian sensibilities emerged incidentally to reveal an independence from the Soviet perspective. The government called on the sinologists to defend its position. Many critical comments were published. Research on the humanities came to a complete halt. The government closely monitored the sinologists to keep them from engaging in pure research. Instead, research on the Chinese Cultural Revolution, China's internal situation, and especially Chinese attitudes toward Mongolia constituted national policy. Violations of these restrictions could result in serious political consequences. As the defense of Mongolian dignity proceeded, the Soviet- and PRC-trained sinologists never abandoned their methodologies or the origins of their scholarship.

In 1968, an Asian research taskforce emerged out of the Department of Asian-African Studies at the Mongolian Academy of Sciences. The taskforce formed a foundation for the Institute of Oriental Studies that was established in 1976. This became the Institute of International Relations in 1991. The former Social Academy of the People's Revolutionary Party Center was also involved in confronting the Cultural Revolution. In line with an assignment by the USSR, Mongolian sinologists became concerned about the political suppression of ethnic minorities along the Chinese border. A number of research projects during the period focused on Inner Mongolia, Xinjiang, and Tibet. Their publication in the early 1980s indicates that even political assignments could be carried out in a fairly scholarly manner as these projects primarily relied on reviews of Chinese literature that had been acquired in China. Mend. Zenee, for example, wrote *The Administrative and Regional Changes in the Inner Mongolia Autonomous Region* (ӨМӨЗО-ны засаг захиргаа, нутаг дэвсгэрийн өөрчлөлт) (1981) and *Oral Literature in Inner Mongolia* (Өвөрмонголын ардын аман зохиол) (1981). D. Maam published *The Sufferings of Tibet under Mao's Policy* (Маогийн бодлогод хэлмэгдэж буй Төвд орон) (1975). Legshid Begzjav published *The Inner Mongolian Autonomous Region of China*

(БНМАУ-ынн ӨМӨЗО) (1981), *The Xinjiang Uygur Autonomous Regions of China* (БНХАУ-ын Шиньжаан Уйгарын автономит район) (1984), and *Conditions in Some of the Autonomous Regions in China, 1976–1983* (БНХАУ-ын үндэстний зарим автономит районы байдал, 1976–1983) (1987).

Because of the Cultural Revolution, sinologists were obligated to express disdain or sarcasm toward China. Even N. Ishjamts, later a member of the Academia, was not exempt.[9] However, he managed to fulfill his duty in a scholarly manner. His criticism rested upon a defense of Mongolian historiography, in opposition to the Chinese claim that historically Mongolia had been an unalienable part of Chinese territory. He then accused "the Chinese past dynasties and the contemporary Maoist authorities" of expansionism "for the sake of China's own power and higher status in Asia." He suspected that, "throughout history," the Chinese "have never given up the idea of a greater China, according to which Mongolia and other Asian nations are part of China." Similarly, Ch. Dalai, who had a deep affection for his sinological subjects, had to adapt to the ideological pressures of the time. However, he was able to retain an academic style in his rebuttal to the Red Guards. He decided to focus on Yuan history and he demonstrated how Mongolian historiography of that period was much greater in scope than Chinese historiography. Along these lines, he published *Mongolia during the Yuan* (Юань гүрний үейин Монгол) (1973), *Mongolia of the 13th–15th Centuries* (XIII–XY зууны үейин Монгол) (1982), *A History of Mongolia, 1260–1368* (Монголын түүх 1260–1368) (1992), *The Great Mongolian Nation, 1206–1260* (Их Монгол улс 1206–1260) (1994), *The All Mongolian Nation, 1101–1206* (Хамаг Монгол улс 1101–1206) (1996), and *The Great Mongolian Nation* (Их Монгол улс) (2006). Note that this series of publications was actually carried out up through the twenty-first century, attesting to their scholarly nature.

The academic consequences of the political intervention cannot simply be discounted in its aftermath. The aversion to China had a momentum, reaching also cultural areas. According to contemporary scholar Chimedtseye, Mongolia is too Westernized to be sufficiently sensitive to the intricate relationships among the Asian nations. He believes that Mongolian people do not know how to deal with China because they actually do not know China. For instance, he finds that the Chinese virtue of modesty is mistaken by the Mongolian people as hypocrisy. He contends that "shielding Mongolia from the influence of sinicization" should only proceed on the basis of a "profound appreciation of Chinese philosophical thought and culture (N. Gantulga, 2012)." Since the 1950s, however, Sinology has lost its legacy and has performed poorly in terms of its mission:

> "Mongolian Sinology lags seriously behind elsewhere. It has no shared systematic or disciplinary mode of research of its own. The product of its research makes no contribution to others. Granted that the Institute of International Relations of the Mongolian Academy of Sciences, along with the universities, are engaging in sinology, in my opinion they are far from the level of ancient sinology during the eighteenth and nineteenth centuries. Contemporary people are showing an increasing interest in Chinese literature, but there have been no translations. The peak period of translation of Chinese literature by Mongolian sinologists was during the seventeenth and eighteenth centuries. Mongolian sinologists during that period translated into the Mongolian language a good deal of well-known Chinese classical literature, such as *A Journey to the West, The Water Margin*, and *The Dream of the Red Chamber*. In the 1950s, the works by new literary figures, such as Lu Xun, Ba Jin, and Guo Moruo, were translated into Mongolian. Now the roots [of that tradition] have been severed."[10]

4. A Lingering of the Russian Legacy? Agenda and Leadership

Despite the demise of the USSR, Russian-trained sinologists continue to lead in the academic instituions as well as in China-related think-tanks or government posts in Mongolia. They assume a legacy that is quite different from the style of scholarship of either much earlier centuries when sinologists focused on the humanities and linguistics or the early years of the PRC when those who were first trained in China returned to teach language. Although many of the China-trained sinologists plunged into studies of history, especially recorded Mongolian history that uses Chinese documents, Russia-trained sinologists are able to tackle contemporary policy issues or current affairs. They are also ready to introduce subjects related to political economy and ethnology. Most importantly, to some extent they have refocused Mongolian sinology on practical issues. If the first generation of sinologists in the 1950s had to make some efforts to adapt to the political dictates of the 1960s–1980s, the Russian-trained sinologists are better prepared to analyze Chinese politics and policy.

Sinologists during the Sino-Soviet conflict studied subjects assigned to them by the USSR in accordance with an overall division of academic labor among the socialist countries. They met annually with sinologists in other socialist countries to report on their research and to listen to reports by others.[11] However, Mongolian sinologists were able to retain the methodology with which they were familiar, namely that of literary reviews. Nevertheless, their subjects were consistently political. This was even true for the PRC-trained scholars. Some examples include *Maoism and the Mao Zedong Faction* (Маоизм ба маогийнхан) (1974), co-authored by N. Ishjamts and D. Maam, and *Events in China, 1973–1976* (Хятад дахь хэрэг явдлын тухайд) (1979), by Ch. Dalai. Additionally, N. Ishjamts published an article entitled "How Has Mao Distorted Mongolian History and its Reality" (Маогийнхан БНМАУ-ын түүхийг гуйвуулж байгаа хийгээд түүхэн бодит байдал) (1982).

In fact, N. Ishjamts painstakingly remained scholarly in his critical position on Chinese historiography. He did this by revealing historically how Mongolia and China were equal in time and power. He showed that during the same period when the first Chinese dynasty, the Qin (220–207 B. C.) was established, nomadic Hun (Xiongnu) established, in 209 B. C., the first grassland dynastic nation in history. The Han dynasty that followed could only handle the intruding nomads by instituting a policy of appeasement which granted Xiongnu a sphere of influence north of the Great Wall.[12] He further challenged the mainstream view that Kublai Khan had learned Chinese and had adopted Confucianism in order to win the hearts of the Chinese. N. Ishjamts focused on Kublai Khan's appeal to Buddhism.[13] Kublai Khan had deliberately tried to avoid an over-reliance on Chinese culture. The Tibetan Pagva Lama helped him to develop new Phags-pa characters. Earlier, his grandfather Genghis Khan sought to enhance his influence among Chinese by receiving the Taoist monk Changchun, but historians, according to N. Ishjamts, mistakenly thought he was only trying to acquire the secret of longevity.[14]

Pedagogically, Mongolian National University began to send students to study in the USSR. For example, Oriental Studies at Leningrad University (later St. Petersberg University) admitted Jamsran Bayasakh, Natsagdorj Ariungua, Noosgoi Altantsetseg, Tsedendamba Batbayar, and Choijamts Battsetseg. After the thaw in Sino-Mongolian relations in 1979, they were among the first students to carry out research on broader topics, such as Northeast Asian international relations, economic reform, ethnic minorities, and bilateral economic issues. One noteworthy example is Ts. Batbayar's *Contemporary Chinese Leaders' Main Policy toward Inner Mongolia, 1976–1984* (Орчин үеийн БНХАУ-ын эрх баригчдаас Өвөрмонголын талаар явуулж буй үндсэн чиглэлүүд 1976–1984) (1987).

Non-USSR trained experts became active again in the 1980s, signaling the beginning of a thaw in the Soviet influence on intellectual thinking. The journal *Oriental Studies* was published by the Institute of Oriental Studies of the Mongolian Academy of Sciences. In February 1982, a joint delegation was sent to investigate the Sino-Mongolian border. For the first time since the 1960s officials from the two sides were able to meet.[15] After 1989, with the dissolution of the Soviet bloc, Mongolia turned toward China for trade. All of a sudden, Chinese goods were replacing Russian goods. China quickly became Mongolia's biggest trade partner. To cope with the rise of practical needs, the quest to attain Chinese-language skills resumed.

Nonetheless, some Soviet-trained Sinologists, several of whom had China connections, were able to retain their competitive positions even after the 1980s. For example, Jamsern Bayasakh's father had been among the first group of sinologists trained in the PRC. They have continued to provide Mongolian rebuttals to Chinese historiography on Mongolia and the history of the Yuan dynasty. Together with the PRC-trained sinologists, they are consistently critical of Han chauvinsm in Chinese historiography. Instead of studying Chinese classical literature or ancient documents, they study contemporary literature. For example, N. Altantsetseg published *Chinese Historiographical Perspectives on the Mongolian Rise Against Manchurian Rule* (Монголын ард түмний манжийн эсрэг үндэсний эрх чөлөөний түүхийг БНХАУ-ын түүхэнд тусгаж байгаа нь) (1985). In the same spirit, she also wrote *How Does China Study the History of the Mongolian National Movement in 1911* (1911 оны үндэсний эрх чөлөөний хөдөлгөөний түүхийг БНХАУ-д судалж байгаа нь) (2001). Jigjid Boldbaatar and Tsedendamba Batbayar co-authored *Some Questions in the History of Mongolian-Chinese Relations* (Монгол Хятадын харилцааны түүхийн зарим асуудал) (2011).

Nevertheless, as long as scholarship is exclusively about China rather than about Chinese perspectives on Mongolia, it does not take a critical stand. For example, USSR-trained J. Bayasakh authored *A Brief History of China* (Хятадын товч түүх) (2002) and in the same year D. Naran authored *Chinese History in the Twentieth Century* (Хятадын түүх XX зуун) (2002). Their works parallel the work by veteran sinologist N. Ishjamts, *A Brief History of the PRC from Ancient Times through 1999* (БНХАУ-ын түүхийн товч тойм нэн эртнээс он 1999) (1999). Nor is a critical stand apparent in Chinese economic studies. D. Batbayar authored *Mongolian-Chinese Economic and Trade Cooperation in the Twentieth Century* (XX зууны Монгол улс, БНХАУ-ын худалдаа, эдийн засгийн хамтын ажиллагаа) (2002), and in 2004, the Institute of International Relations published *The Future Direction of Cooperation in Mongolian-Chinese Economic Relations* (Монгол Хятадын эдийн засгийн харилцаа, хамтын ажиллагааны төлөв байдал).

N. Altantsetseg and J. Bayasakh, two Soviet-trained experts, have taken turns in assuming the leadership of the Institute of International Relations and the Department of International Relations of Mongolian National University. They have also been the leading authors in the institute's journal, *International Relations Studies* (Олон улс судлал). At a younger age, both were once actively involved in the Cultural Revolution polemics on the historiography of China. But it appears that they may have adapted differently to the changing situation in China and in Mongolian-Chinese relations, with N. Altantsetseg much more critical than J. Bayasakh. Under their joint leadership, the institute has developed a focus on the modern and contemporary periods, touching on a variety subjects, such as Monglian independence, Mongolian-Manchurian relations, global politics, the history of Greater Mongolia, diplomacy, Chinese leadership, and so on.

5. The Return of the Sinological Tradition in the Humanities

On the eve of the 1960s, the Sino-Mongolian Friendship Association, in which sinologists have played important roles, was established. Ambassador Sharav was its president and Ch. Dalai served as its secretary general. *The Workers' Road* was published in Mongolian, Russian, and Chinese. The Sino-Soviet conflict did not immediately eliminate its established track of research. Chimedtseren and Jugdernamjil, for example, continued to lecture on Chinese history and philosophy at Mongolian National University. In fact, between 1962 and 1968, fifty experts on Chinese translation completed their training at the College of Foreign Languages and Cultural Literature of Mongolian National University.[16]

Also in the 1960s, translations of Chinese literature continued to focus on contemporary writers, such as Lu Xun, Lao She, Ba Jin, and Guo Moruo. Lu Xun can be considered the most popular one. Bandikhuu and Choi Luvsanjav translated his "Long Lantern" (Мөнх гэрэлтүүлэгч дэнлүү 長明燈), "The Beggar" (Гуйлгын эзэн 求乞者), "The Great Wall" (Түмэн газрын цагаан хэрэм 長城), and "Mr. Lu Xun's Lecture at Huang Pu Military Academy on April 8, 1927"(Лүсины 1927 оны 4 сарын 8-нд Хуанпугийн цэргийн дарга нарын сургуульд уншсан лекц 魯迅先生 1927 年 4 月 8 日在黃埔軍官學校的演講). J. Artur translated his *Diary of a Mad Man* (Галзуу хүний өдрийн тэмдэглэл 狂人日記) and *Biography of Ah Q* (Акьюгийн үнэн түүх 阿 Q 正傳). Meanwhile, U. Lodoidamba translated "A Morning in Shanghai" (Шанхайн өглөө 上海的早晨) by Guo Moruo. Dunger-Yachil translated "Family" (Гэр бүл 家) by Ba Jin. The films, *The White-Haired Girl* (Буурал үстэй бүсгүй 白毛女) (1950) and *Grow in Struggle* (Тэд тулалдаан дунд өссөн юм 戰鬥裡成長) (1957) were also made available in Mongolian.

A significant change that continues the legacy of literary and language studies in the twenty-first century is the restoration of the Chinese class of 1975 in the Department of Foreign Languages at Mongolian National Unviersity. This enabled experienced PRC-trained sinologists to nurture younger generations who would lead sinology into the future. The first group of graduates contained 12 students. By the end of the 1990s, there was a total of 70 graduates in nine cohorts. Initially, Choi Luvsanjav prepared the curriculum and edited two volumes of *Chinese-Mongolian Conversations* (Монгол Хятад ярианы дэвтэр). E. Chimedtseren, Tsedevdorj Bazarragchaa, Chimeddamba Taamaa, Ch. Tumur, and J. Gungaa offered courses on Chinese, Chinese literature, and Chinese studies.[17] Note that the leading sinologists of the twenty-first century, such as Menerel Chimedtseeye, Lashid Begzjav, Yadmaa Ganbaatar, and D. Boldbaatar, are all part of the Chinese class, demonstrating the survival of the Chinese legacy despite the Soviet influence that had lasted for almost thirty years only to end in the 1990s.

Chinese-language teaching picked up again in the 1990s. The Department of Chinese was established at Mongolian National

University in 1993. In the same year, the University of Foreign Languages (Гадаад хэлний дээд сургууль), Normal University (Багшийн их сургууль), and Ulaanbaatar Univerity (Улаанбаатар) all offered Chinese classes. Private universities followed suit. Even high schools stepped up their language teaching. In 2004, the Association for Chinese Teachers (Хятад хэлний багш нарын холбоо) was established. According to its 2007 survey, a total of 50 schools, among which 30 were colleges, offered Chinese classes; 4,500 students, including 1,900 at the college level, were studying Chinese. Among the Chinese teachers, 66 out of 90 were Mongolians.[18] In 2010, 2,300 Mongolian students were studying in China.

Research on China has expanded in scope to include all possible subjects in order to meet the needs of the country in its increasing contacts with China in almost all fields. Added to the nascent interest in Chinese foreign policy, economic reform, politics, local governance, and so forth, a renewed enthusiasm about ancient Chinese records that enables a comprehensive portrayal of Mongolian history is apparent, along with research on other topics in the humanities, including literature, culture, philosopy, and religion. Using Chinese records to write Mongolian history has its roots in the sinology of the 1950s. Ch. Dalai continued this trend throughout his career. Except for his works on the People's Republic of China (1959) and culture and science in the People's Republic of China (1959), he was consistently able to draw on details of Mongolian history from Chinese documents in his *Studies of Sinology in Mongolia* (Монголын хятад судлал) (1960), *Mongolia in the Yuan Dynasty* (Юань гүрний үеийн Монгол) (1973), and *Mongolian-China Relations* (Монгол Хятадын харилцаа) (1945–84). The latter one was also published in Russian in Prague in 1986. In Prague, he additionally published several articles, including, in 1971, twin articles entitled "Mongolian-Chinese Relations during the 13th–14th Centuries" (XIII-XIYзууны үеийн Монгол) and "Translation of the History of the Yuan" (Юань Шигийн монгол орчуулга).[19] Ariungua, as another example, published *Mongolian-Chinese Relations during the 14th–16th Century* (1996).

Continuing the long tradition of Mongolian sinology, literary studies and translations of the classics resumed in the twenty-first century, albeit still limited to an individualized scale. First of all, the 1950s' generation once again resumed its cherished topics. L. Manlajav, who had earned her doctoral degree in 1973 with a dissertation entitled "The Evolution of Mongolian Phonetics of Chinese Characters Used in the Secret History of the Mongols" (Монголын нууц товчоон дахь хятад үсгээр галигласан монгол хэлний өөрчлөлт), since the 1990s has frequented the National Library of the Republic of China in Taipei. Poet Bazarragchaa has been unceasingly devoted to translations of modern as well as classical poems. His scope of interest covers both modern poets, such as Lao She, Mala Qinfu, Zang Kejia, Feng Jicai, and so on, and classical Tang-dynasty poets, such as Li Bai, Du Fu, Wang Wei, and so forth. He even translated *Shi jing* (The Book of Poetry). On the pedagogical front, in 1985 he edited *A Curriculum for Translation* (Орчуулгын сурах бичиг), *Comparative Translations of Mongolian and Chinese* (Хятад монгол хэлний харьцуулсан судалгаа), and *Studies of Mongolian-Chinese Translation* for college teachers who teach Chinese.

The 1970s' generation, who had studied under the 1950s' generation, began to graduate from Mongolian National University in 1979. Most noteworthy is the head of the Confucius Institute in Ulaanbaatar, M. Chimedtseeye, who over the years translated *The Analects*, *Great Learning*, and Sun Zi's *Art of War*. He also published *A Study of the Methodology for Translating Chinese Classical Literature into Mongolian* (Хятадын сонгодог уран зохиолын монгол орчуулгын уран чадварыг шинжихүй) (2006). His colleague Ya Ganbaatar published *Selected Chinese Classic Poetry* (2006) and *Selected Chinese Poems by Mongolians during the Yuan Dynasty* (Юань гүрний үед хятадаар уран бүтээл туурвиж байсан Монголчуудын шүлгийн сонгомол), which was reprinted in 2007, and *Chinese Ancient Literature* (Нангиадын утга соёлын товчоон) (1998, 2006).

Linguistic studies has also resumed with noteworthy momentum. Comparative linguistic studies of Mongolian and Chinese are among the popular doctoral dissertation subjects in the twenty-first century, to an extent that would have been difficult to anticipate even a decade ago. Batmaa wrote "Comparative Studies of Mongolian and Chinese Sentences" (Хятад Монгол хэлний өгүүлбэрзүйн зэрэгцүүлсэн судалгаа) (2002); Ts. Byambatsend wrote "Comparative Studies of Mongolian and Chinese Dictionaries" (Монгол Хятад хэлний тользүйн зэрэгцүүлсэн судалгаа) (2003); and D. Badmaanyambuu wrote "Comparative Studies of Mongolian and Chinese Quantifiers" (Монгол хятад хэлний тооллого үгийн зэрэгцүүлсэн судалгаа)

(2004).[20] Moreover, D. Boldbaatar, who once translated the popular TV series *Princess Pearl* (*Huanzhu gege*) and many other famous Chinese films, wrote a doctoral thesis on "Translation of Idioms in Chinese Movies" (Хятад киноны орчуулгын хэлц үгийн оноолтын уран чадварын асуудалд).[21] All these subjects reflect the relevance and significance of the reconnection with Chinese academic institutions and the return of the humanities to sinology. These studies are taking place along with the rising attention given to current affairs as well as social science research.

Social science research did not arise directly from those of the 1950s' generation. However, the training of these scholars and their connections with Chinese academics similarly reflect the earlier legacy in the humanities. A representative institution is the Institute of International Relations of the Mongolian Academy of Sciences. The institute was formerly the Institute of Oriental Studies which, in 1976, evolved from the Asian Studies Team of the Institute of African-Asian Studies of the Academy, which had first emerged in 1968. In 1991, it became the Institute of Oriental and International Studies.[22] The Institute publishes a bi-annual journal, the *Journal of Northeast Asian Studies*.[23] Although its topics are typically mundane, what allows the Institute to remain embedded in the humanistic traditions is the connection with China as well as with the 1950s' generation. It is noteworthy that Chinese scholars frequently visit the institute. Furthermore, the institute is currently staffed and headed by scholars trained in Mongolia, not in Russia. Although the topics it has covered during the past forty years have consistently been related to contemporary developments in China, the joint production of *Today's China* (Өнөөгийн Хятад орон) with the Confucius Institute in Ulaanbaatar is a straightforward indication of its embedded association with humanistic sinology.

The Confucius Institute is in close cooperation with the College of Foreign Languages and Literature (Гадаад хэл, соёлын сургууль). The college publishes the biannual *Foreign Languages and Cultures* (Гадаад хэл ба соёл). Its strengths include linguistic studies and Chinese culture. The nascent association with the Confucius Institute has enabled the college to develop a focus on Confucian thought and Chinese philosophy.[24] This strength in linguistics has doubtlessly benefited from N. Ishjamts who not only admired Chinese civilization but also promoted Mongolian phonetics of Chinese words in order to release Mongolian sinology from its Russian influences.[25] In the twenty-first century, two sinologists who have carried on the humanistic legacy most actively are perhaps M. Chimedtseye and L. Begzjav.

6. Individual Intellectual Tracks

Born in 1956, M. Chimedtseye encountered Chinese only after he entered college. Later, he graduated from the Chinese class of the College of Foreign Languages and Literature of Mongolian National University. He was able to improve his spoken Chinese during his service at the National Radio. He also translated for the Mongolian president. In 2006, he successfully defended his doctoral thesis "Characteristics of Mongolian Translations of Chinese Literature." In 2011, he received the Performance of Excellence Award granted by the Confucius Institute. He recalled his coincidental admission to the world of Chinese learning:

> "Initially, my major in Mongolian language should have led to continuing my education at Moscow State University in the USSR. The requirement was to pass all the courses with excellence. After receiving a notice from the government about the upcoming exams, I worked day and night in preparation for examination on the History of Socialist Thought in the Soviet Union. In the end, my teacher gave me an F. This shattered my dream of entering the field of international studies in Moscow. From then on, I began my companionship with Chinese and entered the world of the great thought and literature of China. Possibly I have been made for China."[26]

M. Chimedtseye especially enjoyed Chinese literature, Tang-style poetry, and philosophy of thought, believing that an understanding of Chinese culture can be better achieved via reading the literature, from which one learns to appreciate life customs, the characteristics of the times, and the historical trajectories. That is why he was determined to translate as much Chinese literature as possible for the Mongolian public. Personally, he liked the Tang poets Li Bai, Wang Wei, and Du Fu and he admired Confucius. He tried to accumulate as much knowledge as possible about Confucius. He was likely more affectionate toward Chinese culture than any other Mongolian sinologist. He has endeavored to compare Mongolian and Chinese ways of thinking. But his pedagogy stresses the importance of language skills. Without language, one cannot explore Chinese culture in depth or understand China in a broader perspective. His most recent publication, *The China and Chinese Thought and Culture That We Understand and Do Not Understand* (2012), reveals some sense of regret that Chinese culture is not as well-received as it should be in Mongolia.

Lashid Begzjav was also born in 1956 and came into contact with Chinese in his first Chinese class in 1975. He was among the first cohort to graduate during the period of the Cultural Revolution. His direct mentor at the time was Bazarragchaa, a member of the first cohort that studied in China in the 1950s. Starting his career as a research assistant at the Academy of Sciences, he was the Chinese translator of the Mongolian People's Revolutionary Party Guidelines. Only after the reforms began in the 1990s has he been able to work on topics of his own choosing. He has visited Peking University, University of Inner Mongolia, and Shandong University in order to advance his research. He has also taught at Peking University as a visiting professor. Administratively, he once served as the head of China Studies in the Institute of International Studies of the Academy of Sciences.

Before the reforms, for personal reasons he left his positions on seven occasions. But his multilingual skills seem to have guaranteed his rehabilitation each time. Nevertheless, he took his assignments seriously enough during the Soviet-dominated period to be able to grow intellectually. His institute was assigned to conduct research on Chinese ethnic issues. Although later in his career he was able to develop his research in multiple directions, there is a consistent interest in scholarship on Chinese ethnic affairs and local governance, with a specific focus on the Uygurs of Xinjiang. He is also broadly knowledgeable about Chinese relations with its neighbors and border area issues. His publications include works on Hong Kong, Taiwan, Sino-Russian relations, Sino-U.S. relations, Sino-Japanese relations, Sino-Indian relations, and Mongolian-Chinese relations. Instead of adopting sinological methodology from Russia, in the twenty-first century he has also published in Russian. This reversed flow of knowledge would have been unimaginable before the 1990s. He explains the importance of learning the Chinese language in his construction of knowledge about China:

> "[We] must study hard the languages of our neighbors on both sides, especially that of rapidly-growing China which is now open to the world. China should be our lifetime subject of research. We should study Chinese language and culture. This is not the same, as some people claim, that we accept sinicization. We use language in order to reach the great Chinese civilization—its ways of thinking and Han culture."[27]

7. Conclusion

The alleged anxiety about a potential Chinese resumption of sovereignty over Mongolia does not seem to be present among contemporary Mongolian sinologists. The consensus has always been that Mongolian historiography covers a much more extensive scope than Chinese historiography on Mongolia. Chinese classical documents are regarded as useful materials to restore a comprehensive picture of the lives and institutions of the ancient Mongols. To fully utilize the Chinese documents, Chinese language skills are a prerequisite. With China substituting for the Soviet Union as Mongolia's closest economic partner after the dissolution of the Soviet bloc, the importance of studying Chinese language is very much appreciated in Mongolian society. However, Mongolian sinologists worry that such a functional attitude is insufficient to appreciate Chinese civilization.

Nevertheless, this instrumental view of Chinese language is a rather modern consideration. From their pre-modern encounters with Chinese culture, generations of Mongolian sinologists have been fascinated by Chinese literature. Before the recent emergence of instrumental thinking about Chinese language, it was always regarded as an entertaining vehicle via which the nomadic Mongols could gain access to Chinese philosophy, poetry, novels, and so forth. It was only after the 1960s that language skills began to serve politics. But politics has produced a need to study the political and economic realities in China and therefore has broadened the scope of sinological research. In fact, social science as well as policy-oriented research has entered Mongolian sinology in an all-round fashion since the 1980s. Sinology is now taking off in multiple directions.

Although the humanities dominated the sinological agenda in Mongolia before the 1950s, political interventions in the 1960s transformed the style of research. To begin, academic relations with China were severed and, as a result, sinologists received their training in the Soviet Union. Nevertheless, an interest in the humanities lingered on in the style of research carried out by the 1950s' generation and had an impact upon the later development of research through students trained after the mid-1970s. New generations invariably go to China or Taiwan for training and Russia has now completely lost its pedagogical position. However, those trained in the Soviet Union during the Sino-Soviet conflict have continued to hold many leading political and academic positions. Other than perhaps their critical views of the Chinese government, their differences in terms of research and other perspectives are relatively negligible.

Notes

1. Huo Wen, "Meng Zhong guanxi jinxi tan" (A Note on the Past and the Present of Sino-Mongolian Relations), Өнөөгийн Хятад сэтгүүл (Today's China), No. 1 (2009), pp. 59–60.
2. Ya Ganbaatar, Нангиадын утга зохиолын товчоон (Chinese Classical Literature) (Ulaanbaatar: n. p., 2006), p. 426.
3. Ibid, p. 430.
4. Ibid.
5. Chuluun Dalai, Түүвэр зохиол *I* (Collected Works of Ch. Dalai, I) (Ulaanbaatar: n. p., 2000), p. 31.
6. Ya Ganbaatar, Нангиадын сонгодог утга соёлын товчоон (A Study of Classical Chinese Literature) (Ulaanbaatar: n. p., 2006), p. 462.
7. Ya Ganbaatar, Утга зохиолын тухай яриа (A Discussion on Studies of Literature) (Ulaanbaatar: n. p., 2010), p. 80.
8. Interview with Bazarragchaa in February 2010. Available at http://raec.igd. tw/act/InterviewM_Barzarragchaa_guyain_yarilstlaga_M.doc (accessed 11 September 2014).
9. Nyambuu Ishjamts, БНХАУ-ын түүхийн товч тойм (A Brief History of the People's Republic of China) (Ulaanbaatar: n. p., 1999), pp. 1–2.
10. N. Gantulga, "Interview with M. Chimedtseye," Өдрийн сонин (Today's News); Сэтгүүлч Гантулга, "Udriin sonin," 4 June 2012. Available at http://www.dnn. mn/publish/?vid=18364 (accessed 18 October 2013).
11. Noosgoi Altantsetseg and Bat-Yunden Ganchuluun, "Монгол дахь Хятад судлал" (Sinology in Mongolia), in Монгол Хятадын харилцаа жарнаас жаранд (The Sixtieth Anniversary of Sino-Mongolian Relations, 1949–2009), edited by N. Altantsetseg and A. Battsetseg (Ulaanbaatar: Адмон, 2010), p. 129.
12. Nyambuu Ishjamts, "Маогийхан БНМАУ-ын түүхийг гуйвуулж байга хийгээд түүхэн бодит байдал" (The Maoist Distortion of the History and the Historical Facts about the Republic of Mongolia), Түүхийг гуйвуулах маоист аргыг шүүмжлэх нь (The Maoists Who Distort the Historical Facts) (Ulaanbaatar: n. p., 1981), p. 5.
13. Ibid., p. 8.
14. Jamsran Bayasakh, "Академич Н. Ишжамцын Хятад судлалд оруулсан хувь нэмэр" (A Review of Academician Ishjamts' Contribution to Mongolian Sinology and China Studies), Академич Н. Ишжамцын бүтээл

туурвил, Дэд дэвтэр (Collected Works of Academician N. Ishjamts) (Ulaanbaatar: n. p., 2011), vol. 1, p. 165.

15. Mongolian Embassy in China ed., *Youyi hezuo de yijiazi* (Sixty Years of Friendly Cooperation) (Beijing: Mongolian Embassy in China, 2009), p. 149.

16. Chimeddamba Taamaa, "МУИС-Д Хятад хэлний мэргэжилтэн бэлтгэсний товчоон" (A Note on the Preparation of Experts at National Mongolian University), Өнөөгийн хятад сэтгүүл (Today's China), No. 1 (2009), pp. 108–110.

17. G. Eldev-Ochir, "МУИС-ийн Хятад судлалын тэнхим үүсч хөгжсөн түүхээс" (A History of the Establishment of the Department of Chinese at Mongolian National University), in Монгол Хятадын харилцаа жарнаас жаранд (The Sixtieth Anniversary of Mongolia-China Relations, 1949–2009), p. 151.

18. Vanchaarai Batmaa, "Монгол дахь хятад хэлний сургалтын өнөөгийн байдал" (The Conditions for Teaching Chinese in Today's Mongolia), in N. Altantsetseg and A. Battsetseg eds., *Sixty Years of Mongolia-China Relations* (Ulaanbaatar: Адмон, 2010).

19. Chuluun Dalai, Түүвэр зохиол *I*, pp. 107–114.

20. Noosgoi Altantsetseg and Bat-Yunden Ganchuluun, "Монгол дахь Хятад судлал" (Sinology in Mongolia), in Монгол Хятадын харилцаа жарнаас жаранд (The Sixtieth Anniversary of Mongolia-China Relations, 1949–2009), p. 127.

21. Ibid., pp. 127–133.

22. Dugarjav Naran, "Menggu hanxue yanjiu gaikuang" (General Conditions of Mongolian Sinological Research), *Hanxue yanjiu tongxun* (Center for Chinese Studies News), November 2009, pp. 40–43.

23. Lashid Begzjav, "Монгол улсын хятад судлалын уламжлал, өнөөгийн төлөв" (The Tradition and Current Conditions of Mongolian Sinology), Өнөөгийн Хятад сэтгүүл (Today's China), No. 1 (2009), p. 79.

24. Ch. Batsuren, "Күнзийн нутгийн сургууль, боловсрол" (The Academy and Education in Confucius' Home Country), Өнөөгийн Хятад сэтгүүл (Today's China), No. 1 (2009), p. 61.

25. Nyambuu Ishjamts, БНХАУ-ын түүхийн товч тойм, p. 4.

26. N. Gantulga, Interview with M. Chimedtseye, Өдрийн сонин (Today's News); Сэтгүүлч Гантулга, "Udriin sonin," 4 June 2012. Available at http://www.dnn. mn/publish/?vid=18364 (accessed 18 October 2013).

27. B. Tserenjamts, "Interview with L. Begzjav in 'Улаанбаатар Таймс,'" Сэтгүүлч Цэрэнжамц (Ulaanbaatar Times), 19 May 2008.

Chapter 4

Sinology in Poland: Epistemological Debates and Academic Practice

Anna Rudakowska

1. Introduction: Sinology in Poland

The oldest sinological center that exists in Poland today was first founded in the 1933–34 academic year at the Institute of Oriental Studies, University of Warsaw (UW).[1] The work of the institute was interrupted by World War II, but it resumed in 1945. For five decades this course (referred to below as "Warsaw sinology") was the only one of its kind in Poland.[2] It was only after the collapse of communism in 1989 that new Sinology Departments, Chinese-language courses, and lectures on China and Chinese culture mushroomed on the Polish academic map, and Chinese is now taught in primary and high schools, universities, and language schools. At the same time, academic institutions in Poland devoted to Far Eastern, Asian, or East Asian studies, as well as international relations—particularly in Kraków, Gdańsk, Toruń, Lublin, and Łódź—have gradually been introducing language courses and new lectures about China. For example, the Institute of the Middle and Far East at the Jagiellonian University and the University of Gdańsk both offer Chinese-language courses.[3] In 2006 the first institute sponsored by the Chinese government with the goal of teaching the language and spreading the culture—the Confucius Institute (CI)—opened in Kraków, in cooperation with the Jagiellonian University.[4] In 2008 three more CIs were inaugurated in Opole (Opole University of Technology), Poznań (Adam Mickiewicz University), and Wrocław (University of

Wrocław). Moreover, some of the centers that originally taught language courses have now expanded their curricula to include lectures on Chinese culture, history, religion, politics, and so on.

In addition to language courses, many new centers—called Sinology Departments, Chinese Studies, or Chinese Philology Departments— have been established at institutions of higher learning in Poland.[5] Although many of these call themselves "sinology" centers, in addition to the one in Warsaw only two other institutions in Poland are generally recognized in academic circles as offering sinology studies: Adam Mickiewicz University (UAM) in Poznań (referred to below as Poznań sinology),[6] and the Catholic University of Lublin (Katolicki Uniwersytet Lubelski Jana Pawła, KUL, referred to below as Lublin sinology).[7] The others are commonly regarded as language schools.[8]

The question arises as to why only these three Polish institutions are recognized in academia as having "sinology" centers, and what are the necessary characteristics to be recognized as such. Are there particular subjects that denote either sinology or other subjects that distinguish linguistics? This chapter is interested in the approaches of Polish academics conducting research on China to sinology curricula and the organization of the study environment. It examines the evolution of their understanding of sinology as a discipline and how sinology has been studied in Polish universities.

The chapter first introduces the epistemological debates on the study of China and the postulates of the so-called "New Sinology." It then explains its theoretical foundation and methodology, before moving on to an analysis of the interviews. It concludes with a summary of the evolution in the understanding of sinological training among Polish specialists on China against the background of the epistemological debates on the study of China.

2. Epistemological Debates about the Study of China and the "New Sinology"

The first professional and scientific sinology courses in European universities, at the end of nineteenth century, focused on the literary language and on classical literature and philosophy. John Fairbank compares the scientific rigor of the traditional sinological centers to the tradition of evidential research created by the Qing dynasty scholarship of *kaozheng* (考證).[9] The starting point for evidential researchers was that the contemporary understanding of the dominant Confucian ideology was distorted, since it was comprehended through the prism of particular interpretations, each with its own abstract categories. In order to recapture the original meaning, evidential researchers sought to rediscover the ancients by means of a philological analysis of the classical texts. They stressed the value of concrete, verifiable facts, in opposition to research based on creating theoretical constructions.[10] Similarly, traditional sinology concentrated heavily on historical documents, including classical literature, with an emphasis on the acquisition and application of advanced text-reading skills as the basis for scholarship in the areas of literature, philosophy, religion, and history. This method of studying China was developed in France and over time came to prevail in other European universities. It can be characterized simply as a single-discipline polymath approach.[11]

During the first three decades of the twentieth century, following the impact of the social sciences on research in sinology centers mainly in the United States and Australia, traditional European scholarship on China began to face challenges.[12] Chinese Studies moved into the realm of the social sciences and was approached from the perspective of area studies, conducted by specialists in particular fields such as history, politics, art, sociology, or anthropology.[13] China was no longer studied through the reading of classical texts but rather through the application of the methods and theories of a particular discipline.

Students of China today are divided into two camps, those with training in traditional sinology, focusing on the classical texts and those with a disciplinary and social science-based perspective. The two sides—later called generalists and specialists respectively[14]—have engaged in polemics in journals and academic papers and in speeches at conferences and symposia.[15] In 2005, Australian sinologist Geremie R. Barmé signaled a departure in this debate when he proposed an ecumenical approach to sinology studies, the so-called "New Sinology." Barmé explains that the only way to engage with "the Sinophone world in all its complexity" is to draw from both traditions—generalist and specialist—and in research and study to include the classical with the modern, the empirical with the theoretical, and the local and regional with the global.[16] By asking Polish scholars studying China about their understanding of sinology, this research will reveal on which side of this divide they fall.

3. Theoretical Foundation and Methodology

This work is interested in the social processes at work in the construction of sinology as a realm of knowledge. It builds on one of the main premises of constructivist thinking, which is that we do not perceive reality "as it is out there." Instead, we produce meaning and categorizations that are based on our experiences, background, culture, and so forth, and these may change over time. This creation of meaning takes place in social interactions.[17] Thus, knowledge is always produced in specific social and historical circumstances, which depend on past experiences and the culture of the particular group involved.

In order to examine the construction of "reality," this study uses discourse analysis. It recognizes the claims of those discourse analysts who, in line with poststructuralist linguistic philosophy, admit that our access to reality is always through language. We know about the world around us because we ascribe meaning to it.[18] The discourse analysts do not suggest that physical objects do not exist, but rather that they only gain meaning through discourse.[19] In other words, when we talk, or write, we are also "doing" things. In the same way, in the process of communication sinologists are actively engaged in creating meaning.

The adoption of these assumptions has the following implications for this study: 1) There is no fixed meaning of "sinology." Rather, it is constantly reinterpreted over time. The study examines two periods in the history of Polish sinology—the 1950s–1960s in the Communist era, and the years since 1990 after the collapse of communism in 1989—on the assumption that the political situation particular to each period had a distinct impact on the meaning of sinology and 2) Meaning creation is a complex process, which takes place in a social world. It depends on the definitions of participants interested in the creation and (re)interpretation of meaning as well as on certain historical and social circumstances. From this perspective, it makes sense to interview sinologists and specialists in Chinese Studies to determine their own interpretations of sinology.

Three data sets are employed in this study: scientific research, official documents, and interviews. The scientific research provides background information on the epistemological debates about the study of China during the periods under discussion. The official documents include data on the higher education policies of the Polish government and documents issued by universities, such as university and department mission statements, histories of their didactic units, curricula, and information concerning department staff and student grades. The goal of this part of the inquiry is not to verify the interpretations and perceptions of the interviewees, but rather to understand the background to which they are referring.

The interviews are the key source of information for this study. They were conducted in order to determine the subjective opinions of the respondents regarding two main issues: 1) what constitutes knowledge about China, and 2) how should this knowledge be acquired. "Sinology" is treated here as one of Thomas Diez's "discursive nodal points" (DNPs). DNPs are terms that mean different things to different people who, consequently, in discursive practice struggle to invest these contested concepts with different meanings by applying a variety of discursive strategies.[20] This accords with the theoretical assumption in this study: that the meaning of sinology is not fixed, but is constantly being reinterpreted.

During the period from 28 August to 7 October 2013 the author conducted fourteen interviews with seventeen Polish sinologists or specialists in Chinese Studies. There were two main groups of interviewees: the staff in the three Sinology Departments in Poland (nine interviewees), and recognized Polish sinologists or specialists in Chinese Studies who had pursued their academic and/or diplomatic careers outside of these institutions (eight interviewees), including three who had been students of Polish sinology in the 1950s. This selection provided the author with insights into two perspectives on Polish sinology: an insider's view of sinologists ("we," "us") and an outsider's view ("they"), as expressed by researchers on China in area studies and other more "practical hands," such as diplomats and artists. Seven of the interviewees had gone to China in the 1950s and 1960s as recipients of the first PRC scholarships. Permission was granted for the recording of eleven of the interviews. Two discussants did not wish to be recorded but permitted note-taking, and two agreed to a telephone conversation during which notes were taken. The interviews were conducted in Polish, with some words or phrases expressed in Chinese. In order to create a relaxed atmosphere and to enable the respondents to speak freely, all the interviewees remain anonymous. The study thus does not mention their names and refers to them as I1 (for Interview 1), I2 (for Interview 2), and so forth.

In addition, the author had the benefit of using the nine interviews conducted by Dr. Marcin Jacoby and Dr. Ewa Paśnik between 2011 and 2013. Eight of these respondents had been recipients of Chinese government scholarships to the PRC during the period between 1950 and 1966, and one was a Chinese person who had moved to Poland and became a sinologist.[21] Eight of the nine interviews are available online.[22] Table 1 lists the interviewees.

The data from the interviews provide information about the sinology curricula and the relationship between sinology and society during the two periods under discussion. A description of Polish sinology during each period is followed by an analysis of the respondents' interpretations of developments at sinological centers in Poland. According to Diez, these interpretations reveal "rules about what is considered to be a reasonable argument" and, as a consequence, they legitimize particular actions.[23] They are crucial to this study, as they reveal what arguments are recognized as the most relevant in the debate about what should constitute the curriculum of sinological training. The analysis is augmented by selected quotations from the interviews, both for their extraordinary informative value and to provide readers with the possibility of discussing the author's interpretations.

Table 1: List of Interviewees

Interview	Respondent
15	Irena Sławińska (Hu Peifang): Chinese, moved to Poland in 1955, worked in the UW Sinology Department beginning in 1956 as a lecturer in Chinese, translator, and writer
16	Jan Rowiński: Recipient of a scholarship to China, 1954–60, academic and diplomat
17	Krzysztof Gawlikowski: Recipient of a scholarship to China, 1964–66, political scientist
18	Marzenna Szlenk-Iliewa: Graduated from the UW Sinology Department, one of the first recipients of scholarship to China for that department (1956), translator of Chinese literature (interviewed by Ewa Paśnik and Marcin Jacoby)
19	Stanisław Tworzydło: Recipient of a scholarship to China in 1955, artist
20	Teresa Lechowska: Student in the UW Sinology Department from 1950
21	Zdzisław Góralczyk: Recipient of a scholarship to China, 1953–59; Polish ambassador to China, 1994–99
22	Agnieszka Łobacz: Graduated from the UW Sinology Department, among the first recipients of scholarship to China for that department (1956)
23	Bogumił Dąbrowski: Recipient of a scholarship to China, 1950–55, studied oriental studies at the Jagiellonian University, diplomat

Source: Interviews I15–I23.

* Unless otherwise indicated, the interviews were conducted by Dr. Marcin Jacoby between 2011 and 2013.

4. Polish Sinology in the 1950s and 1960s

a. The Curriculum: Sinology as Philological Studies

In the interviews, Polish sinology in the 1950s and 1960s was categorized as philological studies. The UW Sinology Department primarily offered language and literature courses. For example, according to the transcript of a student enrolled there between 1951 and 1956, language classes constituted about 60 percent of all hours offered by the department (not including courses offered by the university) for the entire term of study. Students learned Chinese (67 percent of all language classes), and Japanese (27 percent of all language courses), and took one course on Cantonese grammar (6 percent of all language courses).[24]

The focus was on the classical heritage, with a strong emphasis on classical Chinese. The same transcript indicates that history lectures—including "History of China," "History of Japan," "History of Japanese Literature," "History of Chinese Literature," "Monograph Lecture: History of Contemporary Chinese Literature," "History of Contemporary Chinese Literature," "History of the Chinese Revolution," and "History of the Art of the Far East"—constituted 20 percent of the compulsory hours offered by the department throughout the entire period of study. There were only two courses on contemporary issues in the Far East: "Introduction to the Far East" and "Far East: Contemporary Issues," and no lectures on the culture, society, or politics of contemporary China.[25]

Moreover, the respondents complained that the lectures on modern Chinese taught a passive knowledge of the language. The courses developed students' writing and reading skills, but not their speaking ability. The respondents lamented that, instead of learning the language, they would analyze the grammatical functions of one word for several hours. The 1951–56 student transcript indicates that this theoretical bias existed at the expense of practical linguistic abilities: in the first and second semester of study, two out of the six hours of Chinese per week were devoted to descriptive grammar; while in the third semester, out of a total of eight hours of Chinese per week, two hours were devoted to a descriptive grammar of modern Chinese and two hours were devoted to a descriptive grammar of classical Chinese. In the fourth semester, the proportion of practical Chinese decreased further in favor of theoretical language study, including the same language classes as in the third semester as well as an additional course on "Theory of Translation from Chinese."

Beginning in 1956, Japanese studies and sinology functioned as independent units. Nevertheless, the character of the sinology curriculum remained unchanged, with the prevailing language courses teaching a passive knowledge of Chinese and emphasizing the classics. Along with the department's specialized courses, students of sinology were required to attend some lectures by the philology faculty, such as the "The History of Philosophy," as well as courses that were compulsory for all university students. Some of these, such as physical education and a Western language of their choice, are still compulsory today. The exceptions to this rule were the lectures on Communist ideology, such as "An Outline of the History of the Communist Party of the Soviet Union"[26] and courses on Marxism and Leninism, which were emblematic of the era.[27]

b. In Relation to Society: Sinology as an "Ivory Tower" and Staff Members as an "Intellectually Isolated Group"

The department was described as being relatively detached from political and economic reality and not contributing to society by sharing its knowledge about China. The interviewees characterized the professors and some of the students as an "intellectually isolated group," "outsiders," "refugees," "closed," and "cut off" from the outside world. They hid in the Sinology Department to escape the reality of their personal or political problems.[28] According to the interviewees, the department staff did not organize scientific discussions, seminars, or public lectures, avoided meetings outside of the department, and did not contribute to academic debates or invite outside experts as visitors.[29]

That said, the staff and students were not completely isolated from the political and economic realities of the times. They were vulnerable to Communist censure, monitoring, and repression, and they did not enjoy freedom of speech.

> "People never knew who would denounce whom, so they were scared of one another. ... Even his [Prof. Jabłoński's] position was uncertain ... because he came from a family of landowners." (I18)

5. Discursive Strategies Explaining the Sinology Condition in the 1950s and 1960s

During the 1950s and 1960s—and even, as the respondents mentioned, during the three following decades—epistemological questions about what constitutes knowledge about China, and how and from what sources this knowledge should be acquired, were generally answered by the professors, with the head of department as the main decision maker. The head of the department seemed to have a good deal of leeway in terms of running the program. Apart from some lectures that were compulsory for students in the philology faculty, if not for all university departments, he made most of the decisions about the curriculum, without political or university-level influence. He was not required to consider the students' opinions: "Some of us, including me, objected to not speaking the modern language. We wanted to learn real Chinese, but there wasn't anything like that."[30] Additionally, the cadres were described as ignoring material or financial considerations, as they did not teach practical skills that might have helped students secure jobs later on. One of the interviewees pointed out that the students "weren't prepared for contemporary life because they studied the *I-Ching* ... but couldn't speak Chinese or read a newspaper."[31]

The considerable decision-making power wielded by the department head meant that the management style in the department depended largely on his personality and ability. The interviewees mentioned that sometimes he would even prevent students whom he disliked from pursuing research on China, while he would open career doors for his favorites. He also had great influence in the hiring of new staff and accepting new PhD students:

> "If the head of the department favored a given person, that person would find his/her way up in sinology. If not, there were no prospects—one's knowledge did not count." (I3)

> "Professor Chmielewski said you should respect your superiors, and even if he put a block of wood on a chair, we would have to bow down before it. I replied I was not going to do that. So I stopped working in the department. It was my own decision to quit, but then again, no one persuaded me to stay." (I15)

Similarly, the department head's personal background, knowledge, skills, and interests had a major impact on the design of the curriculum. Respondents claimed that the main reason for the lack of teaching on

modern Chinese was that "there was no one at all to teach it" as even
the professors did not speak it:

> "To be honest, our teachers did not speak Chinese. Jabłoński spoke, but …
> after two years in China we spoke better than the professor!" (I4)

Still, it should be noted that Professor Jabłoński was also described as
the one who, unlike other sinologists at the time, highlighted the importance of teaching practical Chinese and greatly valued contact with the
living language.[32] Only one interviewee attributed the focus on classical
language and literature to the organization of studies "at that time":

> "I think that education really used to be subdivided into units, so you had
> linguistic studies, and nothing but that, ethnographic studies, and nothing but
> that, archaeology, and nothing but that. Right?" (I4)

This also explains why, despite a political environment that theoretically
favored contacts between Polish and Russian sinologists, in reality
Warsaw sinology cultivated the traditions of French sinology.[33] The first
and second heads of sinology in Warsaw—Jan Jaworski (1903–45) and
Witold Jabłoński (1901–57)—had both been educated abroad and had
received their PhD degrees in Paris. Moreover, Prof. Jabłoński had
studied under the most famous French sinologists of his time, including
Henri Maspero, Marcel Granet, and Paul Peliot.[34]

The relative freedom of the department head in the design of the
curriculum does not mean that in the 1950s and 1960s there were no
competing discourses about what constituted knowledge on China or
how it should be acquired. There were indeed students and staff
members, as well as scholars from outside the department, who questioned the priority placed on classical Chinese. One of the respondents
argued that students should first learn modern Chinese and should be
able to read a newspaper, talk on the phone, and communicate readily
in Chinese, and that only then would they be ready to learn classical
Chinese.[35] Furthermore, proponents of the specialist approach criticized
sinologists for their lack of a methodological background and research
tools. For example, one of the respondents stated that sinologists at UW
were unable to conduct historical research as they did not possess a
basic knowledge of the methodology of historical research and did not
understand the fundamentals of historical knowledge.[36] In the 1950s and
1960s, however, these dissenting voices failed to influence the program
of sinological training at Warsaw University.

The Polish government did not intervene directly in knowledge construction in the department. At that time, the authorities priotitized contacts with the Soviet Union and other Soviet bloc countries that were close geographically. Political developments in relations between Poland and China depended on relations between the USSR and the PRC, and the Polish government's interest in China "ebbed and flowed, depending on the political situation."[37] As a result, the Polish government had no strategic plan for educating sinologists in order to build specialist knowledge about China. The respondents questioned whether the Polish authorities had any strategic plan at all for educating those cadres who would be responsible for future contacts with China:

"There was no special political strategy on cultural exchanges, at least on the Polish side. There were simply opportunities." (I23)

"There was this kind of thinking [about building a specialized knowledge base on China], but it wasn't a priority." (I24)

Still, the Polish authorities and the political situation did have an indirect impact on young people interested in the study of China. Interviewees mentioned that they developed an interest in studying China due to the rich cultural exchanges between Warsaw and Beijing and their access to abundant information about the country, generously provided by the Polish media in the 1950s and up until the mid-1960s. China constituted an example of the successful spread of communism around the world, and was "our biggest neighbor's biggest neighbor"[38]— so, during the period of friendly relations between Moscow and Beijing, the Polish authorities spread news from that part of the world.[39] The interviewees assessed the news as having been of a high standard, and they felt that the society was very well informed about and interested in China. They stated that China was "fashionable," "popular,"[40] and a "hot topic"[41] that was "often in the news."[42] Furthermore, the authorities could stimulate interest in the study of China by deciding whether to offer scholarships and career opportunities. First, it was the government that would decide who could benefit from such a scholarship. Immediately after World War II only graduates of high schools were selected for four- or five-year degree scholarships. They usually returned to Poland with an excellent command of Chinese and first-hand information about the country, as experts in their particular field of study; and, in the following decades, as scholars of history or international relations, as artists, publicists and diplomats, many of them contributed greatly to the understanding of China in Poland and to the debates on sinology.[43] Not until 1956, however, could Sinology Department students or graduates hope for a chance to go to Beijing, and then only for a one-year language course.[44] Second, the government prevented some young people from going to China for political reasons. Third, the authorities sometimes selected the country of destination against the will of the relevant scholarship recipients—for example, three respondents who ended up in China had originally applied for scholarships to other countries. Some respondents admitted that their interest in China, and their academic careers in this field, came about only by coincidence:

> "You could say where you wanted to go [on a scholarship]. I put down the USSR because I was interested in it. ... I arrived at the ministry. There was a very nice director there, ... who said ... unfortunately, the USSR is no longer available. Everything is settled. You will be sent to China, and you have two hours to decide whether you want to go." (I16)

Moreover, career opportunities for Polish people at that time were to a large extent regulated by the political machine. This practice meant that people were allocated jobs by the government. One respondent complained that sinology graduates were at a disadvantage, as the government did not allocate jobs for them and they had to seek employment on their own.[45] Furthermore, those who were not party members very often were unable to find jobs or receive promotions:

> "After my graduation in August 1955 I came back [from China] to Poland ..., to Warsaw, where I was immediately allocated work at the Ministry of Foreign Affairs. ... I didn't need to look for work because at that time there were the so-called work allocations." (I23)

> "... when I returned to Poland ... to my great surprise I discovered that I had been expelled from both the university and the party. Such a person could not find employment anywhere." (I17)

The political situation was cited as an important factor in either enabling or restricting development of the department, depending on the state of relations between Beijing and Warsaw (which, as we have seen, depended in turn on Sino-Soviet relations). In the early 1950s, when the Soviet Union and the PRC were friendly, native Chinese-language speakers were invited to teach in Warsaw, and

Chinese-language books, magazines, and newspapers were donated to the library of the Sinology Department.[46] During the same period, young Polish people were awarded scholarships to China—a privilege not offered to students or scholars from Western countries.[47] The situation changed at the beginning of the 1960s when contacts between Poland and China deteriorated, and they ceased altogether between 1962 and 1969 as a result of the Sino-Soviet split.[48] The last group of young Poles went to study in Beijing in the mid-1950s.[49] In 1966 China was shut off from the outside world because of the Cultural Revolution (1966–76), and until 1979 students were barred from studying in China.[50] Language teachers were no longer sent from China to teach at UW and Polish sinology was thus deprived of direct access to first-hand information and resources on China.[51] The end of direct contacts, combined with the critical attitudes of Polish society toward the Cultural Revolution, made China seem even more remote in the eyes of the Polish government and society, and resulted in the further isolation of the Sinology Department. Deprived of direct contacts with China, academics had no option but to focus on what was available at the time. They therefore devoted themselves to the study of the ancient culture, language, philosophy, and literature. According to one respondent, this isolation has had a deep imprint on the character of sinological training in Warsaw:

> "In the 1970s and 1980s, contacts with China were very limited. And opportunities for speaking the language, too, you know? And we were closed in, and China too. So, in Warsaw, classical literature, philosophy and history flourished. … And there were staff who had always specialized in these topics, and perforce still are working on them, so that is why this department has been more traditional [than the one in Poznań]." (I5)

None of the respondents referred to financial considerations (such as future job opportunities or the prospects of good salaries) as factors influencing the design of the sinological training program during that period. Students and cadres perceived sinology as an original but not a practical choice, since graduating from the department did not guarantee job opportunities.[52] According to one interviewee, during the entrance examinations the department head publicly tried to dash the applicants' hopes of lucrative job prospects, with the following words:

> "Ladies and gentlemen, please do not hope that you will get anything after sinology, do not expect any benefits—there will be nothing special." (I4)

6. Polish Sinology: 1990s to the Present

a. Curriculum: Sinology as Modern Philology[53]

Before the 2000s, the most radical change in the sinology curriculum in Warsaw was its separation from Japanese studies; other than this, the curriculum remained more or less intact. The collapse of communism did not give rise to much change in the 1990s, and it was not until the beginning of the 2000s that a transformation gradually began to take place. The changes described by the interviewees can be grouped under three headings: a cultural shift, specialization, and the adoption of a more practical approach. In addition to the linguistics and history seminars offered in the past, students could now choose "more interdisciplinary" seminars, combining cultural topics with literature or literature with history, and could develop their interests in other areas such as the cinema and theater:[54]

> "This idea that sinology can belong with cultural studies is quite new, and the greatest change in recent years is that sinology has moved from philology to cultural studies. So instead of examining language and literature, it analyzes culture—I mean, traditions, cultural anthropology, art, modern culture— these are things you couldn't even mention before, but now this is the key profile." (I4)

This cultural shift was accompanied by an increased focus on particular areas of Chinese studies, such as, for example, Chinese art, religion (a new course "The Main Chinese Religions"), cultural anthropology, various aspects of modern China including culture ("Chinese Civilization—Selected Issues in Modern Chinese Culture"), society and politics ("Chinese Civilization—Current Political Issues in China," and "Chinese Society and Culture"). In addition, there are now lectures introducing the research methodology for a given area of study, such as history (for example, "Introduction to Historical Research").[55] This increased specialization at the departmental level was reinforced by the introduction of new rules and structures in the Faculty of Oriental Studies at UW. Students now attend one of four workshops: on language; literature and culture; philosophy and religion; or history and socio-political issues.[56] In each workshop, students become familiar with the respective research methodologies and they are offered a one-year course consisting of discussions on the main philosophical and religious ideas of East and West.

Furthermore, in addition to the traditional preoccupation with the classics (such as classical Chinese) or subjects traditionally taught as part of sinology (for instance, history and philosophy), the UW department now emphasizes modern Chinese.[57] The new language courses aim not only to improve the students' reading and writing abilities, which constituted the core of the teaching in the 1950s and 1960s, but they also put a heavy emphasis on speaking skills and include both written and oral translation ("Applied Translation Studies," as opposed to the "Theory of Translation from Chinese" that was offered in the 1950s).[58] Together with the recently introduced new teaching methods, this concentration on the modern language equips students with more practical skills.[59] In the opinion of one respondent, Warsaw sinology has undergone a transformation: from study for its own sake to "a discipline that is very practical and that educates people who will find a job."[60]

"For a very long time, it [sinology] has been only study for its own sake. … There are now multiple practical lectures." (I8)

At the same time, Warsaw sinology has not turned its back on its roots. It also continues the old sinological tradition of teaching classical Chinese and lecturing about the past of China.

"[A]nd this is what Warsaw sinology has to stick to: contemporary China, but with very strong roots in traditional classical sinology. It has to be history, history of literature, and history of philosophy." (I1)

"We have kept classical Chinese, literary studies, and history, and at the same time we have added some new elements, and we try to balance [the curriculum]." (I8)

"Sinology should have two pillars: the first is tradition, and the second is modern times." (I9)

b. Sinology's Contribution to Society

The isolation of Warsaw sinologists from the political and economic realities ended with the regime change and the "generational changes."[61] Today the department is open to cooperation with other institutes in terms of publishing, lectures, organizing conferences, and student meetings.[62] Still, the staff admit they are only able to take part in a very limited number of such activities due to financial and time constraints. Respondents agree that there is not much cooperation between the department and similar institutions around the world. Although several academics do collaborate with foreign institutes—for example in Germany or the Czech Republic—these are individual cases, not instances of institutional cooperation.

c. Two New Sinology Centers

The other significant change in Polish sinology during this period has been the establishment of two new centers, one in Poznań and one in Lublin. The institute in Poznań, according to our respondents, is more linguistically oriented than the one in Warsaw, and is described as "strongly linguistic," "philological studies."[63] The focus is on practical, modern Chinese, although lectures on classical Chinese are also compulsory:

> "I think that they [the Sinology Department in Poznań] think in a different way. The emphasis is on very different issues. They do not have this whole package of ... history, philosophy—the classical part. They put priority on practical language abilities." (I1)

> "We have never been as theoretically-oriented as Warsaw. From the very beginning, we have always had less of that. We always used to have more practical courses. And it is still the same now." (I6)

The department's practical approach manifests itself not only in the curriculum but also in its internship program which, according to UAM regulations, is compulsory for undergraduate students in the philology departments, including sinology, Japanese studies, and indology.

The curriculum in the Sinology Department in Lublin is also strongly philological, with a concentration on practical, modern Chinese, accompanied by a small number of linguistic lectures, such as "Translation Studies,""Descriptive Chinese Grammar," and "Introduction to Linguistics." Although "History of China" and "History of Philosophy" are taught, this center cannot really be described as embracing the generalist tradition, as classical Chinese is not offered. Nor does it represent the specialist approach, as the number of specialist lectures is limited to a few topics: "Introduction to Oriental Cultures," "The Literature and Culture of China," "The Ethnology of China," and "The Modern History of China."[64] The approach is very practical, as the students in this department take part in internship programs and the department grants half-year scholarships to China.[65]

In short, since the 2000s sinology in Warsaw has become more pragmatic, more responsive, and more connected to society than it was in the 1950s and 1960s. Nevertheless, upholding the earliest traditions of the department, it strongly defends the core elements of the generalist approach to scholarship on China. At the same time, it has introduced into the curriculum a variety of changes that signal a strong influence of ideas promoted by the specialist camp. This specialization cannot be observed in the two other Polish sinology centers. In Poznań, sinology—described as philological studies—focuses on teaching modern Chinese but also offers classical Chinese, thereby combining the generalist tradition with the practical approach. Lublin focuses on teaching the modern language. Compared to Poznań, it offers a few more courses on Chinese culture, although the number is still too small to be able to speak of the influence of the specialist model. Still, most respondents felt that it is too early to generalize about the department, which was set up only two years ago. The other aspect that differentiates the new approach to sinology in Poznań and Lublin from that in Warsaw is that the former have a compulsory internship program for their students. At this point, it can be concluded that the interviewees mentioned more differences than similarities among the three sinology centers in Poland.

We now turn to the respondents' arguments either defending the traditional approach or justifying the need for change in the study of China. This section focuses solely on sinology in Warsaw, as only this center is involved in the epistemological debates on scholarship on China.

7. The Need for Change in the Warsaw Sinology Department

All the interviewees agreed that change in the department at UW has been unavoidable. Its transformation is presented as a necessity, created primarily by global forces. The department has had to respond to developments in the international economic and political environments, and in particular to the "rise of China," by modernizing the curriculum in order to provide students with a full understanding of these processes. It therefore began to offer lectures on Chinese politics, economy, society, and culture, and their respective international impacts:

"The traditional understanding of sinology is philological studies on the one hand and classical studies on the other, with an emphasis on the classical language, history, and literature … a classical kind of education. Still, we also know that we are in the twenty-first century … and sinology is becoming more open. It now realizes the importance of contemporary China." (I1)

Moreover, the respondents pointed out that sinology has had no choice but to adapt to global and regional trends in education, including the privatization of higher education, adjustments to European norms, marketization, and specialization. Higher education was privatized in Poland during the democratic transformation in the 1990s. This mainly entailed the establishment of non-state universities and the imposition of fees by the state universities on selected groups of students, including part-time, night, and external students.[66] The government granted the public universities more autonomy in terms of research and teaching. It also decreased its spending on education and introduced a system of funding whereby both the institutions and the individual scholars had to compete for grants. These changes put great pressure on the public universities, which now have to compete with the private institutions for students and have to secure the bulk of their financial resources on their own. The changes also give academics, whose salaries at public universities are low, an opportunity to seek additional employment at private schools. The adjustment to European norms stems from various agreements signed by the Polish government, mainly as a result of European integration. The series of agreements, known as the Bologna Process, is something that the respondents regarded as an important factor in shaping developments in the Warsaw Sinology Department.[67]

The interviews indicated that the consequences of privatization and the Bologna Process were important factors leading to heavy administrative workloads,[68] difficulties in dealing with multiple work commitments, including in the private universities, and scarcities of financial resources. The respondents perceived these factors to be the main obstacles to the organization of and participation in scholarly activities outside of the department and to the development of cooperation with other academic institutions around the world:

"There is this chap coming from abroad, and we don't even have the money to take him to lunch." (I8)

"Our salaries are … rather modest, so most of us have to do other things [besides teaching at UW], and, as a result, we have less time. So we try to

> fulfill the minimum requirements, and we have no energy for developing international cooperation." (I8)

Furthermore, privatization and the Bologna Process are associated with a decline in academic standards. Following the guidelines of the Bologna Process, Polish universities now adopt a two-tier system of study, i.e., a BA and an MA, instead of the previous four- or five-year MA degree. This decrease in the length of study required to obtain a university degree allows faster entry into the labor market. Respondents were skeptical about the academic content of the shorter cycle:

> "But this whole idea of university studies with a division into a BA and a MA—it's like a death knell for higher education, for the quality of higher education. What can they learn in three years?" (I2)

Finally, the establishment of a large number of private institutions that compete with public universities for students has ended the latter's monopoly on teaching about China. Students wishing to understand the country and to speak the language now have multiple paths from which to choose. They also have more opportunities when it comes to scholarships, and they are no longer dependent solely on the decisions of the authorities. They can apply for government grants from Beijing or Taipei, as well as from the European Union and private foundations. There are also internship opportunities in Polish and European companies that have cooperative arrangements in China with Chinese firms. Furthermore, some students decide to cover the costs of staying in China or Taiwan by private means—something that would have been unimaginable in the 1950s and 1960s.

Privatization and the introduction of European standards have been accompanied by marketization. Marketization means that higher education functions according to market principles: the university provides services, while knowledge is treated as a commodity and the students as customers. Consequently, university students become important stakeholders in their own training programs. In the interviews, young Poles were described as "business oriented,"[69] mostly "pragmatic,"[70] and people who "want to do business, politics, or diplomacy."[71] The majority of students, it was claimed, "chose this department to make money,"[72] or to "sell underwear to China,"[73] not out of passion. This means that they are not interested in translating the classics or doing research:[74] they demand practical lectures that can improve their chances on the job market, and want to study subjects such as modern Chinese or the Chinese economy, politics, and society. Responding to the more pragmatic students, the UW Sinology Department has taken this focus into account when designing its curriculum, and as a result it has become more practical. Meanwhile, some of these young people with this new perspective on the study of China have joined the staff of the Warsaw Sinology Department, and this "generational change" has naturally led to the introduction of new ideas into the curriculum:

> "Formerly, it seemed … no one thought that the student had to be satisfied or have any expectations, right? … And now, the student thinks 'OK, how can I benefit from my studies? What are my goals in life? Does this lecturer fulfill my expectations? Does he or she give me the product that I'm paying for?' It's a totally different world, entirely different. Now, the roles have changed a bit and the lecturers have to court the students. The student is the important one." (I4)

> "Basically, I had this feeling that the younger generation wanted to go this way [the way of the various other Sinology Departments in Western Europe] … and new PhD students started to work [at Warsaw sinology]. And there is definitely this change of generations, and that's it [the reason for change]. We've been forced to react to China's great success … The world started to notice it and we did too, but a bit later than the rest of the world. To make a long story short, we wanted to adjust to the new environment out of pure pragmatism. It works like this: the students come and they want to learn a profession, knowledge that will enable them to find a job." (I9)

Marketization is also seen as being responsible for changes in academic values. The university has to meet the pragmatic demands and values of the students, which have adjusted to the commercial situation:

> "The introduction of evening studies was a terrific freshening up of our old Sinology Department: it was like a breath of fresh air; it gave us an opportunity to search, while introducing new curricula, selecting new textbooks—it added a commercial dimension. These are the people who are paying, right? It has changed our way of thinking and has helped us adapt to reality, where, according to the new rules, your studies have to provide you with a job, not just develop your knowledge." (I2)

The last of the trends in international education that has required a change in the Sinology Department is the growing popularity of specialization:

"… a sinologist probably cannot be only a sinologist. … And everyone condemns us. On the one hand, we're not really linguists. It's not philology, we're not philologists. And on the other, we're not really students of cultural studies either. We somehow combine the two, and all of those humanists, those ethnographers, and anthropologists, they look down on us a bit, saying that we don't have the complete educational background that we would need in order to understand their area and to pursue research." (I2)

8. In Defense of the Tradition (in the Sinology Department of UW)

This section sets out the arguments adduced to explain the rationale for cultivating the traditional approach to the study of China, in which the sinologist works mainly with language (the generalist approach). The argument runs as follows: although the translation of texts is an important task for sinology, it does not constitute a goal in itself. Instead, it serves as a means of understanding China. The language is thus perceived of as a tool, a key to scholarship on China, and the paramount role here is accorded to classical Chinese. It is believed that familiarity with Chinese history is a prerequisite for understanding modern China, and, consequently, classical Chinese should constitute a fundamental element in sinological training:

"As far as I am concerned, language, which has unfortunately become a goal in itself nowadays, should be used as a way of researching a particular problem I'm interested in—let's say, a humanistic or … whatever kind of problem. Then, if I'm interested in something, I can read first-hand sources in Chinese and understand them." (I2)

"A sinologist has to have a sinological background, that is, has to know the history and the language. If not, he is not a sinologist. He can be an expert on China, but not a sinologist." (I8)

"If a person knows contemporary China and understands its economics, but does not know about the past … I think he or she does not understand everything … If you completely abandon classical Chinese … future generations will not be able to do anything with it … Still, the role of higher education is to educate people who will be able to do research in the future." (I9)

To support the traditional approach to the study of China, respondents referred to the discourse of responsibility. First, they pointed to the particular role institutions of higher education play in society, which, they say, should go beyond preparing students for a future job: they should help students "develop intellectually" and should provide the "fundamentals of a worldview," encouraging certain values. In addition to practical skills, university lectures should therefore offer theoretical and classical knowledge that can be acquired from courses on philosophy, history, and literature:

> "My approach to higher education is that you cannot limit a curriculum to a subject that gives you only practical skills. That would not be a university, but some type of vocational school." (I8)

> "[A]t the undergraduate level, we should somehow find a middle way between, on the one hand, preparing people for their profession, which everyone claims to be the most important, and, on the other, the university, which I believe is a place where people should develop intellectually. The practical dimension of what you teach is not as important as the skills and the kind of general knowledge that will constitute the basis of your worldview in the future." (I8)

Second, sinology is described as a cultural repository of a tradition, whose goal should be to promote the legacy of Polish sinologists in society.

> "I believe it is a kind of responsibility to earlier generations, to generations of Polish intellectuals ... I think that today, in particular, with the total decline of value systems, traditional values, and traditional understandings, sinology ... as part of a certain intellectual Polish heritage, has this responsibility: it is the mission of sinology." (I1)

The third responsibility attributed to sinology, for which a traditional sinological training is a prerequisite, is that of educating society about China. This is described as a particularly important mission, as the respondents contended that among Poles today knowledge about China is very poor. It is suggested that the horizons of both society and government are confined to the United States and Europe, and that knowledge about China is very superficial, even distorted. Society gets information from journalists who do not speak the language and do not understand Chinese society, or from accidental tourists who travel there "for two weeks and write a book about China."[75] As in the 1950s and 1960s, the Polish government has no strategic plan for developing specialist knowledge about China and does not actively promote

Chinese studies or sinology. Even though there are great sinologists in Poland, "no one is interested in them"—neither Polish politicians nor business:[76]

> "It is a huge country, China—1.5 billion people—a global superpower, which, if there are no catastrophes, will sooner or later manage this world. We [Poles], kind of, haven't noticed this fact." (I7)

> "People think we [in the Sinology Department] have a kind of mission. They expect us to organize open lectures, workshops, days about China…That type of thing." (I9)

> "Due to the glut of 'pop culture' interpretations of China, which are very superficial, we have to defend our specific character. This knowledge is usually the result of something like—a person goes to China for two weeks and writes a book about China, becomes an expert. That's it. And we [sinologists] are at the other extreme. We have the right to be there and to defend ourselves [our way of acquiring knowledge]." (I9)

> "Poland does not yet have a global perspective, and it is still parochial. It still suffers from the after-effects of 1989. This means that since Poland joined the EU and NATO it has totally neglected everything else … And our political elites and media are still bogged down in the realities of the past." (I13)

> "When Poland joined the West in the 1990s, and dived into the capitalist and consumerist societies … our mentality changed dramatically: intense cultural life faded away, as did our deep interest in other cultures. We suddenly became mentally 'closed.' Poles could at last travel freely, but their horizons were limited to Europe and the United States." (I17)

The articulation of responsibility constitutes a powerful discursive move undertaken in order to take the issue out of the realm of the strategic and selfish promotion of traditional sinology and to relocate it on the "higher ground" of the morally good. The application of this discourse therefore might be seen as the struggle to construct a realm of knowledge (the study of China) in a way that displays the abilities and knowledge that are characteristic of the UW Sinology Department.

Even though all the respondents agreed that changes in the department are necessary, they differed in assessments of those changes. Two of the interviewees questioned the quality of the specialization and claimed that, despite transforming the curriculum, UW sinologists have not become specialists in areas such as history, culture, or anthropology.

By denying the ability of sinologists to apply the methodologies and tools of the social sciences, they draw a clear boundary between area studies and sinology and limit the role of sinology to the study of language. In their opinion, sinology as such cannot provide an understanding of the social processes in China:

> "The Orientalists have not learnt anything at all about cultural issues or anthropology or social issues. It is only the same old study of literature, classical literature, just a bit more contemporary … [t]hey [at UW] taught it the wrong way, starting with the fact that the history of the Han dynasty at the university [UW] has always been taught as "the chronicles of the Han dynasty." It cannot be a chronicle if it is a history with descriptions and bibliographies—how does that compare with a chronicle!? And they still do it … so if you commit yourself to specializing in the history of China, then you should know at least as much about history as a first-year student in the History Department." (I3)

> "I might add that even today in my country there are still sinologists who look at China through the old propaganda lenses and regard official declarations and appearances as the 'truth'… They are unable to grasp real processes, with their enormous complexity. … A scholar, particularly a historian, should understand and explain foreign or historical realities without imposing on them contemporary values or stereotypes voiced by their country's elite." (I17)

9. Conclusions

The main goal of this study has been to examine the evolution of the understanding by Polish academics of sinology as a discipline against the background of the epistemological debate between the generalist and specialist approaches to the study of China. It has focused on two periods in the history of postwar Polish sinology: first, the 1950s and 1960s, and second, from 1990 to the present. Based on interviews, it provides insights into the understanding of sinology. As a first step, information about the state of Polish sinology during each period, with respect to the curriculum and to relations between the Sinology Department and society, was obtained from interviews, supplemented by an analysis of government and university papers on policies and programs. In the next step, the respondents' explanations of this particular state of affairs in sinology were analyzed. The most important findings are summarized below.

In the 1950s and 1960s, Polish sinology was represented by a single institution—the Sinology Department at the University of Warsaw. This department taught philology focused on the classics, strongly influenced by the French sinological tradition. Studies were pursued for the sake of knowledge, but they did not provide students with practical skills useful in the labor market. The department was relatively isolated from the political and economic realities of the time. Discussions about this particular design of sinological training programs in the 1950s and 1960s revolved around personal and political factors. The respondents pointed out that at the time sinology was shaped by individuals—mainly the head of the department—who made autonomous decisions about the curriculum and employment, and even had an impact on the students' careers. Neither the students nor the wider society contributed to the design of the program. Although the Polish authorities did not intervene directly in knowledge construction in the department, they did limit academic freedom and decide on scholarship and career opportunities for young people. Furthermore, political developments influenced the sources open to the Sinology Department and the information about China available within Polish society. The events with the most marked consequences were the Sino-Soviet split and the Cultural Revolution, which cut Polish society and sinology off from channels of information about China and led to further isolation of the UW Sinology Department.

Not until after the collapse of communism was the UW Sinology Department joined by a number of other Polish centers for the study of China and Chinese language, many of which were also called Sinology Departments. Only two of these newly established institutions, however, are commonly recognized in academic circles as being sinology centers: Poznań sinology at UAM and Lublin sinology at KUL. Still, it is difficult to point to particular characteristics that denote "real sinology," as the three centers offer very different curricula. The sinology course in Poznań consists of traditional philological studies, with lectures on classical Chinese but with a main focus on modern Chinese. The sinology curriculum in Lublin can be described as modern linguistic studies, as it concentrates on modern Chinese and has no courses on classical Chinese. It also offers some lectures on Chinese culture. However, it is still too early to make any assessments about the program only two years after its opening. The Warsaw Sinology Department, after 1990, introduced substantial changes into its curriculum, signaling its acceptance of the ideas promoted by the specialist camp. It has undergone a cultural shift (the introduction of lectures on Chinese culture), specialization (lectures on research methodology, workshops focusing on research in particular areas of study, such as literature and culture, for example, or philosophy and religion) and modernization (lectures on modern Chinese politics, economy, and society, and greater stress upon modern language) in order to equip students with more practical skills. At the same time, the changes do not reflect a desire to abandon the old traditions. On the contrary, the department perceives its mission to uphold tradition. It underscores the importance of a classical education, with classical language, philosophy, and history at its core.

All the respondents agree that Warsaw sinology has undergone a significant transformation. The proponents of the specialist approach to the study of China, however, question whether such changes provide sufficient background knowledge and tools for understanding present-day Chinese society, politics, and culture. The most critical voices claim that China should be analyzed by specialists in particular areas of study, such as history or philosophy, whereas sinologists should confine their research to the study of language.

These different voices demonstrate that epistemological questions about sinology have become the subject of heated debates among Polish scholars who are struggling to establish the meaning of sinology and Chinese studies and, at the same time, are attempting to determine the future of their profession. Of the three Sinology Departments in Poland discussed here, the Warsaw department is an important participant in this debate. Since the 2000s, it has been open to the ascription of new meanings to scholarship on China while simultaneously defending those elements of sinology that differentiate it from other disciplines and that constitute its identity. In practice, it has cultivated the generalist tradition, while at the same time allowing its program to be greatly influenced by the specialist approach. Thus the sinology taught in the Warsaw department, which draws on both traditions, can indeed be called a "New Sinology."

Notes

1. From 1952 it constituted a unit in the Faculty of Philology; in 1969 it came under Foreign Philology, and later, Neo-Philology. See the website of the Faculty of Oriental Studies, University of Warsaw, available at www.orient.

uw.edu.pl/en/history.html (accessed 27 October 2013). In 2008 the institute became the Faculty of Oriental Studies. *Monitor UW*, No. 1, 23 January 2003.

2. The UW unit that teaches sinology has changed its name over time. The official Faculty of Oriental Studies Web site states that in 1933–34 it was a seminar; in 1964 it was one of "seven chairs" at the Institute of Oriental Studies (*katedra* on the Polish Web site); and in 1975 it was called a specialization (*specjalność*). Today it is called a department (*zakład*). However, the different Polish names for units at the university, such as *katedra, zakład*, and *wydział*, are very often translated by the same word in English—"department." The situation becomes even more complicated when we realize that the name of this didactic unit at UW has different names in Polish (*zakład sinologii*—"Sinology Department") and in English ("Chinese Studies Department"). In order to avoid confusion, this chapter uses "Sinology Department" or "Warsaw sinology." See www.sinologia. uw.edu.pl/index/php and www.orient.uw.edu.pl/en/history.html (accessed 8 July 2014).

3. See http://www.wsmip.uj.edu.pl/en_GB/institute-of-the-middle-and-far-east (accessed 21 October 2013).

4. From the perspective of the international community, the role of the Confucius Institutes goes far beyond promoting Chinese language and culture. They are seen as a cultural diplomatic tool for promoting China's international status, and as an important element in China's soft diplomacy (see H. H. Michael Hsiao and Alan H. Yang, "The Rise of Confucius Institutes and the Examining of China's Soft Power Diplomacy," paper presented in International Workshop on Confucius Institutes in Asia and Beyond: Examining China's Soft Power Diplomacy, Taipei, 30 November 2012). They have been criticized as an attempt to "extend Chinese political control activities to Western universities." See Don Starr, "Chinese Language Education in Europe: The Confucius Institutes," *European Journal of Education*, Vol. 44, No. 1 (March 2009), pp. 65–82.

5. See http://fil.ug.edu.pl/oferta_ksztalcenia/kierunki_studiow_0 (accessed 19 July 2014); The Philology Department of Łódź International Studies Academy offers sinology courses, see www.wssm.edu.pl/studia_chinskie. php (accessed 21 October 2013); the Poznań College of Modern Languages opened an undergraduate program in Chinese Philology (sinology), see www.wsjo.poznan.pl/en/ (accessed 21 October 2013); the Faculty of International Relations at Łódź International Studies Academy (LISA) offers degree in sinology, see http://www.wssm.edu.pl/international_relations.php (accessed 11 August 2014).

6. In 1988, a five-year MA course in Chinese Studies was introduced at Adam Mickiewicz University in Poznań. Since the 2007–8 academic year,

undergraduate (i.e., first-level) studies have been offered under a Chinese-language program in the Department of Oriental Studies, and graduate (second-level) studies in the Chinese Literature and Culture Section of the Department of Asian Studies. For more information on oriental studies in Poznań, see Alfred F. Majewicz, "Thirteen Years of the International Institute of Ethnolinguistic and Oriental Studies (IIEOS)," available at http://www.staff.amu.edu.pl/~majewicz/doc/IIEOS_summary.pdf (accessed 21 October 2013).

7.   The third and youngest center to be recognized as a Sinology Department by Polish academics interested in the study of China opened to students on 1 October 2012 at the Catholic University of Lublin, as part of the Institute of Classical Philology in the Faculty of Humanities.

8.   There is also a new sinology center at the University of Gdańsk. The first students enrolled at the center in the 2013–14 academic year. It is not possible to assess the role of sinology in Gdańsk because the first academic year had not yet begun by the time of the interviews (which were conducted between August and October 2013). Moreover, only two interviewees referred to the sinology center in Gdańsk (I8 and I9) and only one considered it important for a discussion about sinology in Poland (I8). The second respondent who mentioned it stated that "the only partner for our kind of sinology [Warsaw sinology] is the Sinology Department in Poznań." She added: "These young sinology centers. … First, there are not many of them, and second, they … perhaps function a bit under the umbrella of other departments" (I9). The other respondents—when they were even aware of its existence—did not regard it as the equivalent of sinology in Warsaw, Poznań, or Łódź. For these reasons, sinology in Gdańsk is not analyzed in this study.

9.   John K. Fairbank, "Assignment for the '70's," *American Historical Review*, Vol. 74, No. 3 (February 1969), pp. 861–879, at p. 865.

10. Benjamin A. Elman, "The Unravelling of Neo-Confucianism: From Philosophy to Philology in Late Imperial China," *Tsing Hua Journal of Chinese Studies*, Vol. 15, Nos. 1/2 (December 1983), pp. 66–88.

11. Chia-Mei Jane Coughlan, *The Study of China in Universities: A Comparative Case Study of Australia and the United Kingdom* (New York: Cambria Press, 2008), p. 114.

12. Fairbank, "Assignment for the '70's."

13. Coughlan, *The Study of China in Universities.*

14. Ibid., p. 140.

15. Examples of prominent contributions to the debate include the following: Frederick W. Mote, "The Case for the Integrity of Sinology," *Journal of Asian Studies*, Vol. 23, No. 4 (August 1964), pp. 531–534; Benjamin

Schwartz, "The Fetish of the 'Disciplines,'" *Journal of Asian Studies*, Vol. 23, No. 4 (August 1964), pp. 537–538; Mary C. Wright, "Chinese History and the Historical Vocation," *Journal of Asian Studies*, Vol. 23, No. 4 (August 1964), pp. 513–516; Maurice Freedman, "What Social Science Can Do for Chinese Studies," *Journal of Asian Studies*, Vol. 23, No. 4 (August 1964), pp. 523–529; Joseph R. Levenson, "The Humanistic Disciplines: Will Sinology Do?" *Journal of Asian Studies*, Vol. 23, No. 4 (August 1964), pp. 507–512; G. William Skinner, "What the Study of China Can Do for Social Science," *Journal of Asian Studies*, Vol. 23, No. 4 (August 1964), pp. 517–522; John K. Fairbank, "Assignment for the '70's"; Andrew J. Nathan, "Is Chinese Culture Distinctive? A Review Article," *Journal of Asian Studies*, Vol. 52, No. 4 (November 1993), pp. 923–936; Giri Deshingkar, "In Defence of Sinology," *China Report*, Vol. 30, No. 4 (1994), pp. 471–473; Hans Kuijper, "Is Sinology a Science?" *China Report*, Vol. 36, No. 3 (2000), pp. 331–354.

16. Geremie R. Barmé, "New Sinology," available at http://ciw.anu.edu.au/new_sinology/index.php (accessed 15 July 2014).

17. Vivien Burr, *An Introduction to Social Constructionism* (London: Routledge, 1995).

18. Thomas Diez, "Europe as a Discursive Battleground: Discourse Analysis and European Integration Studies," *Cooperation and Conflict*, Vol. 36, No. 1 (2001), p. 17.

19. Ernesto Laclau and Chantal Mouffe, *Hegemony and Socialist Strategy: Towards a Radical Democratic Politics* (London; New York: Verso, 1985), p. 108.

20. Diez, "Europe as a Discursive Battleground," p. 16.

21. Marcin Jacoby, "Oral History of China Scholars in Poland: Final Report (2013)," available at http://politics.ntu.edu.tw/RAEC/comm2/InterviewPo00.pdf (accessed 23 October 2013).

22. Department of Political Science, National Taiwan University. See http://politics.ntu.edu.tw/RAEC/act02.php (accessed 23 October 2013).

23. Thomas Diez, "Speaking 'Europe': The Politics of Integration Discourse," *Journal of European Public Policy*, Vol. 6, No. 4 (1999), pp. 598–613.

24. In the years following World War II, the Sinology Department at UW included also Japanese studies. During the first three years, students had to study both, choosing their specialization, either sinology or Japanese studies, in their fourth year.

25. An interviewee who began sinological studies in 1954 mentioned the lecture "General Knowledge about China." It was partly devoted to contemporary China as, according to the interviewee, it provided basic knowledge on the history and geography of China. (I22)

26. I18.
27. I20.
28. I3, I18.
29. I3.
30. I20.
31. I15.
32. Katarzyna Golik, "Witold Jabłoński—Niesłusznie Zapomniany Polski Sinolog" (Witold Jabłoński—The Polish Sinologist Who Does Not Deserve to be Forgotten), *Azja-Pacyfik*, No. 12 (2009), pp. 218–229.
33. I1, I11.
34. L. Kasarełło, "Polska Sinologia: Przeszłość i Wyzwania Współczesności" (Polish Sinology: The Past and the Challenges of Contemporaneity), paper prepared for the 80th anniversary of Warsaw Oriental Studies (forthcoming).
35. I15.
36. I3.
37. I23.
38. I16.
39. I21.
40. I17.
41. I22.
42. I22.
43. I3.
44. I18.
45. I22.
46. Kasarełło, "Polska Sinologia. Przeszłość i Wyzwania Współczesności."
47. I25.
48. Jan Rowiński, "Wahadło: Czyli Stosunki Polityczne PRL-ChRL" (Pendulum: Or, Political Relations Between the PPR [Polish People's Republic] and the PRC), in *Polska-Chiny: Wczoraj, Dziś, Jutro* (Poland-China: Yesterday, Today, and Tomorrow), edited by Bogdan Góralczyk (Toruń: Wydawnictwo Adam Marszałek, 2009), pp. 11–64.
49. According to the interviewees, the last scholarships to China were granted in 1956. One interviewee, however, went to China on a scholarship in 1964 as a result of an agreement on cultural exchanges between the PRC and Poland. He stated that his was the only scholarship to China at that time and he received it because the Ministry of Higher Education appreciated his help to Asian students in Poland (I17).
50. A small number of students began to go to China on scholarships in 1979 (I13). However, official government scholarships were not reinstated until the 1984–85 academic year.
51. Kasarełło, "Polska Sinologia. Przeszłość i Wyzwania Współczesności."
52. I20.

53. On its official Web site, Warsaw sinology refers to itself as "modern philology." See http://www.sinologia.uw.edu.pl/pods/404_o-zakladzie-sinologii (accessed 22 June 2014).
54. I1.
55. Information on the courses was retrieved from the schedules for the 2012–13 and 2013–14 academic years. The schedule for the current academic year is available at http://www.sinologia.uw.edu.pl/pods/405_planzajec (accessed 24 August 2014). The curriculum can be found at http://www.sinologia.uw.edu.pl/pods/372_sprawy-studenckie (accessed 14 July 2014).
56. The Web site of the Faculty of Oriental Studies (Wydział Orientalistyczny Uniwersytetu Warszawskiego, Wydziałowe Pracownie Specjalizacyjne) can be found at www.orient.uw.edu.pl/pl/io/studia/pracownie.html (accessed 22 January 2014).
57. I8, I9.
58. I1.
59. I14.
60. I8, I9.
61. I9.
62. I3.
63. I3.
64. KUL, "Philology–Sinology, Plan of Study," see www.kul.pl/filologia-sinologia, art_34574.html (accessed 25 January 2014).
65. I13.
66. J. J. Smolicz, "Privatization in Higher Education: Emerging Commonalities and Diverse Educational Perspectives in the Philippines, Australia, Poland and Iran," *Journal of Development and Society*, Vol. 28, No. 2 (1999), pp. 205–228.
67. The Bologna Declaration, signed in 1999 by 29 European countries including Poland, launched a process to harmonize the countries' higher education systems, making them "more competitive and attractive" for students both within and outside of the signatory states. See European University Association (EUA), available at www.eua.be/eua-work-and-policy-area/building-the-european-higher-education-area/bologna-basics.aspx (accessed 8 August 2014) and European Commission, http://ec.europa.eu/education/policy/higher-education/bologna-process_en.htm (accessed 15 July 2014).
68. The respondents mainly complained about the heavy administrative workload resulting from changes due to participation in the Bologna Process, such as the credit system (European Credit Transfer and Accumulation System) for assessing study performance.
69. I7.

70. I8: "Students can be divided into one-third people with passion and two-thirds pragmatists."
71. I2.
72. I8.
73. I2.
74. I7.
75. I13.
76. I13.

Chapter 5

The Lifting of the "Iron Veil" by Russian Sinologists During the Soviet Period (1917–1991)

Valentin C. Golovachev

> *Lift not the painted veil which those who live call life....*
> Percy Shelley, 1818

Russian sinologists were restricted in many ways and to a great extent were limited from engaging in professional exchanges with their colleagues in China and other countries during the entire Soviet period (1917–91). Such restrictions resulted in Russian sinologists being divided, isolated, oppressed, discriminated, limited, and confined to their country for many decades. Nevertheless, Russian sinologists still managed to maintain contacts with their colleagues from the "socialist camp" and the global sinology community. There were at least three "outer sinology worlds" existing beyond the domestic world of Soviet sinology and USSR borders, including China, the "socialist camp countries," and the countries of the "capitalist world."

This study utilizes data obtained from interviews conducted in Russia as part of "The Epistemology of China Studies: Oral History Project" (CS-OHP), initiated by Professor Chih-yu Shih at National Taiwan University in 2007. As of the present, more than 20 countries and territories have participated in this project. The collected interviews are published online, in academic periodicals, and in printed volumes.

A total of 40 interviews with elderly and middle-aged Russian sinologists were recorded by the author and his colleague between 2009 and 2013. All interviewees were born during the Soviet period (between 1918 and 1953). In particular, 28 (70 percent) of the subjects were born in 1918 and during the 1920s and 1930s, and 12 (30 percent) were born between 1940 and 1953. Twenty-two interviews had been translated into Chinese by April 2014.[1] Through the interviews, a number of vivid personal accounts were gathered, which are good starting points for initial reflections and conclusions. Soviet sinologists implemented various methods to penetrate the political and ideological "iron veil," to promote their studies abroad, and to participate in international cooperation on China studies. This chapter seeks to demonstrate the uniqueness of professional interviews as a potentially rich source and foundation for further academic explorations into the oral history of China studies.

1. Performing Chinese Studies in China

Among the main circumstances that predetermined the fate of all Russian sinologists during the Soviet period were the closing of the state borders and the restrictions imposed against opportunities to travel abroad. Therefore, the first encounters with China (or the Chinese world more generally) were usually the very first trips abroad for most of those of the elderly and middle-aged generations. These trips highlighted their complicated experience of engaging in personal contacts with foreigners (Chinese colleagues as well as the general public). The nature of this experience depended largely on the various opportunities to travel abroad, such as forced emigration, official visits (e.g., for study, lectures, or research trips), and family outings. Large groups of Soviet sinologists can be roughly grouped according to when they first visited China. The most common features of the people included in each of these groups upon their arrival in China are also noted. The first and the last groups are not included in our study because of the lack of oral interviews.

a. From 1917 to the 1930s: Revolutionaries and Emigrants to China

Following the October Revolution in 1917, the Russian sinological community split into two main groups. The first group included revolutionary emissaries who attempted to introduce the Communist revolution to China. The second group included those who were forced to emigrate to China during or soon after the Civil War (1917–1920s). Isolated from Russia, most sinologists in exile were doomed to spend the rest of their lives abroad (e.g., in China). This group is beyond the scope of the present research, except for Dr. Ceorgy V. Melikhov (b. 1930, Harbin) who was part of the small group of Soviet sinologists who were born in China. Dr. Melikhov began his Chinese studies after his repatriation to the USSR in the late 1950s.

b. From the 1930s to the 1940s: Translators and Diplomats

Only one representative of this group (ac. Sergey L. Tikhvinsky, 1918) was interviewed for the project. Nikolay T. Fedorenko was interviewed for two hours, and the interview was recorded by Taiwan PTV in 1992. A recording of this interview is stored somewhere in the PTV archives. Members of this group of translators and diplomats began their translation, diplomatic, research, and other professional work in China in the late 1930s and thereafter.

c. From 1949 to 1969: Students, Journalists, Teachers and Scholars, and Their Family Members

This large group of prominent scholars (over 12 interviewees) initially visited China as interpreters or journalists (e.g., Deliusin), graduate students, or "aspirants" (e.g., Lapina, Kondrashova [Molodtsova], Kriukov, Kuczera, and Titarenko), visiting scholars and members of delegations (e.g., Bokschanin, Chudodeev, Kychanov, Myasnikov, and Riftin), and visiting family members (e.g., Golovacheva, Kozhin, Usov, and Zhelokhovtsev), among others.

d. From the Late 1960s to the 1980s: Students, Mariners, and Diplomats, Among Others

This group includes a number of research fellows and students who received Chinese-language training at Nanyang University in Singapore in the 1970s (e.g., Larin, Maliavin) or visited Chinese ports as seasonal workers on cargo ships (e.g., Larin) and served as Soviet diplomats and officials (e.g., Rakhmanin, Zhelokhovtsev, and Galenovitch, among others). No official research trips to the PRC or other direct academic exchanges occurred during this time.

e. From 1983 to 1991: Students, Teachers, and Scholars Visiting China after the Restoration of Student and Scholarly Exchanges

These people formed the largest group visiting China for the first time during the late Soviet period (e.g., Garushyantz, Kobzev, and Pisarev), still under strict CPSU (Communist Party of the Soviet Union) and state control.

f. From 1991 to 2014: All Students and Acting Sinologists during the Post-Soviet Period

This group is actively involved in the new era of personal contacts, visits, and professional exchanges, except for two sinologists (for personal reasons). This group is also beyond the scope of this research because their first meetings with China occurred during the post-Soviet period (after 1991).

The first visits to China, as a very first visit abroad to a foreign country during the Soviet period under review (the 1930s to 1991), had a tremendous impact on most interviewees. Living and studying in China was challenging, and many dramatic changes occurred in the personal lives of this group of Soviet sinologists. These visits significantly changed their perceptions of China and Chinese people, also prompting a drastically new awareness about themselves and their profession. Establishing good working relations with Chinese colleagues often became a new cornerstone for further professional progress in their sinological careers. Sergey L. Tikhvinsky (b. 1918) recalls:

> "I spent two years in Chongqing (starting in 1943) and became acquainted with Guo Moruo and historians Hou Wailu and Cao Jinghua. The widow of Sun Yat-Sen gave me some materials. Feng Ziyou, a Guomindang veteran and a member of the "Xing zhong hui," also gave me materials." (Interview with Tikhvinsky, p. 5)

Five years later, in 1948, a young World War II veteran and student, Lev P. Deliusin, was also deeply impressed by his first professional encounter with China:

> "While at the frontline, I wanted, if I survived, to go somewhere in the East and beyond, such as India or China. When we were in our third year, a man came to our institute to form a group of students who would carry out translation work at the KVZD (CER). Of course, it was an unheard of joy to

be able to go to China! For a long time, I had desired to see the real China and to test and practice my Chinese-language proficiency. Harbin City impressed me immensely. For the first time, I regarded myself as being "abroad." In China, we realized the level of our training. By reading newspapers and books, we realized our almost complete ignorance about the country. And we were also unfamiliar with the oral language used by the Chinese public." (Interview with Deliusin, pp. 4, 7, 9–10, 12)

Prof. Zina G. Lapina (b. 1934) from the Institute of the Afro-Asian States, Moscow State University (IAAS MSU) presented a very romantic recollection of her trip to China.

"In autumn 1957 when I went to China, it was a breakthrough! For the first time, we went to the country that had been the subject of our studies. Nobody asked how long we were going to stay there. The question was inappropriate because we were ready for anything. Such was our romantic attitude toward China. What else can I say about staying in China? During the first year, I felt permanent happiness! I was in the country that I was studying and attempting to understand, and I was not disappointed." (Interview with Lapina, pp. 8, 14)

Visiting and studying abroad were extremely rare and complicated in the 1970s. Soviet sinologists (excluding diplomatic officials) had no opportunities to visit the PRC. Only a very few were fortunate enough to obtain year-long Chinese-language training in Singapore. According to Prof. Victor Larin (b. 1952, Russian Academy of Sciences, Vladivostok), opportunities, such as language-training abroad, were a great eye-opening experience.

"I obtained the opportunity to join a group of Soviet trainees to study in Singapore in 1975. At that time, Singapore was probably the only place where Soviet sinologists could study overseas. This was my first experience to live as an independent adult outside of the "Iron Curtain" in the "capitalist world." (Interview with Larin, pp. 8–9)

Therefore, the specific perceptions of Soviet sinologists on China were predetermined by the policy of self-isolation of the USSR and its relations with the PRC. Their initially distant perceptions regarding traditional and modern China were indirectly influenced by Communist propaganda and were relatively idealistic. Their first personal encounters with China became a real turning point, resulting in deep changes in their professional and personal lives. After returning home enriched and transformed by the eye-opening personal experience of living in China, they felt they were in a position to realistically attest to the distinct qualities of China and its people. Moreover, their perceptions of the USSR, themselves, and their profession inevitably changed as well. Unfortunately, only a small group of Soviet sinologists was allowed to visit the PRC before and during the Cultural Revolution. Although they had dedicated their lives to Chinese studies, they were deprived of the opportunity to personally visit the "country they had been studying" for many years (even for decades). Upon arriving in China, especially in the late 1950s and during the worst times in USSR-PRC relations from 1960 to the 1970s, these Soviet sinologists had to dispel with many initial illusions and ideals that they had acquired in absentia during the earlier period of "brotherhood" between the two countries. Their connections with Chinese colleagues and access to research materials were highly restricted. They lost many colleagues, friends, and relatives and were held hostage to the ideological struggle for "pure socialism" for more than two decades. The situation changed for the better only in the 1980s when hundreds of Soviet sinologists (young students as well as venerable old scholars) were allowed to discover and rediscover China. The drama of these first "foreign" encounters is clearly reflected in the interviews. The personal encounters all share many common features, such as those associated with the complicated changes in USSR-PRC and CPSU-CCP relations, as well as the development of crucial events occurring within the USSR and China. Despite all the vicissitudes of fate, most Soviet sinologists were greatly inspired by their first personal encounters in China. Most chose to remain loyal to their profession (sinology) and maintain their sincere and open love for China.

2. Sinological Exchanges and Cooperation Inside the "Socialist Camp"

a. Alumni Relations

During their periods of foreign study in China, Soviet students met students and graduate students, or "aspirants," from other socialist countries (e.g., Albania, Bulgaria, Czechoslovakia, East Germany, Hungary, North Korea, Poland, Romania, Vietnam, and Yugoslavia).

These relations had their limits relative to both language and the current political situations (see Deliusin, Kychanov, and Kuczera). As Professor Kychanov (1932–2013) recalls:

> "Cubans also came to China … The Hungarians were not present at that time, but the Germans and Romanians were there. There was a Romanian guy who liked to watch movies in our embassy. Every time the car came to fetch us, he would lay on the floor to avoid detection by Chinese or Romanians until the car left our school and was at the entrance of the embassy. Many students were Albanians. Relations with Albania were already bad, but the Albanian students treated us very well. We had good interactions with them and they all could speak Russian. The Vietnamese and Koreans ignored us at close range. Only once did a Korean guy approach me in the yard and say, 'Zdravstvuite' [Hello in Russian]." (Interview with Kychanov, p. 13)

After the departure of the alumni to their home countries, some established friendships evolved into good professional collaborations. These close friendships and lifelong periods of cooperation are vividly described by Zina G. Lapina:

> "All of us students from Hungary, Czechoslovakia, Romania, and other countries became very close friends in China, and we maintained our ties for years to come! They all went to China via Moscow, and they all stayed in our apartment. My parents knew them very well. For example, they knew Peter Polonyi from Hungary, Intraut Haynes from the GDR, and Aurelia, a Romanian, who later went to Israel. We corresponded frequently to update one another on what each was doing. Everyone knew the Chinese language very well. However, they found little use for their knowledge about China. Many had difficulties finding work in their home countries. I knew many Czech sinologists. I was in Czechoslovakia twice between 1975 and 1976 and taught ancient and medieval Chinese history to students who were studying to become sinologists at Charles University. Sinologist Marcellus Kubeshova was then the head of the Asia and Africa Department. She often came to Moscow and we jointly published several books on China. We also visited each other by invitation. In general, many relationships remained very close." (Interview with Lapina, pp. 34–35)

Alumni from other socialist states often visited USSR enroute to China or to carry out their doctoral studies or research and to participate in various academic activities. Meanwhile, they also invited Soviet scholars to visit their universities, museums, or research institutes whenever invitations could be arranged. They mainly invited Soviet sinologists for academic and public lectures on Chinese history or on "current events in China" and to participate in scientific conferences (see Chudodeev, Deliusin, Gelbras, Kuczera, Kychanov, and Lapina, among others).

An interesting record about the first meeting since 1975 of the annual conference on "Society and State in China," which was held in Moscow, was obtained from the interview with Professor Deliusin (1923–2013), the recognized founder of the conference:

> "The invitations for the first conference were sent out. Participants arrived from Leningrad, Vladivostok, and Kazakhstan. Some were from Ukraine. My friends were, namely, Feebler arriving from the GDR, Polonyi from Hungary, and Sławiński from Poland. I had become acquainted with these sinologists during their previous years in Moscow. Some came for practice, some came to work in the INION.[2] Some were engaging in Party work in Moscow (e.g., Polonyi). We observed the lack of professional communications in the home countries of my colleagues from the socialist countries. And no "discussion clubs" yet existed in Moscow. … Of course, there was delation about our very first conference, and I had to explain why I was holding an international conference without first obtaining permission. Others accused us of using the conference to deviate from Marxism." (Interview with Deliusin, pp. 33–34)

b. Socialist Mass Media

International magazines, such as *For Lasting Peace, for People's Democracy* and *Problemy Mira i Sotsializma* (*Problems of Peace and Socialism*, or often referred to by its English-language title, *World Marxist Review*), became very important platforms for regular sinological exchanges inside the "socialist camp."[3] According to Professor Deliusin's interview, working at *Problemy Mira i Sotsializma* magazine provided a venue not only for active debates on professional issues (including about China), but also official travel opportunities as correspondents to many socialist and developing countries. These overseas trips were not subject to approval by the International Department of the CPSU Central Committee in Moscow. During his year of working in 1958 as a correspondent for this magazine, Deliusin visited countries such as China, Egypt, India, Indonesia, Iraq, Korea, Mongolia, Sudan, and Syria.

c. Interkit

Another unique and influential platform was Interkit, which established a distinct reputation in the history of professional exchanges and discussions among "socialist camp" sinologists between the 1960s and the 1980s. (See the interviews with Gelbras and Usov, among others.) Interkit received only scant scholarly attention until the 2000s. The initial exploration into Interkit was undertaken by Claudie Gardet in 2000[4] and by David Wolff in 2003.[5] After these initial studies, substantial interest in Interkit was generated. An international consortium of scholars pooled their resources and findings in the hopes of constructing an all-encompassing narrative of different aspects of Interkit. They studied the Interkit phenomenon using archival material gathered from the former Warsaw Pact states, Soviet Asian allies such as Mongolia, and the United States and China. Building on conferences organized in Beijing in 2004 and Budapest in 2003 and 2010 that were dedicated to exploring Sino-East European relations/Interkit,[6] a two-day conference hosted by Péter Vámos was held in Freiburg (May 2011) to study the intricacies of Interkit.[7] Participants at the conference also formulated plans for further documentary and oral history workshops.

As a result of the collective findings of the group, a solid research and documentary volume entitled "The Interkit Story" was published in 2011 as a working paper of Cold War International History Project (CWIHP). The authors state: "In this working paper, we present an initial sampling of translated documents to outline Interkit's shadowy existence, together with a contextual introduction that outlines our current knowledge of the group's existence and raises some key questions about its function and activities."[8]

According to the documentary volume, the name Interkit or "China International" was derived from the words "International" and *Kitai* (the Russian word for "China"). Interkit first convened in Moscow in 1967 and served as a forum in which the International Department of the Soviet Politburo essentially attempted to ensure close coordination and control over the China policies of the Allied states in the socialist camp. The Chinese dubbed Interkit as *fanhua guoji* 反華國際 , or "the anti-China International."

A series of meetings were held interchangeably in the various capitals of the socialist bloc to periodically gather experts on China from the USSR, the Warsaw Pact allies, and a shifting mix of other nations aligned with the Kremlin (e.g., Mongolia, Vietnam, Laos, and Cuba). The participants, who were primarily Communist Party functionaries, but, in some cases, diplomatic and/or academic China "hands," considered the political, economic, ideological, cultural, and other dimensions of handling their problematic former ally. The unannounced meetings of Interkit, held primarily in Eastern Europe but occasionally in more far-flung localities such as Ulaanbaatar and Havana, spanned the last years of Mao Zedong to the transitional period after his death in September 1976, that is, from the brief yet intense succession struggle to the reign of Deng Xiaoping and his policies of modernization and economic reform and opening. As described by the authors of "The Interkit Story," by the mid-1980s when Mikhail Gorbachev assumed power and began a concerted effort to repair Soviet ties with Beijing, the socialist allies of the USSR went their own ways and were less willing to follow the direction of Moscow; Interkit had finally outlived its usefulness.[9]

The first Interkit meeting, convened in Moscow on 14–21 December 1967, was attended by representatives of the International Departments of the Communist Parties of the USSR, GDR, Poland, Czechoslovakia, Bulgaria, Hungary, and Mongolia.[10] The meetings were held almost annually thereafter, at least 15 times, until the last meeting, held in Moscow on 18 February 1985 (see the list of Interkit meetings).[11] The close coordination of China policies was implemented at different levels, including during meetings of top leaders, ministers, and deputy ministers in Moscow or in other capitals, meetings of "friendly" ambassadors in Beijing, regular meetings of the Ministry of Foreign Affairs and officials of the International Department of the Party Central Committee, meetings of experts on China from government organizations and research institutes, and during consultations among Soviet diplomats and government officials and Party workers.[12]

Though the specialists on China from the various research institutes comprised only one level of the multi-level Interkit system, they significantly influenced the system. As stated by the authors of "The Interkit Story," inevitably, the academic discipline of China studies in the USSR and other Communist nations during this period was influenced, indeed warped, by ideological and policy imperatives. The same experts on China who populated the Interkit narrative had the tendency to dominate, or at least heavily influence, both policy toward China and academic studies on China in their own countries. Mikhail S. Kapitsa, Oleg B. Rakhmanin, Mikhail I. Sladkovsky, and Sergei L. Tikhvinsky were considered the "Big Four" and maintained a firm hold on all studies on China from the commanding heights of four interlocking institutions. Two of the "Gang of Four" in sinology, namely, Rakhmanin and Sladkovsky, were also Interkit leaders. As the directors for China policy in the Central Committee and directors of the Institute of the Far East, Rakhmanin and Sladkovsky represented two streams of policy-oriented China monitoring that would be merged into Interkit, shaping elite and popular perceptions of the Middle Kingdom throughout the Warsaw Pact. Gilbert Rozman, the closest student of Soviet sinology between the 1960s and the 1980s, has written: "Only after 1967 was a concerted effort made to explain what had happened and what was happening in the PRC. ... At the end of the 1960s Soviet Chinese studies had reached their maturity. From this time to 1982 they would be marked by voluminous output, stable organization, and a consistent prevailing outlook on Chinese society. This outlook was an amplification of emerging views from the mid-1960s, specifically the absence of fundamental change in thinking for about two decades under Brezhnev's and Suslov's leadership."[13] This was the direction of Soviet sinology during the later years of the Cold War.[14]

We agree with the previously noted assessments as far as "a consistent prevailing outlook" on modern Chinese society during those years is concerned. However, the prevailing outlook on traditional or historical Chinese society, although it was also the subject of political and ideological control and speculation, was more inconsistent between the 1960s and the 1970s because of certain challenges presented by some Soviet orientalists, such as the adherents of the Marxist "Asiatic mode of production" theory.

To illustrate typical academic activities under the aegis of Interkit, we refer to excerpts from the "Protocol Transcript of the Moscow Meeting," held 16–18 May 1973, including the specific recommendations on coordinating policy toward China. The following are the recommendations "in the area of academic work on the China issue": 1) To use conferences, seminars, and international symposia focusing on various issues to explain and propagate the views agreed upon by our parties regarding China; 2) To hold at the end of 1973 or early 1974, a conference of sinologists, along with Marxist theorists and progressive sinologists from various countries, where a thorough analysis of the Marxist-Leninist position would be presented regarding the current state and future trends in Chinese development, including an assessment of the Cultural Revolution and its consequences for the future of socialism in the PRC; 3) To organize closed symposia, joint research, preparation of monographs, academic exchanges, lectures, and doctoral candidates and students to study China within the framework of academic cooperation; 4) To organize an academic symposium on the topic of "The Ideological Basis and Political Practice of Maoism," in particular, on the practice of Maoism during the first quarter of 1974; 5) To consult on the topics of papers and statements on China for participants at the XXIX International Congress of Orientalists to be held in Paris in July of this year; and 6) To create a united and cooperative academic council on Chinese affairs, which will coordinate study and research and invite leading sinologists from various parties.[15]

As the experts have noted, "the existence of Interkit raises some key questions about its functions and activities. Did it actually influence or shape Kremlin policy toward China and perceptions of what was happening there? Or was it primarily a transmission belt that facilitated the spread of propaganda, policy coordination, and enforcement of orthodoxy among the allies of Moscow? To what extent, if at all, did non-Soviet China experts use the regular gatherings, if not the plenary sessions (where disagreements were resolved) and more private bilateral talks to influence others about their own approaches? Were the effects of China's 'differentiation' strategy evident during the Interkit proceedings? These are some of the questions that will be explored in our Interkit project, along with others that may emerge as more evidence is assembled and assessed."[16]

We believe that CS-OHP can effectively provide answers to these questions. Both available and future data from interviews with venerable sinologists from Russia and the East European countries will also be helpful to increase our understanding of the evolution of Soviet/ Russian (and East European and Central European) scholarship on China. Professor Vilya G. Gelbras (b. 1930, Institute of Asian and African Studies) and Professor Victor Usov (b. 1943, Institute of Far Eastern Studies, Russian Academy of Sciences), for example, were actively involved in a series of the Interkit discussions on China. According to Professor Gelbras:

> "At the turn of the 1970s and the 1980s, these discussions inspired German colleagues to gather a group of really competent experts who had been to China and who were engaged in studies on China (e.g., Bruno Mallow,

head of the International Department of the Central Committee of the Sozialistische Einheitspartei Deutschlands [SED]). There was a small group of Polish sinologists (i.e., Roman Slawiński and Jan Rowiński). The Romanians refused to participate in Interkit. A Soviet sinologist, who had married a Bulgarian lady and moved there, participated in Interkit on behalf of Bulgaria. There were also Hungarians (i.e., Barna Tálas and Peter Polonyi). All of them had studied in China and could speak Chinese. They were very interesting and educated people, who could be considered genuine experts on China and who had their own visions and arguments in heated debates about certain events in China. This was very useful and friendly work of great benefit to everyone. Now the connection is broken." (Interview with Gelbras, pp. 43–44)

As noted in the final chapter of *The Interkit Story* (From Mao's Death to the Death of Interkit), 1986 marked "an anachronistic relic of a passing era. … Its records and structures were consigned to archives and fading memories, along with the artificially imposed Soviet-East Central European coordination of research on modern China and conformity, which it struggled to promote."[17]

In fact, the academic and personal exchanges between the "socialist" sinologists were never limited to the Interkit activities. Sinologists were not associated with Interkit before 1967 and they survived it in the years after 1985. Many Russian (former Soviet) sinologists had never even heard of Interkit. Although not all-inclusive, during the period of its existence Interkit still represented a very important form of sinological exchanges in the socialist countries. Despite various ideological limits, the professional exchanges inside the "socialist camp" (both formal and informal) could at least partially offset the isolation and compensate for the acute lack of information available to Soviet sinologists. Although the Eastern European countries were much more open to the outside world, communications with Soviet colleagues significantly compensated for the shortage of precious professional exchanges and research materials for sinologists from other socialist countries.

3. Encounters with the Non-Communist "Capitalist World"

The encounters of Soviet sinologists with the sinology community in the non-Communist "capitalist world" can be briefly described from at least three perspectives, including 1) personal encounters, cooperation, friendship, and correspondence; 2) international scientific forums as a platform for personal encounters; and 3) teaching/lecturing, scholarships, and other research trips abroad.

Academic exchanges among countries of the "capitalist world" were generally subjected to the most strict controls, restrictions, and regulations in the Soviet Union. In this area, much more distinct was the fine line between the so-called "exit-able" and "non-exit-able" Soviet scientists. This line was essentially unrelated to their academic performance. The so-called "exit-ables" (those with permission to travel outbound) refer to sinologists as acting or retired diplomats (e.g., Tikhvinsky, Rakhmanin, and Fedorenko), journalists specializing on international affairs (e.g., Deliusin), world-renowned scientists, experts, and socially correct and "loyal" scientists. One of the key criteria and guarantees for the loyalty of the "exit-ables" was whether they were members of the CPSU.

"Non-exit-ables," or persons with no permission to travel outbound or those who were prohibited from going abroad, included groups such as the *otkazniki* (lit. denied persons), referring to applicants for emigration to Israel who were denied permission by the Soviet authorities, including Vitaly A. Rubin (1923–1981) and *podpisanty* (lit. signatories), referring to those who signed various opposition petitions, such as Eugenia V. Zavadskaya (1930–2002). Among the "non-exit-ables" were also individuals with "dubious" social (e.g., repressed) and ethnic backgrounds (mainly Jews, according to the "nationality"—the odious "5th column" on the personal data forms of Soviet citizens) or those people with "improper" performance (in terms of official or Party bosses). (See the interviews with Deliusin, Garuschyantz, Gelbras, Kozhin, and Krol.)

In many cases, official invitations to participate in various scholarly trips abroad emerged as a result of long-time personal contacts (Deliusin, Kychanov, and Tikhvinsky). An excerpt from the interview with Professor Evgeny I. Kychanov provides one of the best illustrations of such a personal encounter that fortunately evolved into a professional cooperation:

> "Honestly speaking, I was lucky in terms of Western contacts. During the Congress of Orientalists in 1960, there was an exhibition of manuscripts.[18] A group (including myself) was formed among those who hosted the participants at the Congress ... and we showed them everything there. Eventually, I had a detailed talk with two people. One of them, Demiéville, was a French sinologist who asked many questions about how I was studying

the Tangut language.[19] The second person was Sir Gerard Clauson who was involved in Central Asia and earlier in Tangut language studies.[20] ... He had published a long article, "The Future of Tangut Studies" in Asia Major, in which he excessively praised and positively promoted me. I was corresponding with Clauson afterwards.[21] ... Then, I met Louis Gambise, who also treated me well.[22] I visited him in Paris, at Rue du Cardinal Lemoine, where the Institute des Hautes Études Chinoises is located. Later, I met Herbert Franke, who was the vice president of the Academy of Sciences in Western Germany and who studied the Manchus.[23] So, I had fairly good contacts. I have been to Hungary at least four or five times. I also spent a month in Copenhagen in 1978. I have also visited Japan many times. You know, in principal, I was an "exit-able," even though I was unable to leave on several occasions." (Interview with Kychanov, pp. 16–17)

A small number of Soviet sinologists had individual visiting scholarships abroad (e.g., Chudodeev, Kychanov, Kriukov, and Maliavin). Some joined official delegations to participate in international academic forums, such as the World Congress of Orientalists or the World Congress of Historians. Taking part in the largest international academic forums at home and abroad constituted an important component in the history of professional exchanges between Soviet and "alien," "Western," "bourgeois," or "capitalist" sinologists (see Kychanov, Myasnikov, and Tikhvinsky, among others). According to Tikhvinsky, participation by Soviet Orientalists at the World Academic Forum in the early 1950s produced a big sensation:

"When I was a counselor at the embassy in London, the 23rd International Congress of Orientalists was held in Cambridge in August 1954. The event was attended by over 900 scholars from 32 countries. A delegation of 21 Orientalists from the USSR were among them. ... Since the late 1920s, international scientific contacts with Soviet Orientalists had been virtually cancelled. After more than 20 years of absence, we decided to renew contacts between Soviet and foreign Orientalists. As the Congress ended, the London *Times* reported on 30 August 1954: 'The most significant thing about the 23rd International Congress of Orientalists in Cambridge was, without a doubt, the presence of the Russian delegation.' I met English and Western sinologists there, including Lattimore and Fairbank. We established contacts and fruitful relations were established with Lattimore, Fairbank, and Swedens. ... We attempted to avoid the problems of modern history as a field of dispute. We were trying, after all, to explore history." (Interview with Tikhvinsky, p. 11)

Over time, the presence of Soviet delegations in overseas forums became an ordinary matter. Yet they were often seen by both sides as not only purely academic, but also political affairs. Judging by the Protocols of the 1973 Interkit meeting in Moscow, the Soviet delegates and their East European allies had "to consult on the topics of papers and statements on China for the participants of the XXIX International Congress of Orientalists to be held in Paris in July of this year." Meanwhile, the mere presence of Soviet sinologists at such international forums was treated suspiciously and could sporadically become an excuse for tricks and sensationalism. An interview with Ac. Vladimir S. Myasnikov (b. 1931) contains a striking account of a typical "Cold War" incident, which occurred during the XXIX Congress in Paris:

"I visited the West for the first time in 1973. They were holding the XXIX International Congress of Orientalists at the Sorbonne and I was part of a group, not as a delegate but as a so-called 'scientific tourist.' Nevertheless, I gave a report about publishing early documents on Russian-Chinese relations. … It inspired great interest. … My Paris adventures did not end with that presentation at the Sorbonne. Every day, I attended the Classical China section that included approximately 80 scientists from Taiwan. On the last day of the Congress, a scared female interpreter approached our delegation, holding a copy of *Le Monde* newspaper. An article in the paper reported that of greatest interest for the Congress was the presence of a Soviet scientist, V. S. Myasnikov, who was in constant touch with the Taiwanese. The final question by the French journalist of the article was: 'Does this mean that the Soviet Union is conducting secret talks with Taiwan?' Thus, life had taught me to be cautious toward journalists, who are ready to use any means to sensationalize a particular news topic." (Interview with V. S. Myasnikov, pp. 18–19)

Participation in overseas forums and individual academic trips were often restricted by elaborate official bans (Kychanov), delays (Deliusin), early revocations, and so on. Participation depended on both general considerations and evaluations of the personal performance by certain scholars. As evidenced by Professor Kychanov:

"I also had lecture experience. But my greatest lecture project had failed. I was invited by Gambise to the Sorbonne for one month to present three lectures. I had already ordered a French translation. But they did not allow me to leave because of objections by the Communist Party. They also did not allow me to go on another occasion when Franke arranged a very prestigious trip to the United States where a conference was being held on nation-states within the territory of China. In addition to attending that conference, I was given money for four weeks travel to visit the main universities in the United States. Once again, they did not allow me to leave. ... That was in 1978." (Interview with Kychanov, pp. 16–17)

Even the most seasoned "exit-ables," such as the former CPSU Central Committee staff member, Professor Deliusin, also occasionally encountered such obstacles:

"I had to pass through a dressing-down at the Central Committee of CPSU. But I cannot blame fate. There were people who had been friendly to me and my views both in the International Department and in the department where I worked before. However, perhaps as punishment (there were different people working in the Central Committee), a trip to China or somewhere abroad, to a conference or lecture, sporadically encountered delays on the day of departure." (Interview with Deliusin, p. 36)

Aside from such restrictions on traveling abroad, bringing home foreign books, journals, music discs, and so on were heavily restricted. Moreover, Soviet sinologists, while staying abroad, were regularly approached by the Soviet secret services who attempted to use their personal contacts as another source of special information. According to Professor Deliusin:

"When I was working in Prague and carrying the books I purchased there, they seized a suitcase of my Chinese books (there was no such practice on my return trip from Harbin in the 1940s, and there were no confiscations of Chinese books at the border). So I had to write a letter on behalf of the editorial board of the magazine, claiming that the books were intended for the library of Pravda (of course, I never gave these books to any library). Later, I had to use similar letters to retrieve other books that had been sent to me as gifts from abroad. ... Not only did we have to inform the relevant organizations about our working trips and meetings with foreigners, but also, with an awareness of upcoming meetings of this kind (possibly as a result of wire-tapping of the telephone calls in embassies or hotels that hosted foreigners), staff agents would ask us specific questions of interest to their service. Sometimes, we had to forcefully refuse to answer such questions if the questions were absolutely inconsistent with our interests and the proposed questions could cast doubts on our reputations as scholars." (Interview with Deliusin, p. 32)

In sum, the history of professional encounters of Soviet sinologists with the "capitalist world" still awaits future research. This is an interesting topic for future studies.

4. General Conclusions

A number of major observations can be highlighted from this chapter. First, like all other citizens of the USSR, Soviet sinologists were true victims and hostages of the "closed borders," or the "Iron Veil" policy. Although Soviet sinologists were not totally isolated, most did not have freedom to make regular and independent professional trips abroad.

Second, "exit-able" scholars, who could regularly leave the USSR, only comprised a small fraction of the entire Soviet sinology community. Most colleagues had extremely rare opportunities to travel abroad. Dissidents and scholars with "improper" social backgrounds, personal profiles, and behavior were usually banned from trips abroad. Moreover, a considerable segment of Soviet sinologists without any formal bans had never attempted to travel abroad, except to visit China, because they assumed that such trips were not feasible. Even the renowned "exit-able" scholars often encountered different forms of official restrictions. The extent and choice of these restrictions depended on both general (political and ideological) considerations as well as the personal loyalties and performance by certain scholars.

Third, traveling to China and other socialist countries was easier than visiting or maintaining professional contacts in the capitalist countries. Official controls were imposed on foreign exchanges, implemented simultaneously by the Communist Party system and the academic administrations. The severity of the political and ideological restrictions gradually began to fade during the 1980s. Eventually, such restrictions (the "Iron Veil") were lifted and abolished after the fall of USSR and the CPSU in 1991.

Fourth, different forms and types of professional exchanges took place between Soviet and foreign sinologists, such as individual and group activities, formal, semi-formal, or informal contacts, and cooperation and disputes. However, these exchanges were usually based on mutual sympathy and respect. According to the CS-OHP interviews, once personal contacts with Soviet colleagues were established, foreign sinologists (both socialist and capitalist) usually made great efforts to maintain them and to assist their colleagues in various ways. They sent books and magazines on China studies to the USSR and tried their best to invite Soviet scholars to their countries to participate in official academic forums, lectures, or research trips. Consequently, Soviet scholars could provide support to the global sinology community by their valuable expertise, published works, and rare historical materials and sources.

Therefore, contacts of Soviet sinologists with colleagues from each of the "three outer sinology worlds" were quite specific, asymmetric, and tended to be subject to drastic changes, depending on time, space, and circumstances. Despite all kinds of artificial limits and predicaments, some space was allocated for personal sympathy, friendship, cooperation, discussions, and, as a matter of fact, ideological struggles. Nevertheless, whatever complicated the "Interkit" relations, they were still based on real, although often too implicit (or disguised), mutual respect. After all, love of China and true scholarship pushed all sides to lift the Soviet-style academic "Iron Veil" and to establish personal rapprochements and professional cooperation in international China studies.

Notes

1. See http://politics.ntu.edu.tw/RAEC/act02.php (accessed 8 September 2014).
2. INION is the Russian abbreviation for the Institute of Scientific Information on Social Sciences.
3. *For Lasting Peace, for People's Democracy* is an organ of the Information Bureau of Communist and Workers Parties, it was issued in 1947–48 in Belgrade and in 1948–56 in Bucharest. Until September 1949, it was a weekly magazine. Thereafter, it became a fortnightly. It was closed, along with the Information Bureau, in 1956. *Problemy Mira i Sotsializma* is a joint ideological magazine of Communist and workers parties around the world. Founded and based in Prague in 1958, it existed until 1990. Each issue had a circulation of more than 500,000, which was read in some 145 countries. At its height, the magazine was translated into 41 languages, and editors from 69 Communist parties worked in its office in Prague. The master copy of the magazine was the Russian-language edition, *Problemy Mira i Sotsializma*, guided by the International Department of the Central Committee of the CPSU.
4. Claudie Gardet, *Les Relations de la république populaire de Chine et de la république démocratique allemande (1949–1989)* (Bern: Peter Lang, 2000).

5. David Wolff, "Interkit: Soviet Sinology and the Sino-Soviet Rift," *Russian History*, Vol. 30, No. 4 (2003), pp. 433–456.

6. In 2010, there was a second Budapest workshop: "China and the Communist World in the Second Half of the Cold War: New East-Central European Evidence on 'Interkit' and the Sino-Soviet Split, 1967–1986," Budapest, 26–28 February 2010. The workshop was hosted by Dr. Péter Vámos and focused on Interkit and Sino-Soviet relations. Its purpose was to gather international perspectives from the archives in the region and beyond, collect oral history testimony from Hungarian participants in the Interkit process, and brainstorm future activities. Hungarian, Polish, Czech, and Mongolian documents were added to the already available German and Russian materials. See James Hershberg, Sergey Radchenko, Péter Vámos, and David Wolff, "The Interkit Story: A Window into the Final Decades of the Sino-Soviet Relationship," CWIHP Working Paper No. 63, February 2011, pp. 4–5, 142–143. Available at http://www.wilsoncenter.org/sites/default/files/Working_Paper_63.pdf (accessed 8 September 2014).

7. Péter Vámos, "'Interkit': An International against China? Policy Coordination and National Interests in the Soviet Bloc in the Second Half of the Cold War" (Freiburg imBreisgau, 2011). Available at http://hsozkult.geschichte.hu-berlin.de/tagungsberichte/id=3737#note5 (accessed 8 September 2014).

8. Hershberg et al., "The Interkit Story," pp. 3–5.

9. Ibid., pp. 3, 9–10.

10. See the records of the Interkit meetings, ETH Zurich's Parallel History Project on Cooperative Security. Available at www.php.isn.ethz.ch/collections/colltopic.cfm?lng=en&id=19550&navinfo=16447 (accessed 11 September 2014).

11. Here is a list of Interkit Meetings: 14–21 December 1967, Moscow; 28–31 January 1969, Berlin; 10–13 March 1970, Warsaw; 15–18 February 1971, Sofia; 3–5 July 1972, Prague; 16–18 May 1973, Moscow; 25–26 March 1974, Budapest; 24–28 June 1975, Ulaanbaatar; 15–16 June 1977, Berlin; 11–13 December 1978, Havana; 11–13 June and October 1980, Mierki (Poland); 11–12 May 1982, Sofia; 6–7 December 1983, Prague; 30 October–1 November 1984, Tihany (Hungary); 18 February 1985, Moscow. (Source: Hershberg et al., "The Interkit Story," pp. 140–141.)

12. Hershberg et al., "The Interkit Story," p. 10.

13. Gilbert Rozman, *A Mirror for Socialism: Soviet Criticisms of China* (Princeton, NJ: Princeton University Press, 1985), pp. 42–43.

14. Hershberg et al., "The Interkit Story," pp. 6–7.

15. Ibid., pp. 92, 97–98.

16. Ibid., p. 5.

17. Ibid., p. 31.

18. The 25th International Congress of Orientalists was held in at Moscow State University from 9 to 16 August 1960. Over 2,000 scholars and observers from 48 countries attended the Congress. But, naturally, the majority of the delegates were from the USSR.
19. Paul Demiéville (1894–1979).
20. Sir Gerard Leslie Makins Clauson (1891–1974).
21. Gerard Clauson, "The Future of Tangut (Hsi Hsia) Studies," *Asia Major* (New Series), Vol. 11 (1964), pt. 1, pp. 54–77.
22. Louis Gambise is a French Orientalist and Mongolist. He is the author of several works on Khitans.
23. Herbert Franke (1914–2011).

Chapter 6

Soviet Sinology: Two Conflicting Paradigms of Chinese History

Alexander Pisarev

1. Theoretical Background to Soviet Sinology: Feudalism vs. the "Asiatic Mode of Production"

Discussions about the nature of traditional Chinese society in Soviet historical studies were based on the Marxist paradigm of world history, generally known as "historical materialism." This is the reason why, in order to present Soviet scholars' theories of Chinese history, the author of this chapter focuses on the main concepts of Marxism. However, the primary objective of this chapter is neither Marxism nor its Soviet version. The emphasis is on the changing views of Soviet historians about China under the framework of the Marxist historical paradigm, as this paradigm remained the only ideologically legitimate approach to understanding China.

The key concepts in the Marxist theory of history, widely utilized in Soviet historical and social studies, includes such terms as "productive forces," "productive relations," "mode of production," and "social-economic formation." To this list one could also add some other important concepts, such as the ruling class and the exploited class. The meanings and interrelations among these concepts are important to understand the polemics among Soviet sinologists. Productive forces are mainly understood as the economic foundation of social life, which determines other spheres, in combination with the productive relations (or relations between the ruling and exploited social classes) that constitute different modes of production. In turn, the mode of production of social-economic life, according to this theory, determines the nature of different social-economic formations. The latter term refers to the patterns of society in its totality, and includes social-economic factors in sphere such as ideology, politics, culture, and so on. Another important feature of the paradigm of historical materialism is the emphasis on the historical continuity between different modes of production.

According to Marx (though this view was challenged by some Soviet Marxist theoreticians), there were five modes of production which represented different stages in the development of human history: primitive society, the "Asiatic mode of production," ancient, feudal, and the capitalist social-economic formation. Each of the subsequent modes of production, excluding primitive society, manifested a different type of social-political contradiction between the ruling and exploited classes. Under the "Asiatic mode of production," it is the opposition between a communally organized society and an oppressive state, in ancient society it was the struggle between slave owners and slaves that determined social-political life, under feudalism it was the fight between feudal landlords and serfs, and the social contradictions in the "capitalist mode of production" were characterized by the confrontation between the bourgeoisie and the working class. The Marxist theory of the Communist revolution (or future studies in Marxism) postulated that the transition from feudalism to capitalism was impossible without the serfs' fight against feudal landownership for personal freedom and land (the agrarian revolution). The transition to the "post-capitalist mode of production" (the "Communist social-economic formation"), according to this approach, was marked by the expropriation of the capitalists and the total abolition of private property.

The roots of Marxist historiography in Soviet Russia can be traced to Lenin's views on Russian social history as a part of a global transition to communism. Though it was based on the sophisticated paradigm of the "modes of production" designed by Marx, there are sufficient differences between the two. If for Marx, as noted above, world history was represented by the two major trends (the "Asiatic mode of production" in the East and the succession of different social-economic formations in the West), for Lenin the Western model of historical development became a universal pattern applicable to both West and East. One of the most important outcomes of this Euro-centric approach was Lenin's conclusion that the "feudal mode of production" was a universal stage in historical development, typical to all the more or less developed civilizations, including both the Western and Eastern realms of the universe.[1]

Lenin began with the application of the feudal paradigm to his analysis of rural society in Russia after the Great Reform of 1861, though this view contradicted the views on Russian history of the majority of professional Russian historians at that time. They argued that behind some superficial similarities, the historical route of traditional Russia was different from that in the West.[2] Later on, Lenin applied this approach not only to studies of traditional and semi-traditional Russia, but also to an understanding of the historical development of the Eastern world as well. This remarkable shift in Marxist history and political science is quite evident in Lenin's classic article, "Democracy and Populism in China" (1912), which later became the theoretical framework in Soviet historiography for studies of history and the revolutionary process in the East. In this article, Lenin's analysis of the nature of the Chinese revolution of 1912 and its driving social forces was entirely based on the feudal paradigm and actually modeled on the Bolshevik theory of revolution in Russia, which in turn followed the European political and social context after the Great Revolution in France. Lenin characterized the Xinhai Revolution in China as "bourgeois-democratic," whereas its historical role was defined as the destruction of feudalism "in all its manifestations," which meant liquidation of the system of feudal land ownership and the distribution of land among the peasantry.[3]

Lenin suggested a similar approach to the delegates of the Second Congress of the Communist International (CI) in 1920. In the section of Lenin's draft resolution dedicated to perspectives on the revolutionary movement in the East, he specifically emphasizes the role of the struggle of the peasantry against the feudal landlords as a driving force behind the revolutionary process. Thus, the initiation of the agrarian revolution became one of the most important goals, for both the democratic and Communist movements in colonial and semi-colonial countries.[4] It is worth noting that due to disagreements among the delegates at the Congress on social-economic relations in the countries of the East, in the final version of the resolution the term "feudal landlords" is not mentioned, but in later publications in the Soviet Union of the documents of the Second Congress, Lenin's version of the resolution was restored.[5]

Although the feudal paradigm was legitimized by the leader of the Bolshevik revolution, in the mid-1920s it was challenged by the theory of the "Asiatic mode of production." Its partisans also appealed to Marx, arguing that his views on traditional and semi-traditional Asian societies did not include the feudal approach. One of the most important reasons behind this theoretical shift was the failure of actual implementation of the concepts of feudalism and the agrarian revolution in China in the 1920s. In fact, the disintegration of the First United Front (1925–27) between the Communists and the Nationalists was a clear signal that the strategy of the CI based on the initiation of a massive peasant movement against feudal landlords was in jeopardy. Soviet scholar and prominent Communist, Ludvig Madyar, attempted to apply the theory of the "Asiatic mode of production" to an analysis of the Chinese revolution, but, even though his research was based on a vast variety of primary sources, it was not an obvious success. Madyar failed to accommodate the views of Marx (the dominance of state institutions in combination with the system of rural communities under the "Asiatic mode of production") with the realities of social-economic relations in early twentieth-century China.[6]

By the 1930s, the concept of the "Asiatic mode of production" was proclaimed "anti-Marxist" and had lost its legitimacy. In fact, it was abolished. Some scholars, however, continued to support the concept of the "Asiatic mode of production" as a more convincing theory in terms of traditional and semi-traditional Chinese society. Sergei Dalin, a leading Soviet expert on East Asian affairs and an influential scholar in the 1920s, mentions in his memoirs that he had been using a feudal approach to Chinese history while teaching this subject in Moscow. But when, in the mid-1920s, he went to China for the first time, he had the chance to observe the realities of Chinese rural society firsthand and his views changed completely. According to his recollections, he saw the "remnants not of the feudal, but of the Asiatic mode of production, in Asian society."[7]

It may well be that there are two major reasons for the abolition of this theory in the USSR: if it had been accepted by the Soviet political and academic establishment, it might have led to a search for more complicated answers to the challenges confronted by the revolutionary movements in Asia at that time. In addition, any deviation from the logically unshakable, as it seemed, paradigm of succession of the "modes of production" in their ascension to the Communist phase threatened the sustainability of the entire theory. Moreover, there were some purely political reasons for labeling the concept of the "Asiatic mode of production" as anti-Marxist. By the end of the 1920s, the most important rival to Joseph Stalin in internal party struggles, Leon Trotsky, had been defeated. Some of his close associates had declared that the feudal concept did not meet the realities of China and should be substituted by the theory of the "Asiatic mode of production." Among these close associates was Boris Lominadze, the 1927 CI representative in China.[8]

The triumph of feudalism over the concept of Asiatic society in Soviet historical studies led to some further contradictions in the accepted version of the modes of production paradigm. Soviet scholars had to find answers to new theoretical challenges: why was feudal China lagging behind feudal Europe in terms of social-economic development? Why was the emergence of capitalism in China characterized by obvious differences with Europe? Last but not least, why was the path of the Chinese revolution so specific and not modeled after the experiences of the revolutions in modern Europe? The search for answers to these questions led in two directions that sometimes intersected with one another. Some historians focused on the peculiarities in the historical development of Chinese feudalism, whereas others emphasized the specific features of Chinese feudalism. Grigorii Grinevich, for instance, stressed characteristics such as the feudal mode of production in China, the bureaucratic nature of the ruling class, and the absence, unlike in medieval Europe, of institutionalized social boundaries in terms of acquisition of landed property. As for the most important reason, that is, why Chinese feudalism was unable to give birth to modern capitalism, Grinevich attributed this to particular feature of Chinese history, the congruence between periods of higher development of trade capital and the political disintegration of the society, which rendered the emergence of the sprouts of the bourgeois mode of production unlikely.[9]

Other Soviet scholars during the prewar period attempted to explain the backwardness of China by referring to its specific model of feudalism, which made Chinese society in the Middle Ages less flexible and more conservative in terms of historical development. They specified features in the Chinese model of feudalism, such as the merger between industry and agriculture on the basis of the system of rural communities and the impact of the powerful Chinese state, which they characterized as a modification of Oriental despotism.[10] It should be noted that the arguments of the partisans of the specific model of feudalism in traditional China were quite close to the ideas of the supporters of the concept of the "Asiatic model of production."

2. Post-World War II Soviet Sinology: From "Eastern Feudalism" to Feudalism

After World War II, Soviet historians, like their predecessors, continued the search for an answer to the issue of the backwardness of Chinese feudal society; some emphasized the peculiarities of the historical process in China, whereas others focused on specific features of the Chinese version of the feudal mode of production. For instance, in an edited monograph on the history and aftermath of the seventeenth-century Manchurian conquest of China, which was the first comprehensive study on Chinese history of this period in Soviet historiography, the disastrous impact of the Manchurian invasion was primarily to blame for undermining the sprouts of capitalism already evident during the Ming dynasty.[11]

Studies by prominent scholar Oleg Nepomnin focused on the economic and social history of China during the Qing dynasty. In his early works, this leading sinologist relied on the concept of feudalism in China, but he emphasized specific features of Chinese feudal society, which were evident in the form of agriculture, the predominance of economic forms of exploitation of the peasantry, the absence of serfdom, and feudal landlord estates.[12]

A certain liberalization of the social sciences in the Soviet Union in the early 1960s had a positive influence on Oriental and Chinese studies in the USSR, as Soviet scholars were permitted to discuss theoretical issues, which several decades earlier had been considered to be ideologically unacceptable. One such ideologically sensitive topic was discussion of the "Asiatic mode of production," which in the 1960s was actually initiated not by Russian but by foreign scholars, the French in particular, who were close to the Communist movement. It is interesting to note that some interviews, conducted as part of an oral history project, reveal that for some Soviet sinologists the initiation of the discussion on the "Asiatic mode of production" in traditional China was not only a way to broaden the horizons of scientific debate, but also contained obvious political allusions.[13] The concept of a powerful state dominating over an enslaved society, which was a part of this theory, could easily be applied to the realities of the socialist countries. It was not accidental, in this sense, that the annual conference, which had been organized for several decades by scholars in the Sinology Department of the Institute of Oriental Studies (the Russian Academy of Sciences) under the leadership of liberal-minded, Lev Deliusin, was entitled "State and Society in China." It is also interesting that after relaxation of the ideological pressures in the PRC in the 1980s, similar discussions on the nature of feudalism were conducted by Chinese historians in China. As Arif Dirlik argues, they were quite uneasy, as it had been their Soviet colleagues, about identifying the basic features of feudalism in traditional China, whereas attempts to imply the "Asiatic mode of production" approach to Chinese history were unwelcome because of ideological considerations.[14]

Though the majority of Soviet scholars who participated in this debate agreed that Marx's approach to the "Asiatic mode of production" was the most important in analyses of Eastern societies, they concluded that the feudal theory should be used as the main instrument for understanding the "mysterious" East. This "old-new" approach once again became quite popular in Chinese studies and some scholars, despite the ideological pressures, declared that they were supporters. Since the 1960s, prominent Russian scholar Professor Leonid Vasiliev has been coherently relying on this concept in his studies of traditional China. In his view, the "Asiatic mode of production" dominated in China throughout Chinese history up until the period of the Western invasion, and it was based on the predominance of state institutions in the form of a merger between the system of political power and property institutions.[15] As an outstanding scholar of traditional China, Vasiliev paid less attention to social-economic relations in pre-modern Chinese society. Consequently, certain aspects of the "Asiatic mode of production" theory in its application to late imperial China remained unclear. Among these one can cite the problematic rural community, the "landlord economy," the nature of the ruling class in China and its relations with the peasantry and the state, and so forth.

During the 1970–1980s the majority of Soviet historians of China, due to growing ideological pressures, especially after the Soviet invasion of Czechoslovakia in 1968, were still trying to accommodate the feudal theory with facts in Chinese history. In the 1980s Oleg Nepomnin constructed his own version of a specific pre-capitalist mode of production in China, which, although based on the feudal paradigm, challenged its main traits. He borrowed some definitions from the concept of the "Asiatic mode of production," but he defined them as binary feudalism. Nepomnin argued that the Chinese version of feudal society was based on an equilibrium between the private, or semi-feudal, pattern of social relations (landed tenancy) and the impact of powerful state institutions. This unique composition was not only different from classic European feudalism in which the private domi-nated over the collective, but it sufficiently limited the potential for development in the direction of capitalism, which was founded on private institutions.[16] It is worth noting that in his review of Nepomnin's monograph, one of the leading Soviet sinologists, Arlen Melixetov, stresses that the way in which Nepomnin portrays Chinese semi-traditional society strengthened the argument of those scholars who insisted on the predominance of the state over society in pre-modern China and, in this sense, the existence in China of a mode of production different from the classic European model of feudalism.[17]

Professor Vladimir Pavlov, a famous Soviet scholar in the field of the history of pre-colonial and colonial India, formulated another sophisticated theory aimed at explaining the differences between medieval Western and Eastern societies. Though he relied mainly on Indian historical sources, Pavlov considered his approach applicable to other traditional Oriental societies, including China. His theory was quite different from that of his predecessors because he viewed "Eastern feudalism" from the perspective of the different stages of development in this social-economic formation. In Marxist studies of traditional soci-eties, the "feudal mode of production" was supposed to proceed through three definite stages: early, developed, and late feudalism, whereas the latter in the European historical context was accompanied by the emer-gence of the sprouts of capitalism. According to Pavlov, the specificity of the Eastern pattern of feudalism was the outcome of its inability to move from an early stage to a developed phase, the result of which was the absence of obviously identifiable traces of modern capitalism in pre-colonial Oriental societies.[18] Although this theory permitted an explanation of the backwardness of the East in comparison with the modern West, it brought to light another key question: Why was "Eastern feudalism" fatally incapable of moving on to a more developed phase? Needless to say, this and the other obvious contradictions in the "Eastern feudalism" approach were eagerly emphasized by its critics.[19]

In terms of logic, in order to exhaust the explanatory potential of the feudal paradigm, its supporters had to move in the direction of a different possible model. In the mid-1980s, Soviet historiography formulated the concept of over-developed feudalism in the East and in China. For the proponents of this theory, the Oriental version of the feudal mode of production appeared to be so sophisticated in terms of traditional societies that it simply did not need to proceed to modernity.[20]

Another outstanding Soviet sinologist, Vasilii Iliushechkin, highly praised by his colleagues for his research on the history of the Taiping uprising in the mid-nineteenth century, tried to solve the contradictions in the application of the feudal paradigm to China in his own way. If other scholars were searching for a definition of a specific Chinese (or Eastern, in a broader sense) pattern of feudal society, or defined it in terms of different stages in the development of the feudal mode of production, Iliushechkin put the issue in a broader historical context. In his view, there was no taxonomic interrelationship between different patterns of exploitation in traditional societies (slavery, serfdom, or landed tenancy). Rather, they were related typologically. In other words, there was only one mode of production in pre-modern societies, either European or Eastern, which Iliushechkin identified as an "estate-social class" society. In different historical contexts, and in different parts of the world, he argued, different forms of exploitation could play a dominant role, and sometimes landed tenancy was succeeded by slavery, serfdom, or vice versa.[21] This attempt to solve the contradictions in the application of the feudal model to traditional China, this time in the form of "everlasting" feudalism, failed to address the key issue that Soviet sinologists had been discussing for decades: that is, why did certain "estate-social class societies" proceed to the capitalist mode of production whereas others did not?

Although Emiliya Stuzhina did not participate directly in the debates on the definition of the mode of production in traditional China, her outstanding contribution to studies of the urban economy during the Ming and Qing dynasties obviously supported the theory of the "non-feudal" nature of social relations in late imperial China. She argued that the similarities between urban social institutions in pre-modern China and Europe were only superficial, as there was no independence from imperial supervision of city life in China. Unlike medieval Europe, urban dwellers in China, like their rural counterparts, were subjected to strict control by government officials, and they did not enjoy any special status as there was no jurisdiction protecting their rights. As a result, private property was not guaranteed by law and, in Stuzhina's opinion, this constituted the main obstacle to the transition to modern capitalism.[22]

Another topic, which can be put under the framework of discussions on social-economic formations in traditional and semi-traditional China, was the debate in Soviet sinology on the nature of "agrarian relations" in early twentieth-century China. From this, two principal themes emerged: the problematic communitarian institutions in China's countryside, and the social characteristics of the feudal landlord economy. For Marxist historians, the issue of the typology of a village commune in traditional society was essential, as the founder of "historical materialism" made it the starting point for his analysis of the pre-capitalist mode of production. In Marx's view, the "Asiatic mode of production" was based on the system of "Asiatic" communes, which were characterized by the dominance of social relations founded on clan structures, whereas the Germanic type of village commune—the basis of European feudalism—was free from the constraints of archaic blood-related ties.[23]

For some Soviet sinologists, the village commune miraculously disintegrated during the early period of Chinese history (though it managed to survive in medieval Europe).[24] Others insisted that there were no traces of the village commune in late-imperial China.[25] Scholars who acknowledged the existence of communitarian institutions in the late nineteenth and early twentieth centuries in China characterized them as similar to the Germanic type, which seemed quite logical under the paradigm of a feudal society in traditional China, but sounded quite extravagant.[26] In contrast, their opponents, relying on historical sources from early twentieth-century China, drew attention to the social institutions associated within Chinese clans, members of which were not only related by blood, but also shared property, including commonly owned arable land.[27]

The constraints of the feudal approach in its application to early twentieth-century semi-traditional China made it difficult, if not impossible, for Soviet historians to comprehend the salient features of the Chinese peasant movement, especially after the Chinese Communist Party (CCP), under the guidance of the CI, proclaimed the agrarian revolution to be the chief instrument for acquiring political power. Logically, from the point of view of the theory of feudalism, as previously argued, the social split between the peasantry and the feudal landlords (if it really existed) could be naturally transformed into a political struggle to confiscate the landlords' estates in favor of the poor. Understandably, as the actual history of the Communist movement in China testifies, this was not the case—the agrarian revolution as a spontaneous struggle by the peasantry against feudalism did not occur. Soviet scholar Lev Deliusin was the first to clearly show this in his monographic research on the history of the peasant movement during the Chinese revolution of 1925–27.[28]

The answer to the question of why the peasant movement in China was so different from the European and Russian cases was formulated in the works of influential Soviet sinologist, Anatolii Mugruzin. Using broad statistical data, from both Guomindang and Communist sources, he demonstrated that the so-called "feudal landlord's monopoly on land" in China was a myth created by Soviet and CCP theoreticians in order to come up with a conceptual foundation for the "agrarian revolution." In fact, different kinds of landlords, including rich peasants, controlled more than 40 percent of the cultivated land, but not more than 70–80 percent, as had been argued before.[29] In his later research, Mugruzin showed that in the first part of the twentieth century rural capitalism was at an initial stage of development in China, thus making the agrarian revolution quite unlikely.[30] Addressing the issue of the nature of peasant movements in China, he argued quite convincingly that the main aspirations of Chinese peasants were not associated with confiscation of the feudal estates (that actually did not exist) but rather with the regulation of state-imposed taxes, which in the first part of the twentieth century, due to the system of warlordism, became the chief burden suffocating the rural economy.[31] Without exaggeration, this was a revolutionary reconsideration of the approaches in the previous historiography.

It is quite obvious that in order to find answers to the problems of the backwardness in traditional China and of the specific features of the revolution in China and other colonial countries, Soviet sinologists tried to utilize all logically possible approaches under the framework of the social-economic formations of the feudal paradigm: feudalism, "Eastern feudalism," "early feudalism," "over-developed feudalism," and "everlasting feudalism." But all of these efforts, although solving some contradictions in the previous models, resulted in new puzzles that had to be addressed. Surprisingly, the picture of traditional Eastern societies drawn by supporters of different modifications of the feudal paradigm in its application to a non-European world appeared to be quite similar to the arguments formulated earlier by supporters of the concept of the "Asiatic mode of production."

It may appear to be another historical peculiarity that by the late 1980s not only the agnostic capabilities of the feudal approach to traditional China had been exhausted, but the social-economic potentials of the "Communist social-economic formation" had been exhausted as well. But the Soviet sinologists' search for a logically sustainable model to understand traditional and semi-traditional China, under the framework of the paradigm of the social-economic formation, was not entirely in vain. Though the results were negative as Soviet historians failed to find in China fundamental characteristics of the "feudal mode of production" such as a rural community similar to that in the European societies in the Middle Ages and the system of landownership based on a hierarchically organized large landlord economy, which dominated the rural community through serfdom, they discovered something else. Namely, traditional Chinese society was not a distorted reflection of the feudal West, but instead it was its own unique entity.

3. Post-Soviet Russian Sinology: The Concept of "Traditional Chinese Society" vs. "Feudalism in China"

The disappearance of ideological constraints in post-Soviet Russia was, to a large extent, equal to a shock for the social sciences, as scholars were permitted to formulate any concepts they wished. However, they were not ready for new theoretical breakthroughs. Some of the sinologists insisted, as did the influential scholar of late imperial China, Alexei Bokschanin, that the "social-economic formations" paradigm had to be complemented by a "civilizational" approach.[32] Other scholars refrained from the social-economic formations vocabulary and mainly used neutral terms, such as "traditional China" (meaning Chinese society prior to the Opium wars), in their historical research. But in some publications traces of the latent debate with the partisans of the feudal theory are quite evident.

In the first collected research on the general history of China published in post-Soviet Russia, the authors distance themselves completely from the problematic of the social-economic formations and instead address Chinese history as its own unique entity. Chronologically, they divide the history of China into two major parts: traditional China and Chinese society after the Western invasion, or modernizing China. Traditional China is portrayed as a civilization in constant cultural development, though, starting with the formation of imperial China, its main social institutions remained stable. They were represented by the powerful state, which not only enjoyed supreme economic and judicial rights, but also merged with the semi-religious institutions of Confucianism. The social basis of traditional Chinese society was characterized by a system of clan-organized rural communes, while the ruling class was comprised of strata of bureaucratic officials not necessarily associated with landed property. Under this social system, city life was also subjected to strict bureaucratic regulations. Addressing the issue of the social-political dynamics in traditional China, the authors rely on the concept of the dynastic circle, which, they argue, brought the society to its social foundations. This type of historical development was not necessarily destined to result in modern capitalism. The starting point of modernization, they conclude, coincided with the invasion of the Western powers and, in fact, was forced upon traditional China.[33] It is quite evident that this presentation of imperial China is much closer to the main conceptions in the "Asiatic mode of production" than it is to the theory of feudalism.

Although comparisons between trends in Russian and Western historiography of China are not the subject of this chapter, still it is appropriate to refer to the quite lengthy citation in one of the recent publications by Francis Fukuyama. Fukuyama is neither a historian (though it is he who coined the famous term the "end of history"), nor is he a sinologist, but his approach to China is close to that of Russian historians, as he follows general trends in world history and attempts to find China's place in these general trends. His conclusion is quite similar to views of Russian scholars of traditional China: "There was no landed, independent aristocracy, no independent cities. The dispersed gentry and peasantry could passively resist the government's orders, and periodically broke out in violent uprisings that were suppressed with great savagery. But it was never able to institutionalize itself as a corporate group to demand rights from the state, as the peasantry in Scandinavia was to do. ... Religion continued to be a sectarian phenomenon that was viewed with suspicion by the orthodox Confucian authorities and never represented a powerful social consensus that could limit the state's power through its custodianship of law."[34]

One can find a similar approach in an edited monograph on rural China and the agrarian policy of the National Government during the 1920s–1940s. The authors argue that the feudal theory failed to explain the nature of the social structures in early twentieth-century rural China and the driving forces of the Chinese revolution. Feudal landed estates, unlike in pre-modern Europe and Russia, did not dominate social life in the Chinese countryside, and the majority of a village's population was comprised of an independent peasantry. Under these circumstances, the initiation of the agrarian revolution as the main instrument of modernization and the transition to socialism, as the CI insisted, proved to be ineffective. This was mainly due to the fact that the chief social conflict in the countryside was not between "feudal landlords" and "serfs," but rather inside the clan communities themselves. Some of the arguments formulated by the supporters of the "Asiatic mode of production" obviously resonate with the ideas of the authors of this volume, though only in the sense of the existence of a "non-feudal" society in China, as they specifically stress.[35]

Judging from some of the most recent publications by Russian sinologists, one can conclude that the paradigm of "social-economic formations" and the theory of feudalism in China are no longer the main focus of Russian theoretical thought.

In the collection of essays published after the conference on the impact of the Xinhai Revolution on modern Chinese history (December 2012), the concept of Chinese traditional society is dominant. In an article by Russian historian, Yurii Chudodeev, pre-modern China is depicted as a traditional society, subject to evolution according to the mechanism of the dynastic circle that, in fact, excludes the possibility of a transition to capitalism on its own basis.[36] In a paper by another patriarch of Russian sinology, Leonid Vasiliev, whose works are mentioned earlier, the author refers to his previous conclusions on the "non-feudal" nature of traditional society in China, which was not supposed to make a transition to modernity without the Western impact. Vasiliev argues that due to the Confucian cultural legacy, China successfully managed to accommodate itself to the challenges of modernization by the end of the twentieth century.[37] Thus, it is tempting to conclude that today at least some of the arguments of the partisans of the "Asiatic mode of production," under the framework of the concept of "Chinese traditional society," are gaining momentum.

4. Conclusion

The theoretical foundations for studies in Soviet sinology were established by Lenin who reformulated Marx's views on social-economic formations. According to Marx, there were two trends in world history—Western and Eastern—each of which represented different historical experiences. While in the West the mode of social-economic development included a succession of different modes of production from less to more technologically developed, the "Asiatic mode of production" in the East did not experience drastic changes in terms of patterns in social relations. Eastern societies, according to Marx, remained stuck in their social development, and this was the main reason for the superiority of the capitalist West. Unlike Marx, Lenin advocated the universality of the succession of the modes of production in all traditional developed countries, including China. Consequently, he characterized the mode of production in early twentieth-century China as feudalism. According to Lenin, in order to modernize Chinese society needed a bourgeois revolution, the driving force of which would be the peasants' agrarian revolution against their feudal landlords. In the late 1920s, supporters of Lenin's theory defeated the partisans of the "Asiatic mode of production" who tried to draw attention to specific features of social relations in the traditional East, and Chinese feudalism became an official concept in Marxist historiography.

Attempting to accommodate the principles of the feudal approach with the historical realities of China, Soviet scholars applied all logically possible modifications of the feudal theory: feudalism, "Eastern feudalism," "early feudalism," and even "over-developed feudalism," in order to come up with explanations for the "peculiarities" of the "feudal mode of production" in China. However, based on the feudal approach, they failed to build a sustainable theory.

After the removal of ideological controls over the social sciences in post-Soviet Russia, historians gradually began to return to certain aspects of the theory of the "Asiatic mode of production." However, this time it was not on the basis of the paradigm of "social-economic formations," but rather it was based on the framework of the concept of "Chinese traditional society." Contemporary Russian sinologists are more interested in understanding the realities of pre-modern society in China than they are interested in constructing universal and essentially theological schemes of human development.

Notes

1. Viktor Nikiforov, *Sovetskie istoriki o problemah Kitaya* (Soviet Historians on the Problems of China) (Moscow: Nauka, 1970).
2. Nikolai Pavlov-Silvanskii, *Feodalism v Rossii* (Feudalism in Russia) (Moscow: Nauka, 1988), p. 28.
3. Vladimir Lenin, *O natsional'nom i natsional'no-kolonial'nom voprose* (On National and National-Colonial Questions) (Moscow: Izdatel'stvo politicheskoi literaturi, 1956), p. 58.
4. Ibid., p. 517.
5. Alexander Pisarev, "The Second Congress of the Communist International and the Revolutionary Movement in China," *Issues and Studies*, Vol. 36, No. 3 (2000), p. 172.
6. Ludvig Madyar, *Ekonomika sel'skogo hozyaistva v Kitae* (Rural Economy in China) (Moscow-Leningrad: Gosudarstvennoe izdatel'stvo, 1928); On Marx's views on traditional Eastern societies, see Karl Marx and Friedrich Engels, *Sobranie sochinenii* (Collected Works) (Moscow: Politizdat, 1968), Vol. 46, Part 1.
7. Sergei Dalin, *Kitaiskie memuari* (Chinese Memoirs) (Moscow: Nauka, 1982), pp. 271–272.
8. Richard A. Thornton, *The Comintern and the Chinese Communists, 1928–1931* (Seattle: University of Washington Press, 1969), p. 15.
9. Grigorii Grinevich, "K voprosam istorii kitaiiskogo feodalisma" (On Feudalism in China), *Problemi Kitaya* (Problems of China), No. 14 (1935), p. 259.
10. Lazar Duman, *Novaya istoriya Kitaya* (A Modern History of China) (Leningrad: Leningrad University, 1939).
11. Sergei Tikhivinskii, ed., *Manzhurskoe vladichestvo v Kitae* (Manchurian Domination in China) (Moscow: Nauka, 1966), p. 6.

12. Oleg Nepomnin, *Genezis kapitalizma v sel'skom hozyaistve Kitaya* (Genesis of Capitalism in Chinese Agriculture) (Moscow: Nauka, 1966), p. 10.

13. Interview with Yurii Garushyanz, Moscow, December 5, 2009. Available at http://www.abirus.ru/content/564/623/626/11544/11548.html (accessed 12 August 2014).

14. Arif Dirlik, "The Universalization of a Concept: 'Feudalism' to 'Feudalism' in Chinese Marxist Historiography," *Journal of Peasant Studies*, Vol. 12, Nos. 2–3 (1985), p. 199.

15. Leonid Vasiliev, "Fenomen vlasti-sobstvennosti: K probleme tipologii dokapitalisticheskih struktur" (Phenomena of Power-Property: On the Typology of Pre-capitalist Societies), *Tipi obschestvennih otnoshenii v srednie veka* (Types of Social Relations in the Middle Ages) (Moscow: Nauka, 1982), p. 96.

16. Oleg Nepomnin, *Sotsial'no-ekonomicheskaya istoroya Kitaya* (A Social-Economic History of China) (Moscow: Nauka, 1980), p. 7.

17. Arlen Melixetov, "Retzenziya na monografiu O. Nepomnina" (Review of O. Nepomnin's Monograph), *Narodi Azii I Afriki* (Peoples of Asia and Africa), No 2, (1981), p. 223.

18. Eugenii Zhukov, Michail Barg, and Vladimir Pavlov, eds., *Teoreticheskie problemi vsemirno-istoricheskogo protsessa* (Theoretical Problems in the Global Historical Process) (Moscow: Nauka, 1979), p. 236.

19. Andrei Fursov, "Vostochnii feudalism i istoriya Zapada: kritika odnoi inter-pretatsii" (Eastern Feudalism and the History of the West: Critique of One of the Interpretations), *Narodi Asii I Afriki* (Peoples of Asia and Africa), No. 1 (1984), p. 97.

20. Leonid Alaev, ed., *Evolutsiya vostochnih obschest: Sintez traditsionnogo i sovremennogo* (Evolution of Eastern Societies: Synthesis of Tradition and Modernity) (Moscow: Nauka, 1984).

21. Vasilii Iliushechkin, *Soslovno-klassovoe obschestvo v istorii Kitaya* (Estate-Social Class Society in Chinese History) (Moscow: Nauka, 1986).

22. Emiliya Stuzhina, *Kitaiskoe remeslo v 17-18 vv.* (Chinese Craftsmanship in the Seventeenth-Eighteenth Centuries) (Moscow: Nauka, 1970), p. 100.

23. Marx and Engels, *Sobranie sochinenii*, Vol. 46, Pt. 1, pp. 462–463.

24. *Iliushechkin, Soslovno-klassovoe obschestvo v istorii Kitaya*, p. 222.

25. Nepomnin, *Genezis kapitalizma v sel'skom hozyaistve Kitaya*, p. 43.

26. Nadezhda Tyapkina, *Derevnya i krestyanstvo v sotsial'no-ecnomicheskoy sisteme Kitaya* (Village and Peasantry in the Social-Economic System of China) (Moscow: Nauka, 1984), p. 236.

27. Alexander Pisarev, *Problemi tipologii kitaiskoi obschini* (Issues of Typology of the Chinese Commune) (Moscow: Moscow University Press, 1981), p. 37.

28. Lev Deliusin, *Agrarno-krestyanskii vopros v politike KPK* (The Agrarian-Peasant Question in the Policy of the CCP) (Moscow: Nauka, 1972), p. 14.

29. Anatolii Mugruzin, *Agrarnie otnosheniya v Kitae v 20-40-h gg. 20v.* (Agrarian Relations in China in the 1920s–1940s) (Moscow: Nauka, 1970), p. 22.

30. Anatolii Mugruzin, *Agrarnii vopros v Kitae v pervoi polovine 20 veka* (The Agrarian Question in China in the First Part of the Twentieth Century) (Moscow: Nauka, 1988), pp. 2–3.

31. Anatolii Mugruzin, "O tipe kitaiskogo krest'yanstva: Problemi krestyanskogo dvizheniya v noveishee vremya" (On the Type of Chinese Peasantry: Problems of Peasant Movements in Modern Times), in *Sotsial'no-ekonomicheskoe polozhenie Kitaya v kontse 40 i v 50-h godah 20 v.* (The Social-Economic Situation in China in the 1940s and 1950s) (Moscow: IMRD RAN, 1977), pp. 182–183.

32. Alexei Bokschanin, *Sovremennie istoriki KNR o problemah feodalisma v Kitae* (Contemporary PRC Historians on the Problems of Feudalism in China) (Moscow: IV RAN, 1998), p. 128.

33. Arlen Melixetov, ed., *Istoriya Kitaya* (A History of China) (Moscow: Moscow State University, 2004), pp. 283–290.

34. Francis Fukuyama, *The Origins of Political Order: From Prehuman Times to the French Revolution* (London: Profile Books Ltd., 2012), p. 313.

35. Andrei Karneev, Vitalii Kozirev, and Alexandr Pisarev, *Vlast i derevnya v respublikanskom Kitae* (State and Rural Society in Republican China) (Moscow: Sovero-print, 2005), p. 20.

36. Yurii Chudodeev, "Sinhaiskaya revolutsiya i krah monarhii v Kitae" (The Xinhai Revolution and the Fall of the Monarchy in China), in *Sinhaiskaya revolutsiya i respublikanskii Kitai* (The Xinhai Revolution and Republican China), edited by Valentin Golovachev (Moscow: IV RAN, 2013), p. 25.

37. Leonid Vasiliev, "Ot nevnimaniya k Zapadu k triumfu vesternizatsii v Kitae" (From Ignoring the West to the Triumph of Westernization in China), in *Xinhaiskaya revolutsiya i respublikanskii Kitai*, edited by Valentin Golovachev (Moscow: IV RAN, 2013), p. 81.

Chapter 7

Chinese Studies in Post-Soviet Russia: From Uneven Development to the Search for Integrity

Alexei D. Voskressenski

There has always been a search for interdisciplinarity and integrality in international Chinese Studies, especially given the relatively long history of research on China and its national ambitions [1] The same has been, and still is, true for Russian Chinese Studies, a discipline that has always also had a practical side due to the two countries' common border and their long and complex bilateral relationship. Two more salient reasons come to mind. First, in order to delve into Chinese studies one really needs to be interdisciplinary because the language itself is not enough to understand the history, culture, or politics of China; and vice versa, knowledge of its history, political science, or anthropology is useless without being acquainted with its language and cultural specificity. Second, China has been at the forefront of world politics, especially after it became the second largest global economy, with influence far beyond its borders, arousing the interest of a much larger scope of people than merely sinologists and businessmen. This second consideration presupposes interest in experimenting with new integral methods of modern social sciences that did not exist even thirty or forty years ago.

In explaining the traditional idea of the complexity and interdisciplinarity of Chinese studies, Vassili Mikhailovich Alekseev, arguably the most renowned and intellectually influential Russian sinologist of the twentieth century, has noted that China is a cultural/civilizational complex in and of itself, thus making sinology a scholarly discipline in the traditional sense of the word.[2] Though it seems provocative in terms of the modern hierarchy in the social sciences, Alekseev's idea reflects some pragmatic academic problems that confront anyone who begins research in Chinese Studies today: how to combine a necessary advanced methodological framework with a very specific object since China must be broader than any simple disciplinary framework. This problem is still not always resolved.[3] There is also the need to use primary and secondary sources written by an army of professional historiographers whose task was—and still is, but with new advanced methods—to create a "correct" history written with Chinese characters that require years to study and are very different from alphabetical texts. The specifics of China as a research object lies today in the impossibility of understanding it within a single disciplinary frame-work. This relates to Alekseev's idea of China being a cultural/civiliza-tional complex that lies at the intersection of different realities and thus different disciplines.

In the twentieth century every well-established Chinese Studies program usually had a *xiansheng* (先生) of Chinese origin who helped with the texts and their interpretation in the context of another culture. Although Russia also used this "tool," it also had an original tradition of understanding China "from the inside," by professionally trained sinologists (old China hands or dragomans) who had lived in China for as long as several decades, felt China to be their native country, and could speak and read Chinese including *wenyan* (文言), the written classical language analogous to Latin in Europe. In Russia this trend began even before the Russian ecclesiastical mission that was founded long before any Russian or Western embassy or any other longstanding commercial or military missions. Other nations followed suit and "old China hands" who can explain what is going on in China are still in demand. However, in modern times when the social sciences (and Chinese Studies as one branch of the social sciences) have become "an industry of knowledge," the ability to create a complex and integral vision of one's research object relates to many other spheres: How deep is the nation's academic tradition? How extensive is its material and social capital, and whether it can be used intensively and effectively, as well as how modern is its organizational structure for producing and disseminating knowledge? Inadequate material and social capital or outdated organizational structures will lead to uneven development of the academic disciplines and the knowledge within them, thus influencing or even hindering the appearance of interdisciplinary or integral research.

All this sets the stage for the birth of a field whose complexity presupposes its interdisciplinarity, though at different times it was understood differently. Many Chinese Studies programs in universities all over the world accordingly were created as interdisciplinary ventures and thus stood outside any specific disciplinary framework in the modern university structure. This tradition was followed by Russian universities. However, in Russia the situation was even more complex since the discipline of Chinese Studies was treated historically as a species of "practical knowledge." Oriental linguistics and diplomatic history were needed for the Ministry of Foreign Affairs to pursue diplomatic and commercial relations with a society that was distinctly non-Western and thus arguably required special skills to master it. This was a reciprocal process since China was also becoming closer to Russia, mostly through an infusion of translated books, some exotic goods, and later special missions. The conquest of Siberia and Central Asia brought to China's attention another pragmatic necessity—the need to understand the military dimensions of Russia's relationship with Asia. Following this trend the Russian General Staff began to finance geographical expeditions, headed mostly by brilliantly educated military men (Przhevalsky, Obruchev, Mannerheim, Kozlov, and so forth,) who could combine geographic explorations and ethnographic findings with military or economic analyses of these faraway territories, albeit with a new strategic perspective due to the rivalry of the Great Powers in Central Asia and China. At that time, interdisciplinarity was understood as a historical description of a combined geographical, economic, military, and ethnological reality.

Another very important impetus for the search for interdisciplinarity and integrality in Russian Chinese Studies occurred after the 1917 Bolshevik Revolution, resulting in the creation of a Soviet state with rapidly growing political ambitions and military capabilities, whose newly created political elites desired to change the world, create new states, and reconfigure old ones in favor of the new Russian Red Empire whose sphere of interests included Eastern Europe, Mongolia, China, and later Vietnam, Korea, and Cuba. This resulted in the predominance of economy-centered but simplified Marxist analyses of all research domains, including history and ethnology.

This situation was reversed in the 1990s after the collapse of the Soviet Union, creating yet a new impulse for pragmatism and real interdisciplinarity in post-Soviet Chinese Studies in Russia. Less ideologically biased but still economy-centered analyses prevailed, though in certain segments of knowledge they were substituted by sociological, political science methods, or civilizational approaches. Geopolitical change now coincided with a sudden lack of research funds, degenerating research structures, and the migration of people from research to business or other commercially or administratively profitable fields. This period was also marked by decreasing material and social capital in Chinese Studies as well as a loss of interest in China because of economic problems at home but at the same time by the rise of innovative intellectual efforts by sinologists themselves. However, these innovative attempts were not well received by the public.

Only by the mid-2000s did the broader research community, as well as the wider public in Russia, become more interested in China than they had ever been during the Soviet era. The general public ("ordinary" readers) was fascinated by the notion of "sacred" philosophical knowledge as communicated by the *wushu* masters. The new political elite, after the collapse of the Soviet version of socialism, saw China as the only large and authentic socialist country, though it had generally been hostile to the Soviet Union, as well as, for some, was the last hope against triumphant Western liberalism. Another part of the Russian political elite, and the research community allied with it, saw in China a successful model of modernization and reform based on skillfully moderated social consensus and gradual de-Sovietization through careful political restructuring. The idea of Soviet-Chinese normalization and, later on, a Russo-Chinese partnership, the ups and downs in Russo-Chinese relations from hatred to partnership and later to an over-reliance on each other exposed the need for Russo-Chinese studies to become a kind of new integrated field combining international relations, international political economy, and strategic studies. This was in order to ensure Russo-Chinese regionalization for the purpose of modernizing the economic, military, and technological spheres in both countries. The complexities of the modern age, which combine uneven globalization with a global economic recession and a patchy economic recovery, became the basis for analyzing international interconnectedness, both its positive and its negative sides.

All the aforementioned factors—the specifics of China Studies, linguistic as well as disciplinary, internal developments in Russia and its politics toward China, China's initial success in modernization that resulted in its rise, as well as the complexities of the modern age—necessitated a break from the traditional methods of research and inquiry and the application of new interdisciplinary and integral approaches to this object of research or inquiry. It is still unclear how Chinese Studies in a post-Soviet Russia, still mostly a traditional discipline within the realm of history and descriptive economics where political affairs are seen as an extension of the official course, can resolve this important practical task. However, due to the "new fields" of inquiry (juridical studies, political economy, sociology, political science, and politics) combined with the achievements of the Soviet school (linguistics, historical studies, and economics), post-Soviet Chinese Studies seem methodologically better equipped for this task than during Soviet times, notwithstanding the lack of research funds, an outdated administrative structure, and an ongoing brain drain to business.

The above-mentioned "disciplinary approach" implies an approach connected to the traditional academic disciplines of history, political science, economics, sociology, geography, and anthropology. Some of these academic disciplines in their modern forms are still underdeveloped in Russia or under-represented in specific segments of area studies; others are especially underdeveloped in post-Soviet Chinese Studies. However, an integrative, comprehensive, and interdisciplinary approach to the issue of global importance—the rise of China—has not yet evolved anywhere, Russia included, mostly because it is so challenging to bring about. Hence, a rising China, its possible place in a new world, and the consequences of this process are dealt with mostly in the field of ideology. This situation is prone to instability and the possibility of mistakes or miscalculations when it comes to choosing the right political course. Thus, given the practical considerations involved, further attempts at interdisciplinary and integral research on China will continue.

This chapter will briefly overview the development of Chinese Studies in post-Soviet Russia, particularly the historical roots of the foreign policies in question, Chinese economic history, and the political and legal background for the development, reform, and modernization of China. International politics is an essential component of any international studies agenda. This reflects the idea that any analysis of world events has to take into consideration their political nature, i.e., the government institutions and human interactions that feature both power and conflict. The analysis in question borrows the definitions of Sheldon Anderson, Jeanne A. K. Hey, Mark Allen Peterson, Stanley W. Toops, and Charles Stevens in their *International Studies: An Interdisciplinary Approach to Global Issues*, where they point out that "The power-and-conflict definition encompasses all governmental decisions and actions and also decisions and actions that occur outside government purview but that are nonetheless intensely political."[4] This chapter will also look at what was written in the field of political history as central to understanding current international relations. Another issue on the agenda is the economic history of China as this provides insights into economic trends in today's China and the development and future of its economy. Illustrating the development of these fields inside post-Soviet China Studies may explain the deficiencies of the field, but will also reveal the portion of the literature that might be referred to as interdisciplinary or integral research on China. This research informs overall perceptions of China among the research and analyst in all major geographical centers of sinology located in Russia—Moscow, St. Petersburg, Novosibirsk, Chita, and Vladivostok.

1. Research on the Historical Roots of the Foreign Policy Doctrine and an Overview of the Historical Process

Research on the historical roots of the foreign policy doctrine and the relationship between history and foreign policy in the Soviet Union was a distinct subfield of Chinese political history because it arguably provided a possibility to explain current foreign policy developments and to resolve practical questions related to the border issues between the USSR and China. The flourishing of this subfield can be explained by the Soviet-Chinese split—the disagreements between the two Communist powers, one of which was the leader and the other of which was considered to be the follower—on the path to socialism. This resulted in the conclusion by Soviet analysts that the Chinese Communists had reverted to the foreign policy behavior of the Chinese emperors and thus had clearly betrayed "the cause of communism." This idea partially freed research on Chinese foreign policy from Communist ideological indoctrination and helped bring more professional Soviet sinologists to this field, and sometimes to foreign policy as well. Two schools dedicated to research on Chinese foreign policy flourished, both in Moscow. One, the Institute of Oriental Studies, relied on research on ancient, medieval, and imperial sources in all their complexity; the other, the Institute of Far Eastern Studies, took a more pragmatic and modern approach to solving the problems in current Sino-Soviet relations and border questions, as understood mostly through the mainstream ideology. A third school, the Leningrad School of sinology, also engaged in fundamental research but it focused mostly on the ancient and medieval aspects of the Chinese foreign policy doctrine that were not very well covered in Moscow, such as China-Tibet relations in the seventeenth to eighteenth centuries, China's relations with the nomadic states of Central Asia, and so forth. All three schools are still the most influential in post-Soviet Russia together with the rival Vladivostok Sinological School, though little by little new centers of Asian studies are emerging in other regions. They do not necessarily focus on China, but the popularity of rising China presses them to pay more attention to sinological themes and to hire or prepare China specialists. However, due to the overall financial centralization of the Russian state, the small regional centers or emerging new centers still cannot rival the major centers of sinology.

The importance of tradition in the late Soviet Union enabled the transfer of knowledge and research stimuli from generation to generation as well as the appearance of a new wave of research in this field in the early 1990s by students of well-known professors, such as Sergai Tikhvinsky, Vladimir Miasnikov, Boris Gurevich, Oleg Nepomnin, Leonard Perelomov, and so forth, who had started to specialize in this field in the early or mid-Soviet era. This older generation (except for Boris Gurevich who died in the 1990s) continues with projects elaborated on in the 1980s: Sergai Tikhvinsky and Vladimir Miasnikov with the publication of a series of diplomatic documents on Russian-Chinese and Soviet-Chinese relations as well as a summary of research on Chinese border policy (together with Ye. Stepanov).[5] The younger generation has published books based on their PhD dissertations that were prepared during the final years of the Soviet Union or shortly after 1990.[6]

However, up until the end of the 1990s new publications on the subject were sporadic compared to Soviet times, and even current Chinese foreign policy doctrine and practices are less researched than they were previously. Rare exceptions to this trend are the books written by Yuri Galenovich. Galenovich belongs to the medium-old generation of Soviet sinology. Although most of his books were published in the 1990s and 2000s, Galenovich addresses most current issues related to Chinese foreign and internal policy and Russian-Chinese relations. He has authored *Blank Spots and Trouble Zones in the History of Soviet-Chinese Relations*, another book on the subject that was extended into a four-volume edition, *The History of the Relationships between Russia and China*, two other volumes on current relations between Russia and China, a series of books on Chinese-American and Chinese-Russian relations, his books on the triangular Russia-China-U.S. relationship, as well as his books on the hottest topics in their Russian and Chinese contemporary histories, including inter-party relations and the mainstream Chinese party vision of Sino-Soviet and Sino-Russian relations.[7] So, amazingly, one author over the period of two decades (1990–2010) covered the questions most often raised regarding Chinese foreign policy and Sino-Soviet and Sino-Russian relations from a perspective that was fundamentally different from most of the research in the field during the Soviet era. Books by Galenovich greatly contributed to the creation of an integral vision of China, although in reality he concentrated on specific segments of China lore.

The most important work on border issues in Sino-Soviet and Sino-Russian relations is a volume on Chinese border policy that summarizes all the research on the topic during the Soviet era.[8] Further research on the history or current situation on the Sino-Russian border practically stopped in post-Soviet Russia due to a lack of interest by the Russian government because of the interim border agreements signed by the two countries as well as the dearth of researchers due to natural attrition and departure from the field.

2. Research on Political Culture and the Cultural Roots of Modernization in China

Post-Soviet sinology has been more successful in explaining the political culture of modern China. The reason for this has been interest among

Russian politicians as well as researchers in the ideas that helped formulate a political course leading to successful reform. The major idea that evolved in the course of this research is that uninterrupted development helped formulate in China a unique civilization that arguably influenced the major historical processes in the Far East due to the dissemination of Chinese material and spiritual culture. China's influence has been explained by its capacity over the centuries to accumulate knowledge of governance and principles of social organization, which were frequently mimicked by the Far Eastern regions that subsequently adopted them. One of the most interesting findings in Russian research on the political culture of modern China is that Confucian ethical principles lessened social aggressiveness, thus creating a new type of historical impetus: through consensus and social accommodation rather than the resolution of antagonistic conflicts through revolution, as arguably associated with a Western type of development.[9] The major research question in this connection developed also as a political question: how to overcome cultural resistance to badly needed reforms, especially in view of the theory of Chinese spiritual and material supremacy. The underlying political motivation was how to ensure the move to a new stage of Russian development not by another revolution, as in 1917, but by the Chinese way as shown by Deng Xiaoping: rather than returning to the past with its compromised Soviet- or Chinese-style communism, by introducing reforms while preserving the social stability of the enormous state with millions of impoverished people. One of the conclusions is that in 1912 the core question for China was what should be taken into the future and what should be left in the past. This question was not resolved and became the reason for the civil war. In 1978, however, unlike in the 1920s and 1940s, China resolved this question primarily through the advent of Confucianism in the economic and political practice of reform. Such important research and political questions resulted in a series of books related to the early period of Guomindang (GMD)-PRC political competition in China, and especially the publication of documents related to the Comintern's heavy involvement in China.[10]

The period of publicizing documents on the Comintern's activities and GMD-Chinese Communist Party (CCP) programs and their actual implementation in mainland China resulted in several original works. Andrei Karneev, Vitalii Kozirev, and Alexander Pisarev's book (with an introduction by Arlen Meliksetov), *Power and Village in Republican China*,[11] explains the tactical political mistakes of the GMD in Chinese villages that resulted in its loss of power and withdrawal to Taiwan. Another book, authored by Vladimir Men'shikov and Oleg Nepomnin, focuses on an explanation of the structural factors in China's situation during the 1930s and 1940s, and especially the differences between the Nanjing, PRC, and Taiwan models of modernization as well as how the inconsistency of the reforms in Nanjing led to the defeat of GMD on the mainland.[12] Historical explanations of the struggle for Communist reforms in China and their later model presented by Deng Xiaoping are presented by Mikhail Titarenko in his book of articles and presentations at scholarly congresses, entitled *China: Civilization and Reforms*.[13] Another series published by the Institute of the Far Eastern Studies also develops along this line, whereas Leonard Perelomov focuses on analyses of Confucianism and its role in the evolution of different developmental doctrines in China.[14] Perelomov argues that the specific ethical principles of Confucianism and their implementation in China's political struggle after Deng Xiaoping's return to political power enabled the country to establish a progressive political consensus that pushed forward its economic development. The above arguments are summarized in a book dedicated to the Chinese model of modernization, in which the author, a scholar at the Institute of Far Eastern Studies in Moscow, argues that at certain periods of Chinese history the evolving model of political consensus and Confucianism helped to create a new Chinese identity that actually enabled the country to proceed with the reforms during these years.[15] The ideas in the book indirectly point to the policies of Russian reformers whose actions polarized their society, whereas the Chinese political elite were able to ensure stable reform and development without major political clashes.

3. Reconsiderations of Recent Chinese History

Not only are the cultural and political histories of modernization and its relationship to foreign policy a point of interest for post-Soviet historians. In the early 2000s interest peaked in a reconsideration of Communist China's past and the role of the Soviet Union in this historical process. There have been several reprints of the classic Chinese history textbook, edited by Arlen Meliksetov, written at the end of the

Gorbachev era but published in the 1990s.[16] Later, two other versions of Chinese history appeared. One, authored by Victor Usov, heavily relies on the mainland Chinese vision of the country's contemporary historical development.[17] The other book, by Oleg Nepomnin, presents a much more objective vision of China's development in light of the two "versions" of history, Communist and GMD.[18] It is clear that periods of history not wholly covered by the primary sources attract much attention. Thus, Alexander Pantsov published his *A Secret History of Sino-Soviet Relations*, Nikolai Riabchenko concentrated on the years of confrontation, and Tatiana Zaozerskaya studied the role of Soviet specialists in the formation of the Chinese military-industrial complex.[19]

This research resulted in an alternative and probably more objective vision of the reform process in China as a politically conflicted process, with successes as well as defeats for certain political factions. Yuri Galenovich published a pioneering series of books on the Tiananmen crisis and later in his other works also refers to the political struggles in China: from his detailed foreword to *The Unofficial History of the Chinese Reforms* to the translation of Chen Yizi's memoirs *China: A Decade of Reforms*, as well as on Liu Shaoqi's predicament during the Cultural Revolution.[20] He has also published on China's modern life, Chinese attitudes to Deng Xiaoping, his unofficial appraisals of the Chinese reforms, and Mao Zedong.[21] These monographs present a more objective vision of the new China. His book *Novoye Litso Kitaya* (The New Face of China) analyzes three dimensions of reforming China: the situation in the Communist Party, the situation in society and Hu Jintao's political and economic program.[22]

The general vision of political development in China to a certain extent has been distorted by the overlap between these two contradictory modes—one biased toward the CCP vision that coincides with the Soviet version of Chinese political history before the split and another that favors the less official or even unofficial underlying sources, including the reasons for internal political struggles on both the mainland and Taiwan, which were censored before 1990. Thus in post-Soviet Chinese Studies both visions are present but cannot be easily reconciled. This situation contrasts greatly with the Soviet era. There were a number of books published on the system of state norms and legislative acts, as well as books on China's current system of political governance.[23] The system of state governance in China was researched mainly by the following authors: Konstantin Yegorov, Leonid Gudosh-nikov, with his thorough chapters on the political systems of the mainland and Taiwan in the book *Vostok I Politika,* and Boris Doronin and Galina Stepanova on the relationship among the different parties in China.[24]

In the political history of the last ten years, the formation and development of the two major political parties in China—the GMD and CCP—attracted particular attention. In the history of the GMD, the most interesting question for Russian researchers was how a corrupt and politically and militarily defeated party could rejuvenate itself in such a way as to defend the island part of China and later create a "Taiwanese miracle." It is clear that after its defeat the GMD could not retain a democratic platform and needed to lean on the authoritarianism already introduced during its mainland period. The Taiwanese history of the GMD up to the 1980s clearly shows the theoretical effectiveness of the many things tried in mainland China in the 1930s–40s that none-theless failed. However, the GMD and its leaders managed to rethink the political experiments of the so-called "Nanjing model of political development" during its history on Taiwan not only regarding economic issues—strongly supported by American economic advisers—but also in politics, the authentic model of political development. The GMD managed to rethink Sun Yat-sen's political legacy and correct many mistakes in China during the period from 1920 to 1940. The course that was elaborated upon by Chiang Kai-shek in 1947 was fully imple-mented on the island. Albeit with many difficulties Chiang managed to increase the role of the party in the overall governance of the island in such a way as to ensure central governance by the newcomers from the mainland through Taiwan's Administrative Chancellery. At the same time, the local governing process was led by the Taiwanese population. Though the system developed some cracks at the end, it could be seen as a tool to ensure the speedy development of the island. The GMD reform from 1950 to 1970 led to a reconsideration of overall policy during the Chiang Ching-kuo period in Russian Chinese studies. In this connection the Taiwan multi-party system from 1990 to 2000 was of particular interest. Several books were published on Taiwan's political history and political system,[25] and others dealt with the Taiwanese multi-party system.[26]

It should be noted that overall Taiwanese political and economic development was the object of particular attention. One book was dedicated to an overview of the Taiwanese way to democracy and another presented an overview of Taiwanese political and economic development.[27] In addition, a Taiwanese citizen who studied in Russia wrote a PhD dissertation, though not published as a book, on the political development of Taiwan.[28] In 2001 the Institute of Far Eastern Studies published an overview of research on the Taiwanese modernization model and also initiated a yearly publication of analytical materials on political and economic developments in Taiwan.[29]

4. The CCP and Modernization in China

Notwithstanding these important publications, it is clear that the GMD was not at the center of official mainstream political research on China in post-Soviet Russia. Much more attention was paid to research on the Chinese Communist Party, starting from the Third Plenum of the CCP (1978). Two questions were of utmost interest: 1) How did the party, which was an offspring of the Communist Party of the Soviet Union, manage to develop and change? 2) How did a party based on principles shared by both the CPSU and the CCP manage to reform itself and the entire society while the CPSU collapsed together with the Soviet Union itself? For this purpose, CCP history was divided into two major periods, with the latter, starting after the Third Plenum (1978), being considered structurally different since the party managed to elaborate on the main principles of China's development by formulating the theory of "socialism with Chinese characteristics." The reforms in China were seen as having established the harmony of "systemic modernization." According to this idea, preserving social stability in China necessitated overseeing the development of the social sphere as formulated in the politics of "balanced development." This "balanced development" worked toward both socio-economic change and the transformation of the party itself. The transformation of the party comprised party reform, reform of the people's representative system, and reform of the government, particularly the juridical and law enforcement systems. This led to the growth of intra-party democracy as well as the policy of oversight of cadres and the party control system. State and party interests in development helped formulate this essence of party policy: the evolution of the system of governance from the direct governance of the revolutionary era to indirect governance, the split between the government and party structures, and a new cadre policy that eliminated the existing gerontocratic system of governance and helped form a new mechanism for running the country. In order to formulate and research all the aforementioned topics a body of CCP literature was translated into Russian—documents from all the major party congresses and plenums as well as troves of Chinese research literature. This helped to create major research monographs, such as *How China is Governed*, as well as many others on similar topics.[30] This body of Russian research literature provided a better understanding about the political process in China as well as about the logic of reform, including the logic of political restructuring.

5. Appraisals of the Legal Basis for Modernization in China and its Economic Successes

Issues pertaining to an understanding of the traditional and modern Chinese legal systems were traditionally understudied in the Soviet Union. Indeed, there were only two or three Soviet scholars specializing in Chinese law. Intriguingly, although the number of scholars on the Chinese legal system did not increase very significantly in post-Soviet Russia (there are currently about ten), the subject can no longer be considered under researched because of the many series of books on this topic published during the last twenty years. The desire to understand the logic of the successful reforms and China's political and economic restructuring accentuated the need to study how the traditional legal system in China worked. The latter encompassed a system of ethical and moral considerations, a system of social control for violations of ethical norms and the law, as well as a system of repercussions for breaking the law. Research on the traditional legal system in the 1990s formed the basis for the modern Chinese legal system in such a way that the modern legal system can be seen containing two organic parts: the first part being the traditionalist view of the world together with the traditionalist subjective legal system, and the second part being the objective modern legal system and its subjective component in the sense that it is supported by the European legal system. This view of the Chinese legal system was developed by legal specialists in a series of books on Chinese jurisprudence, e.g., by Yevgeni Kumanin; El'dar Imamov; and Alexander Petukhov and summarized in Yevgeni Paschenko's book *Economic Reform in China and the Civil Law System*.[31]

Analysis of traditionalism from the point of view of the legal system is important because it shows that traditionalism as a crucial part of Chinese life was changing the norms of modern law, therefore the declared juridical norms did not correspond to the real relationship between the authorities, the power elites, and the citizens. It is important to address these topics in view of the social and economic reforms that are going on in China. It is not clear from the research literature already mentioned how an analysis of this problem will deal with legal corruption since that relates to politics and the pitfalls of the modern political regime in China. However, as applied to historical development in China it could explain the defeat of the GMD and the victory of the CCP in 1949, or at least provide some important explanations. These explanations have been presented in the scholarly work by Andrei Karneev, Vitalyi Kozirev, and Alexander Pisarev, with an introduction by Arlen Meliksetov.[32]

The aforementioned approach is also related to an analysis of the development of the juridical system in the People's Republic of China. The evolution of the legal system in China and the amendments to the existing laws resulted in the creation of a new situation whereby amendments pertaining to the establishment of "socialism with Chinese characteristics" transformed Communist China into a "market economy regulated by the state." These amendments became fixed in the Chinese Constitution. The transformation of the Chinese juridical system is reflected in Russian introductions to translated compilations of the Chinese criminal and civil laws as well as monographs on the modern Chinese legal system.[33]

An attempt was also made to summarize China's development during the years of reform, starting especially in 1990 when the Soviet Union began to collapse. This work began with a book by Vladimir Portiakov on Chinese economic politics during the Deng Xiaoping era in which he presents summaries of all the varieties of China's extensive development.[34] Amazingly enough with regard to Chinese economics—arguably the area that receives the greatest international coverage—Portiakov's book is the only such major monograph in post-Soviet China studies of the 1990s. Books on the Chinese economy, other than those by Yakov Berger and Vilya Gel'bras,[35] were dedicated primarily to the historical formation of the CCP's fiscal policy. Analyses of Chinese economic policy that has catapulted the country to be the second largest economy in the world were published only ten years after the volume by Vladimir Portiakov.

The fourth major book on Chinese economics published in Russia during the last twenty years is by Eleonora Pivovarova.[36] This work explains China's economic development by using the terminology and concepts of socialist political economics, which dominated such discussions in the Soviet Union during the 1970s and 1980s.

Another major book, in which China's overall development is summarized in a more complex way, includes chapters by several scholars at the Institute of the Far Eastern Studies and is edited by Mikhail Titarenko, director of the Institute.[37] In 2004, for the fifty-fifth anniversary of the People's Republic of China, there was yet another attempt to summarize China's development.[38]

6. Instead of a Conclusion: From Uneven Development to a New Level of Interdisciplinarity?

The first complex Russian research work on China and Russo-Chinese relations was written in English outside of Russia, but a Russian version of the book was published four years before the English version.[39] While the English-language research community paid less attention to the book, in Russia it generated serious or critical comments on its methodological and theoretical basis as well as on the possibility of combining theory with substantive empirical evidence cited as "proof." The criticisms were raised by Russian political scientists and historians, but the arguments for and against split according to which branches of the discipline the reviewers belonged—in reality at the center of the criticism was the idea of balancing China. The book has undergone two editions in Russia and after fifteen years is still on the reading list for students in international studies in Russian universities. Though the importance of complex research on modern China is never directly mentioned in this book, its methodology led to two more practical books of complex research on China—the first and, to date, the only joint Russian-Chinese-American research on China's evolving international role to be published in Russian.[40] The subsequent study *Energy Aspects of International Relations in East Asia* promoted a complex understanding of East Asia and the Chinese role in the region as well as the possibility and consequences of reorienting Russian energy relations from West to East.[41]

However, the general trend of uneven development in post-Soviet Chinese studies combined with the ongoing search for a complex understanding of China's development resulted in the appearance of integral works in the 2000s. These attempts are worth being analyzed because of the pitfalls as well as the strengths of such complex interdisciplinary research in Russia and also because of their political implications. In 2006 Mikhail Titarenko and Boris Kuzik produced a significant volume *Russia and China 2050: Strategy for Co-Development* on the basis of research done by thirty academics at the Institute of Far Eastern Studies as well as the Institute of Economic Strategy that paved the way to an elaboration of the political concept of joint Russian and Chinese development up to 2050.[42] The book became a practical though unofficial guide for Russian official policy toward China in the coming years, probably up to 2010–11 or even later. Subsequently, it was subjected to severe criticism by many researchers, the most trenchant being by Alexander Khramchikhin, who analyzed the provisional results of the so-called co-development of Russia and China dating back at least ten years. He argued that these provisional results as well as the new global situation in the era of a rising China are detrimental to Russia's interests.[43] Khramchikhin tried to sum up his own vision of China, regarding China's internal problems, including conflicting concepts of history, migration, geopolitical strategy, military modernization, ideology, the Russo-Chinese relationship, and so forth, as a challenge to Russia.[44] However, he never criticized the methodology of this research; instead he concentrated mostly on the empirical evidence. Meanwhile, a body of researchers headed by Mikhail Titarenko and Boris Kuzik created an original framework called a "methodological matrix" that, as they argued, enabled them to combine qualitative and quantitative research on Russia and China in such a way as to put forward the concept of Russian-Chinese co-development. Though the methodology itself is questionable, it created the possibility of building a concept substantiated by empirical arguments.

Another criticism of the methodological matrix—its intrinsic optimistic bias that led to Russia and China being seen as equal economies—was correctly pointed out by Khramchikhin because at the time of its publication, seven years after the work by Titarenko and Kuzik, the empirical evidence sharply contradicted its conclusions. However Khramchikhin, not being a sinologist and not constructing a structural methodological concept, created an interpretive work based on subjective statements that were seen as contradictory to Titarenko and Kuzik's conclusions, thus rejecting the concept of Russian-Chinese co-development up to 2050. Khramchikhin's most intriguing point was that a year earlier than Titarenko and Kuzik's book a group of researchers at the Institute of Far Eastern Studies, headed by the Institute's deputy director, Vassili Mikheev and in collaboration with Moscow's Carnegie Center, published a study entitled *China: Threats, Risks, and Challenges to Development*.[45] This book presented complex and integral interdisciplinary research that correctly identified all the major risks facing China as it developed and analyzed such risks from the point of view of Russian national interests. Kramchikhin stated that the authors' conclusions of these books arguably may be connected to some commercial or political interests of certain financial groups in Russia and China but he never further openly elaborated this issue. Notwithstanding the weakness of Khramchikhin's arguments, he correctly pointed out that the lack of transparency in the research grant system enabled—and still enables—vested political and financial interests to influence the conclusions. This makes such conclusions unreliable, notwithstanding the correctness of the methodology matrix or the objectivity/subjectivity of the arguments cited. Therein possibly lies the reason for the dearth of complex research in analyzing the rise of China vis-à-vis Russian national and state interests as compared to international research that has already analyzed this problem in regard to Europe and America. This type of research did not begin to appear in Russia until 2013–14. Among this new wave should be mentioned another book by Vladimir Portiakov,[46] which combines historical and economic analyses of China's development during the last ten years in view of China's evolving possibilities to act as a responsible global power, and also two books edited by Alexei Voskressenski that place China's recent development and rise in an international methodological framework of controlled focused comparisons and give it a global and regional context.[47] However, the influence of this new wave of interdisciplinary and integral literature on the post-Soviet Russian research community as well as on its diplomatic and political practitioners is still to come.

Notes

1.   David Shambaugh, ed., *American Studies of Contemporary China* (Armonk, NY: M. E. Sharpe, 1993).

2.   Vassilii Alexeev, *Nauka o Vostoke* (Science of the Orient) (Moscow: Nauka, 1982), p. 120.

3.   Marlène Larouelle and Sèbastien Peyrouse, *The Chinese Question in*

Central Asia: Domestic Order, Social Change, and the Chinese Factor (London: Hurst & Company, 2012), pt. II, ch. 8, pp. 144–150.

4. Sheldon Anderson, Jeanne A. K. Hey, Mark A. Peterson, Stanley W. Toops, and Charles Stevens, *International Studies: An Interdisciplinary Approach to Global Issues* (Boulder, CO: Westview Press, 2008), p. 12.

5. Sergai Tikhvinsky and Vladimir Miasnikov, eds., *Russko-Kitaiskiye Otnosheniya Sovetsko-Kitaiskiye Otnosheniya Ofitsialniye Dokumenti* (Sino-Russian and Sino-Soviet Relations: Collected Official Documents) (Moscow: Nauka, 1958–2013); Vladimir Miasnikov and Yevgeni Stepanov, eds., *Granitsi Kitaya: Istoriya Formorovaniya* (Chinese Borders: The History of Their Formation) (Moscow: Pamiatniki Istoricheskoi Mysly, 2001).

6. Alexei Voskressenski, *Diplomaticheskaya Istoriya Russko-Kitaiskogo Sankt-Peterburgskogo Dogovora 1881* (Diplomatic History of the St. Petersburg Treaty of 1881) (Moscow: Pamiatniki Istoricheskoi Misli, 1995); Alexei Voskressenski, *Diplomatic History of the St. Petersburg Treaty of 1881* (New York: Nova Science Publishers, Inc., 1996); Andrei Chernishev, *Obschestvennoye I Gosudarstvennoye Razviviye Oiratov v 18 Veke* (Social and State Developments of Oirats in the Eighteenth Century) (Moscow: Nauka, 1990); Oleg Zotov, *Kitai I Vostochnii Turkestan v 15-18 Vekakh* (China and Eastern Turkestan in the Fifteenth to Eighteenth Centuries) (Moscow: Glavnaya Redaktsiya Vostochnoi Literaturi, 1991); Dinara Dubrovsakaya, *Sud'ba Sinjiana: Obreteniye Kitayem Novoi Granitsi v Kontse 19 veka* (Xinjiang's Destiny: China's Possession of the New Border at the End of the Nineteenth Century) (Moscow: Institut Vostokovedeniya, 1998); Marina Isayeva, *Predstavleniya o Mire I Gosudarstve v Kitaye v 3-6 Veke* (Perceptions of the World and the State in China during the Third to Sixth Centuries, BC) (Moscow: Institut Vostokovedeniya, 2000).

7. Yuri Galenovich, *"Beliye Piatna" I "Boleviye Tochki" v Istorii Sovetsko-Kitaiskih Otnoshenii* ("Blank Spots" and "Troubled Zones" in the History of Soviet-Chinese Relations) (Moscow: Institut Dal'nego Vostoka, 2 vols., 1992); Yuri Galenovich, *Rossiya I Kitai: Shest' Dogovorov* (Russia and China: Six Treaties) (Moscow: Muravei, 2003); Yuri Galenovich, *Rossia-Kitai-Amerika: Ot Sopernichestva k Garmonii Interesov* (Russia-China-America: From Rivalry to the Harmonization of Interests) (Moscow: Russkaya Panorama, 2006); Yuri Galenovich, *Istoriya Vzaimootnoshenii Rossii I Kitaya* (History of the Relationship between Russia and China) (Moscow: Russkaya Panorama, 4 vols., 2011); Yuri Galenovich, *Tchetiresta let Sosedstva s Kitayem* (400 Years in the Neighborhood of China) (Moscow: Vostochnaya Kniga, 2011); Yuri Galenovich, *O Kitaisko-amerikanskih I Rossiiski-kitaiskikh Otnosheniyakh v Svete Vstrech Ziang Zeminya s B. Klintonom i B. Yeltsinim* (On Chinese-American and Russian-Chinese Relations in View of the Jiang Zemin-Clinton and Jiang Zemin-Yeltsin

Meetings) (Moscow: IDV RAN, 1998); Yuri Galenovich, *Prav li Deng Xiaoping? Ili Kitaiskiye Inakomisliaschiye na Poroge 21 Veka* (Is Deng Xiaoping Right? Or the Chinese Dissidents on the Eve of the Twenty-first Century) (Moscow: Izograf, 2000); Yuri Galenovich, *Gibel' Liu Shaoqi* (The Peril of Liu Shaoqi) (Moscow: Vostochnaya Literatura, 2000); Yuri Galenovich, *Kitaiskoye Chudo ili Kitaiskii Tupik?* (Chinese Miracle or Chinese Deadlock?) (Moscow: Muravei, 2002); Yuri Galenovich, *Prizrak Mao* (The Ghost of Mao) (Moscow: Vremia, 2002); Yuri Galenovich, *Rossiya I Kitai: Shest' Dogovorov* (Russia and China: Six Treaties) (Moscow: Muravei, 2003); Yuri Galenovich, *Kitaiskiye Pominki po KPSS i SSSR* (The Chinese Funeral of the CPSU and the USSR) (Moscow: Vostochnaya Kniga, 2011); Yuri Galenovich, *Novoye Litso Kitaya* (The New Face of China) (Moscow: Institut Dal'nego Vostoka, 3 vols., 2008).

8. Miasnikov and Stepanov, eds., *Granitsi Kitaya: Istoriya Formorovaniya*; see also the partial explanations of these problems in the Russian academic literature in Alexei D. Voskressenski, *The Difficult Border* (New York: Nova Science Publishers, Inc., 1996).

9. Andrei Vinogradov, *Kitaiskaya Model' Modernizatsii: Poiski Novoi Identichnosti* (The Chinese Model of Modernization: In a Search of a New Identity) (Moscow: Institut Dal'nego Vostoka, 2005).

10. Raisa Mirovitskaya, *Kitaiskaya Gosudarstvennost' I Sovetskaya Politika v Kitaye* (Chinese Statehood and Soviet Policy in China) (Moscow: Pamiatniki Istoricheskoi Misli, 1999); Natalia Mamayeva, *Komintern and Guomindang* (The Comintern and the Guomindang) (Moscow: ROSSPEN, 1999); Natalia Mamayeva, *Partiya i Vlast': Kompartiya Kitaya i Problema Reformi Politicheskoi Systemi* (Party and Power: The Communist Party of China and the Problem of the Reform of the Political System) (Moscow: Russkaya Panorama, 2007); *VKP (b), Komintern I Kitai* (VKP (b), Comintern and China) (Moscow: ROSSPEN, 5 vols., 1994–2007).

11. Andrei Karneev, Vitalyi Kozirev, and Alexander Pisarev, *Vlast' I Derevnia v Respublikanskom Kitaye (1911–1949)* (Power and Village in Republican China [1911–1949]) (Moscow: Severo-Print, 2003); Andrei Karneev, Vitalyi Kozirev, and Alexander Pisarev, *Vlast' I Derevnia v Respublikanskom Kitaye (1911–1949)* (Power and Village in Republican China, 1911–1949) (Moscow: Izdatel'stvo IKAR, 2005).

12. Oleg Nepomnin and Vladimir Men'shikov, *Sintez v Perekhodnom Obschestve: Kitai na Grani Epokh* (The Synthesis in the Interim Society: China on the Edge of the Epoch) (Moscow: Nauka, 1999).

13. Mikhail Titarenko, *Kitai: Tsivilizatsiya I Reformi* (China: Civilization and Reforms) (Moscow: Institut Dal'nego Vostoka, 1999).

14. *Ideologicheskii Kurs KPK na Sovremennom Etape Provedeniya Reform* (The Ideological Course of the CCP on the Modern Stage of Reforms) (Moscow:

Institut Dal'nego Vostoka, 2000); Leonard Perelomov, *Konfutsianstvo i Sovremennii Strategicheskii Kurs KNR* (Confucianism and the Modern Strategic Line of the PRC) (Moscow: School of World Politics, Moscow State University, 2007).

15. Andrei Vinogradov, *Kitaiskaya Model' Modernizatsii: Poiski Novoi Identichnosti* (The Chinese Model of Modernization: In Search of a New Identity) (Moscow: Institut Dal'nego Vostoka, 2005).

16. Arlen Meliksetov, ed., *Istorita Kitaya* (A History of China) (Moscow: MGU, 2002).

17. Viktor Usov, *Istoriya KNR* (History of the PRC) (Moscow: Vostok-Zapad, 2 vols., 2006).

18. Oleg Nepomnin, *Kitai v 21 Veke* (China in the Twenty-first Century) (Moscow: Kraft, 2011).

19. Alexander Pantsov, *Tainaya Istoriya Sovetsko-Kitaiskikh Otnoshenii* (A Secret History of Sino-Soviet Relations) (Moscow: Muravei, 2001); Nikolai Riabchenko, *KNR-SSSR: Godi Kontfrontatsii (1969–1982)* (PRC–USSR: The Years of Confrontation, 1969–1989) (Vladivostok: Dal'nauka, 2006); Tatiana Zaozerskaya, "Sovetskiye Spetsialisti i Formirovaniye Voenno-promishlennogo Kompleksa Kitaya" (Soviet Specialists and the Formation of the Chinese Military-Industrial Complex), St. Petersburg State University, unpublished manuscript, 2000.

20. Yuri Galenovich, *Protivostoyaniye: Peking, Tiananmen* (Juxtaposition: Beijing, Tiananmen) (Moscow: Istitut Dal'nego Vostoka, 3 vols., 1995); Chen Yizi, *Kitai: Desiatiletiye Reform* (China: A Decade of Reforms) (Moscow: Institut Dal'nego Vostoka, 1996); Yuri Galenovich, *Gibel' Liu Shaoqi* (The Peril of Liu Shaoqi) (Moscow: Vostochnaya Literatura, 2000).

21. Yuri Galenovich, *Noviye Tendentsii v Dukhovnoi Zhizni Kitaya* (New Trends in the Spiritual Life of China) (Moscow: Institut Dal'nego Vostoka, 2000); Yuri Galenovich, *Prav li Deng Xiaoping? Ili Kitaiskiye Inakomisliaschiye na Poroge 21 Veka* (Is Deng Xiaoping Right? Or the Chinese Dissidents on the Eve of the Twenty-first Century) (Moscow: Izograf, 2000); Yuri Galenovich, *Kitaiskoye Chudo ili Kitaiskii Tupik?* (Chinese Miracle or Chinese Deadlock?) (Moscow: Muravei, 2002); Yuri Galenovich, *Prizrak Mao* (The Ghost of Mao) (Moscow: Vremia, 2002).

22. Yuri Galenovich, *Novoye Litso Kitaya* (The New Face of China) (Moscow: Institut Dal'nego Vostoka, 3 vols., 2008).

23. Leonid Gudoshnikov, comp and ed., *Sovremennoye Zakonodatelstvo Kitaiskoi Narodnoi Respublki* (Modern Laws of the PRC) (Moscow: Zartsalo-M, 2004); *Kak Upravliayyetsia Kitai: Evolutsiya Vlastnikh Struktur v Kontse XX–Nachale XXI Veka* (How China is Governed: Evolution of Power Structures at the End of the Twentieth to the Beginning of the Twenty-first Century) (Moscow: Pamiatniki Istoricheskoi Misli, 2004).

24. Alexei D. Voskressenski, ed., *Vostok I Politika* (The East and Politics) (Moscow: Aspect Press, 2008); Konstantin Yegorov, *Predstavitel'naya Systema Kitaya: Istoriya i Sovremennost'* (The Chinese Parliamentary System: History and Modern Times) (Moscow: Spark, 1998); Boris Doronin, *Konstitutsii i Politicheskaya Systema Kitaiskoi Narodnoi Respubliki* (The Constitutions and China's Political System) (Sankt-Peterburg: Izdatel'stvo Sankt-Peterburgskogo Universiteta, 2007); Galina Stepanova, *Sistema Mnogopartiinogo Sotrudnichestva v Kitaiskoi Narodnoi Respublike* (The System of Multi-Party Cooperation in the PRC) (Moscow: Institut Dal'nego Vostoka, 1999).

25. Petr Ivanov, *Ocherki Istorii Taiwania. Sovremennii Taiwan* (Sketches of Taiwan's History: Modern Taiwan) (Irkutsk: Irkutskoye Izdatel'stvo, 1994); Leonid Gudoshnikov and Konstantin Kokarev, *Politicheskaya Systema Taiwania* (Taiwan's Political System) (Moscow: Komarm, 1999).

26. Yevgeni Batchaev, *Pravovoye Regulirovaniye Deyatel'nosti Politicheskikh Partii na Taiwane* (Juridical Regulation of the Activities of the Political Parties on Taiwan) (Moscow: Institut Gosudarstva i Prava RAN, 2003); Leonid Gudoshnikov, comp. and ed., *Mnogopartiinost na Taiwane* (Taiwan's Multiparty System) (Moscow: Institut Dal'nego Vostoka, 1999).

27. Alexander Larin, Dva Prezidenta, *ili Put' Taiwania k Demokratii* (Two Presidents, or Taiwan's Way to Democracy) (Moscow: Academia, 2000); Andrei Ostrovskii, *Taiwan Nakanune 21 Veka* (Taiwan on the Eve of the Twenty-first Century) (Moscow: Vostochnaya literatura, 1999).

28. Huang Yaoyuan, *Politicheskaya Istoriya Kitaiskoi Respubliki (1986–1995)* (The Political System of the Chinese People's Republic, 1986–1996) (Moscow: Institut Dal'nego Vostoka, 1998).

29. *Problemy Modernizatsii Taiwania* (Taiwan's Modernization Problems) (Moscow: Institut Dal'nego Vostoka, 2001); *Sovremennii Taiwan* (Modern Taiwan) (Moscow: Institut Dal'nego Vostoka, 2005–2012).

30. *Kak Upravliayyetsia Kitai: Evolutsiya Vlast'nikh Struktur v Kontse XX–Nachale XXI Veka* (How China is Governed: Evolution of Power Structures at the End of the Twentieth Century and the Beginning of the Twenty-First Century) (Moscow: Pamiatniki Istoricheskoi Misli, 2004); Konstantin Kokarev, *Politicheskii Rezhim i Modernizatsiya Kitaya* (Political Regime and China's Modernization) (Moscow: Institut Dal'nego Vostoka, 2004); Mamayeva, *Partiya i Vlast*; Leonid Gudoshikov, et al., *Politicheskaya Systema I Pravo KNR v Protsesse Reform (1978–2005)* (The Political and Legal Systems in the PRC during the Reform Process, 1978–2005) (Moscow: Russkaya Panorama, 2007).

31. Yevgeni Kumanin, *Yuridicheskaya Politika i Pravovaya Systema Kitaiskoi Narodnoi Respubliki* (Law Policy and the Legal System in the PRC) (Moscow: Nauka, 1990); El'dar Imamov, *Ugolovnoye Pravo Kitaiskoi Narodnoi*

Respubliki: Teoreticheskiye Voprosi Obschei Chasty (The Criminal Law of the PRC: Theoretical Questions about its General Part) (Moscow: Nauka, 1990); Alexander Petukhov, *Sovremennoye Ugolovnoye Zakonodatel'stvo Kitaiskoi Narodnoi Respubliki* (The Modern Criminal Law System in the PRC) (Moscow: Intel-Syntez, 2000); Yevgeni Paschenko, *Ekonomicheskaya Reforma v KNR i Grazhdanskoe Pravo* (Economic Reform in China and the Civil Law System) (Moscow: Institut Dal'nego Vostoka, 1997).

32. Karneev, Kozirev, and Pisarev, *Vlast' I Derevnia v Respublikanskom Kitaye* (1911–1949) (2005).

33. Leonid Gudoshnikov comp. and ed., *Sovremennoye Zakonodatel'stvo Kitaiskoi Narodnoi Respublki'Ugolovnii Kodeks Kitaiskoi Narodnoi Respubliki* (The Criminal Law of the PRC) (St-Petersburg: Izdatel'stvo Sankt-Peterburgskogo Universiteta, 2001).

34. Vladimir Portiakov, *Ekonomicheskaya Politika Kitaya v Epokhu Deng Xiaopina* (China's Economic Policy during the Deng Xiaoping Era) (Moscow: Vostochnaya Literatura, 1998).

35. Yakov Berger, *Ekonomicheskaya Strategiya Kitaya* (China's Economic Strategy) (Moscow: Ekonomika, 2009); Viliya Gel'bras, *Ekonomika Kitaiskoi Narodnoi Respubliki* (The Economy of the PRC) (Moscow: Kvadriga, 2010).

36. Eleonora Pivovarova, *Sotsializm s Kitaiskoi Spetsifikoi* (Socialism with Chinese Characteristics) (Moscow: Forum, 2011).

37. Mikhail Titarenko, ed., *Kitai na Puti Modernizatsii i Reform. 1949–1999* (China on the Path of Modernization and Reform, 1949–1999) (Moscow: Institut Dal'nego Vostoka, 1999).

38. Mikhail Titarenko, ed., *KNR 55 let. Politika, Ekonomika, Kultura* (China, Fifty-five Years: Politics, Economics, and Culture) (Moscow: Institut Dal'nego Vostoka, 2004).

39. Alexei D. Voskressenski, "Russia and China," Ph.D. dissertation defended at Manchester University, 1997; Alexei Voskressenski, *Kitai: Teoriya I Istotiya Mezhgosudarstvennikh Otnoshenii* (China: Theory and History of Inter-State Relations) (Moscow: Institut Dal'nego Vostoka, 1999); Alexei D. Voskressenski, *Russia and China: A Theory of Inter-State Relations* (London: RoutledgeCurzon, 2003).

40. Alexei Voskressenski, ed., *Kitai v Morovoi Politike* (China in World Politics) (Moscow: ROSSPEN, 2001).

41. Anatoli Torkunov, gen. ed. and Alexei Voskressenski, comp. and ed., *Energeticheskiye Aspekti Mezhdunarodnikh Otnoshenii v Vostochnoii Azii* (Energy Aspects of International Relations in East Asia) (Moscow: Navona, 2007).

42. Boris Kuzik and Mikhail Titarenko, *Kitai-Rossiya 2050: Strategiya Sorazvitiya* (Russia and China 2050: Strategy for Co-development) (Moscow: Institut Ekonomicheskikh Startegii, 2006).

43. Alexander Khramchikhin, *Drakon Prosnulsia* (The Dragon is Awaken) (Moscow: Klutch-S, 2013), ch. 7.
44. Ibid., ch. 2.
45. Vassili Mikheev, ed., *Kitai: Ugrozi, Riski I Vizovi Razvitiyu* (China: Threats, Risks, and Challenges to Development) (Moscow: Moscow Carnegie Center, 2005).
46. Vladimir Portiakov, *Stanovleniye Kitaya kak Otvetstvennoi Globalnoi Derzhavi* (China's Formation as a Responsible Global Power) (Moscow: Institut Dal'nego Vostoka, 2013).
47. Alexei Voskressenski, ed., *Mirovoye Kompleksnoye Regionovedeniye* (World Regional Studies) (Moscow: Magistr, 2014); Alexei Voskressenski, ed., *Praktika Zarubezhnogo Regionovedeniya I Mirovoi Politiki* (Practicing World Regional Studies and World Politics) (Moscow: Magistr, 2014).

Part II

Being Sinologists in Post-Communist Societies

Chapter 8

Polish Sinology: Reflections on Individualized Trajectories

Bogdan J. Góralczyk[1]

According to popular wisdom, "Homeland is my destiny." The same can be said regarding the issue of one's mother tongue, with the exception of some minorities or individuals—really a very few until the recent era of globalization—born or educated in their youth on foreign territory. Only recently, during about the last three decades, has the number of people commuting and surfing across borders, continents, and cultures quickly grown due to the new compression of territory and time, and this new wave of globalization, as properly characterized by sociologist Manuel Castells, has produced a "networked society."

As is well known, China is a world of its own. With her unique language and system of writing, calligraphy, and painting, or, in fact, with the entirety of her rich cultural heritage in which the presence of the past is constantly felt, a serious treatment of the Middle Kingdom by any foreigner requires lifelong devotion, not merely a blind repetition of the homeland experience, wherever or whatever it is. Thus, in the Chinese context, the notes of the distinguished scholar, a true Renaissance man of the globalization era (a Belgian who lived in Australia) Simon Leys (Pierre Ryckmans) have special value, even if severe in content. As he writes: "No scholar can escape his original condition: his own national, cultural, political, and social prejudices are bound to be reflected in his work."[2]

This observation should be popular knowledge and the real starting point for all China-watchers throughout the world. Like it or not, due to her uniqueness, most if not all of the China-watchers treat China as a "special animal," which, for personal reasons or because of their backgrounds, they either like or dislike, hate or love, and almost never are neutral or objective. They judge it from their own—and not the Chinese—perspective, which is usually very different from theirs. This initial observation seems also to be relevant to Polish studies of China.

Another sharp statement by Simon Leys is also called for. As he notes: "The intellectual and physical boundaries of the Chinese world are sharply defined; they encompass a reality that is so autonomous and singular that no sinologist in his right mind would ever dream of extending any sinological statement to the non-Chinese world."[3] In other words, China is always special, not to be easily compared with anything else.

1. Turning Points in Recent Polish History

In 1944, when the Soviet Army encroached upon its territory, Poland became part of the Eastern bloc. This was a very unique experience, as even during the—fortunately short—Stalinist Era (1949–53), the Poles were constantly watching the West, while remaining part of the East. Ideologically and politically Poland was a so-called Communist country, whereas culturally and psychologically it always wanted to be part of the West.

Yes, Josef W. Stalin was right when he famously declared that "giving communism to the Poles is like saddling a cow." From this ambiguity arose the constant tension which led to frequent eruptions of social or political turmoil and upheaval, unprecedented in the entire bloc, occurring (counting only the major cases) in 1956, 1968, 1970, 1976, and 1980–81.

Two of these upheavals had true fault-line value. In the autumn of 1956, Poland provided an example for Hungary, and in both countries there were anti-Communist uprisings. As we know, Hungary unfortunately became engulfed in blood, whereas Poland—probably due to her recent harsh and painful memories of the Warsaw Uprising of 1944— emerged from this turning point as a unique country in the Eastern bloc.[4] Thereafter, with an individual agricultural sector and an almost independent Catholic Church, it became the most liberal country in the

Eastern bloc, its "most joyful barracks," according to a popular saying (though in the 1970s it was surpassed by Hungary under János Kádár).

This specific background led to both the election of a Polish Pope, John Paul II, in the autumn of 1978, and later, in August 1980, to the world famous Solidarity Movement, which, until martial law was declared on December 13, 1981, became an experience of freedom long enough to be one of the major forces that undermined both the Soviet regime and communism as an ideological force (the fateful "Gorbachev factor" emerged several years later). The domestic reforms of *glasnost'* and *perestroika* of the Gorbachev era in the USSR and the resurrection of the Solidarity Movement in Poland led to the *annus mirabilis* of 1989 and the final collapse first of the Berlin Wall and soon thereafter the entire Communist bloc.

The Polish dream—like the Czech, Slovak, or Hungarian dreams, as we know from a famous essay by Milan Kundera[5]—to become part of the West was finally realized. A new democratic era was built on the corpse of real socialism. This led to a socially painful and politically and economically difficult transition and transformation, as an all-dimensional—political, psychological, and economic—departure from "socialism." This process was once famously described in the following joke: Introducing communism was like preparing fish soup from a live fish, whereas bidding farewell to communism and returning to democracy was nothing but an attempt to prepare a fish from fish soup. However, the popular Polish definition of communism—that it was nothing but a long and winding road from capitalism to capitalism—is also valid. Finally, we had achieved what we really wanted.

2. The Chapters in Polish Sinology

This short introduction to modern Polish history is absolutely crucial to understand the history of Polish sinology, established—but still weak— prior to World War II. It did not fully bloom until after the war because, as we shall see, of the Polish Communist experience.

For this reason, a description of the various stages of Polish sinology is required. These stages were not historical thresholds, but highly individual and voluntary phases, as I describe below.

2.1. The Great Wave (1950–57)

When Mao Zedong proclaimed the establishment of the People's Republic of China (PRC) on October 1, 1949, Poland was among the first, on October 7, to establish diplomatic relations with the new Communist regime.[6] At the time, it seemed that both countries—for the first time in history—were not only friends, but real political allies.

One of the obvious results of this strategic choice for both sides was the initiation of the study of Chinese in Poland and the inauguration of bilateral exchange programs.[7] The first group of nine politically approved young Poles went to China in September 1950 to study at academic institutions, beginning with language training at Qinghua University.[8] In March 1951, a second group and in November 1953 a third, and the largest, group of twelve Poles went to China to study. According to meticulous research by a member of this group, later Polish ambassador to the PRC, Zdzisław Góralczyk, between 1950 and 1955 five groups of Polish students were sent to China.[9] These groups included many of the major personalities during period of bilateral political and academic relations, including future ambassadors to China such as Ksawery Burski and Z. Góralczyk, important diplomats such as Bogusław Zakrzewski, ambassador to Thailand, Portugal, and Brazil, and scholars such as Jan Rowiński (a member of the fourth group) and Roman Sławiński (a member of the second group).

This was an unexpected experiment. For the first time in history Poland had a group of people who had been fully educated in China, with enormous personal experience and in-depth knowledge of the Chinese people, culture, and civilization. It comes as no surprise then that this became an influential resource that would be exploited for decades to come, continuing to this very day.

2.2. A Cautious Friendship (1958–66)

There were major political changes on both sides in the fall of 1956, with the uprisings in Hungary and Poland and Mao Zedong's launch of the Great Leap Forward. For instance, the famous Polish historical essayist and writer Paweł Jasienica managed to write his unique and important travel report from China only due to the fact that he had gone there in late 1956 when China had not yet become engulfed in the turmoil of the anti-rightist campaign. Meanwhile, freedom immediately after the thaw in the fall of 1956 led to many Polish publications with honest descriptions of China. However, for domestic reasons on both sides, this situation would last only several months (Jasienica's second edition could not be published until 2008).[10]

The political situation in China and the Sino-Soviet ideological dispute and political split had an immediate negative impact on the exchange programs. Thus, during the next decade, groups of Polish students no longer were studying in the PRC. From China's orthodox Maoist perspective, Poland was quasi-liberal and more open to the West and was already suspect and would soon be labeled revisionist. For Polish authorities, still under strict orders from Moscow, especially in the international arena, China was a revisionist state that no longer followed the ideological course of the Soviet bloc.

Some exchanges, however, did continue, although not without trouble and problems of a different nature, mainly arising from the different internal political situations in the two countries. During this time, the exchanges were based on individual agreements, involving only one or two carefully selected students. The students who went to China during this period included personalities who would be important to future bilateral relations, such as future diplomats Stanisław Pawełczyk and Agnieszka Łobacz, and scholars such as Mieczysław J. Künstler, Tadeusz Żbikowski, and Krzysztof Gawlikowski who was the last Polish student to be sent to China (in late 1964) before the upheaval of the Cultural Revolution.

2.3. The Great Vacuum (1966–82)

The Cultural Revolution (1966–76) created a great vacuum in bilateral relations, affecting all aspects of the exchange programs. Additionally, Poland, after the brief interlude of the 1956 thaw, returned to the group of "honest followers" of Moscow's political and ideological line. This of course included a strong and growing anti-Maoist ideology.

The political atmosphere ended not only the exchange programs but also other earlier initiatives. For instance, the monthly journal *Chiny* (China), which began in the early 1960s to spread knowledge on Chinese culture and literature, ended publication. The official Polish-Chinese Friendship Society was no longer promoted, even though its club on Senatorska Street in Warsaw remained almost the only place (the other was the Shanghai restaurant) where one had an opportunity to eat Chinese cuisine. China once again had become a faraway, exotic country.

The official line of the Polish authorities was to condemn the Chinese revisionists. Publications included Soviet literature on China, of varying value, but all ideologically biased and strongly anti-Chinese.[11] It was a period when many anti-Chinese prejudices and stereotypes (a poor country where everyone wears uniforms, etc.) were created.[12] Accurate knowledge about China, which had been constantly growing during the 1950–66 period became almost non-existent, while the Polish media condemned China with ideological fervor. China virtually disappeared from Polish public discourse, and the best Polish specialists, including those who earlier had been educated in the PRC, were either silenced (the only sinology faculty in the country at the time, at Warsaw University, under the leadership of M. Künstler, made no effort to study post-1919 China), or invisible (Jan Rowiński at the Polish Institute of International Affairs tried to continue his publications under the pen name of Andrzej Halimarski).[13]

The death of Mao Zedong did not bring any dramatic changes because with the breakthrough of President Nixon's trip to China, Beijing condemned Soviet revisionism even more strongly. This rhetoric continued after the establishment of diplomatic relations with the United States in 1979 and the Soviet invasion of Afghanistan at about the same time. Similarly, Moscow continued to dictate its anti-Chinese discourse to all Soviet bloc countries, Poland included.

The Solidarity Movement of 1980–81 did not bring any major changes to Sino-Polish bilateral relations because the leaders of the movement were deeply focused on the volatile domestic situation, thus their attention to international events was limited. Therefore, their obvious anti-Soviet stance did not affect Chinese affairs.[14]

These factors led to a period of dormancy in the small Polish sinological world, with very little interest in Chinese affairs or in exchange programs.[15] The two countries, similar to the situation prior to 1950, were a world apart. A. Łobacz, a Polish "old China hand," has aptly described the situation: "Because of the Cultural Revolution, there was a gap in interest and research on China, and not only in Poland."[16] This was the case throughout the world, but especially in the Soviet bloc.

Nevertheless, this was still a significant era for Polish sinology. Those knowledgeable about China had no interest in participating in the ideological schism and tug-of-war, nor were they willing to openly condemn China (with the exception of a small group of students devoted to Maoist China who were followers of Ché Guevara). Condemnation of China would indicate acceptance of either the Soviet Union or of Maoist extremism. Neither choice was tempting, thus the dormancy, as noted above.

2.4. Same Bed, Different Dreams (1982–89)

Surprisingly, a chance to change the mood, especially in the context of bilateral Polish-Chinese relations, came in the early 1980s after the Solidarity Movement was crushed. At this time, after ending the Democracy Wall Movement and imprisoning Wei Jingsheng for advocating democracy as a fifth modernization, Deng Xiaoping introduced his "four cardinal principles."[17]

General Wojciech Jaruzelski and Deng Xiaoping, both autocratic rulers, with the latter personally afraid of the rise of trade unions and any Solidarity-style upheaval (*luan*), found themselves in the proverbial same bed. However, their political agendas were somewhat different. Poland, still following Moscow's course, was not initiating anything similar to China's "Four Modernizations" program.

Real change in bilateral Polish-Chinese relations came during the "Gorbachev phenomenon" when both countries engaged in reform programs. Since the mid-1980s official relations have been constantly improving, both politically and economically. In September 1986 General W. Jaruzelski visited China,[18] the first high-level visit since the 1950s (Mikhail Gorbachev visited China three years later, in May 1989, during the democracy movement on Tiananmen Square).[19]

After Jaruzelski's visit, high-level exchanges resumed.[20] As a result, other exchange programs that had been frozen for almost two decades were re-established. The bilateral Agreement Between the Government of the People's Republic of Poland (PRP) and the Government of the People's Republic of China on Cultural and Scientific Exchanges, signed in Beijing on September 30, 1986 during General W. Jaruzelski's visit was especially important.[21] Even though the initial exchanges were not as fruitful as expected, at least they marked a new beginning.[22]

Growing interest led to the establishment of some Chinese centers outside of Warsaw. The first was the sinology faculty established in Poznań in the late 1980s. From the beginning, this faculty was very different from the well-known Sinology Faculty at Warsaw University. The former, until today, is more of a vocational school (in a positive sense), focusing on teaching Chinese language,[23] philology, and ethnic minority issues, whereas the latter remains an ivory tower of classical Chinese, with very little interest in contemporary issues.[24] In 1987 a Faculty of Japanese and Chinese Studies was also established at Jagiellonian University in Cracow, Poland's oldest university. It initially specialized primarily in Japanese studies (its first director [until 2004], Professor Mikołaj Melanowicz, was a well-known translator of Japanese literature), and only recently has it introduced some sinological studies, mainly literature (under Professor Lidia Kasarełło). Its current director, Romuald Huszcza, a professor of linguistics and a Japanese translator, is also rather Japan-oriented.

All of the new sinology faculties typically dealt with literature, culture, language, and linguistics. Modern history, economics, sociology, and especially contemporary China were almost non-existent, as the PRC was still politically suspect, either due to its Maoist ideology or due to its reformed socialism. It was only when Mikhail Gorbachev came to power in the USSR that there was visible growth in public interest about China, but an institutional framework in sinological circles was still lacking. Modern China, and especially the PRC, remained marginal in the sinology faculties in Poland.

2.5. Children of Tiananmen (1989–2008)

The expectations of the late 1980s were greater than what was provided by the reality. This was mainly due to domestic issues on the Polish side. In fall 1988, the Solidarity Movement (no longer the trade union) re-emerged on the political stage as an official partner with the Communist authorities. Roundtable discussions ended in partially free elections on June 4, 1989. As a result, on September 12, 1989, Poland became the first country in the former Soviet bloc to have a non-Communist prime minister, Tadeusz Mazowiecki. This led to the beginning of the tortuous and painful, especially with respect to the economy, path of post-Communist transformation.[25]

As is widely known, the Chinese took a different route. Instead of dialogue, the authorities declared martial law to deal with the demonstrators in Tiananmen Square. Thereafter, eight octogenarian elder statesmen, including Deng Xiaoping, chose to crush the largest pro-democracy demonstrations in the history of the PRC.[26] The bloodshed took place in the night of June 3–4, just a few hours prior to the Polish elections that ended Communist rule. Due to this mere coincidence,

Poland, the only post-Communist country, had a strong, emotional reaction to the bloodshed in Tiananmen Square,[27] presenting a serious obstacle to a renewal of relations. Weeping for "the children of Tiananmen"[28] reached the banks of the Vistula River.

This was a decisive and fateful moment that affected the course of Polish-Chinese relations for the next two decades. A fault-line in the bilateral relations led each partner in a different direction. Poland became democratic, whereas China remained authoritarian. Poland joined the Western institutional framework, whereas China (especially under the leadership of Zhu Rongji), although entering the global capitalist economy under its opening-up policy (*kaifang*), rejected any pro-Western solutions suggested by the economic and ideological Washington Consensus.

As a newcomer to the democratic world, the Polish approach to China was strongly motivated by ideology. The former productive bilateral relations resumed, especially after the post-Communist camp returned to power in Poland in mid-1993 (primarily due to the economic turmoil during the first stage of the transformation process). The president of this camp, Aleksander Kwaśniewski (1995–2005), made an official visit to the PRC in November 1997, and Poland welcomed President Hu Jintao to Warsaw in June 2004.

However, the official line was not followed by public opinion, and the mainstream media emphasized that China remained a Communist autocracy that did not respect human rights, especially for its Tibetan minorities, and did not abide by international business and trade conventions, for instance selling poor quality and fake products. After 1989, Polish authorities, as well as the political and media elites, were waiting, in vain, for a democratic breakthrough in China.

Polish sinology at the time faced some difficult decisions. With respect to those who were products of the 1950s and had long been involved in diplomatic activities, Martin Jacoby correctly notes: "None of the eminent Polish scholars chose to defend the PRC's policies after 1989.... Most decided to speak cautiously yet critically of China."[29] Of course, former diplomats, whose careers were interrupted but not yet finished, were even more cautious, in both words and deeds. (Both Z. Góralczyk and K. Burski were to become Polish ambassadors to China in the 1990s, i.e., during a period of democratization, and J. Rowiński returned to the diplomatic world to become DCM in Beijing in the 1990s.)

A more radical change took place after the collapse of communism. Academically, several initiatives were introduced to focus on contemporary rather than ancient China. Finally, there were no longer any political obstacles to the study of modern China, even though the Tiananmen events presented a strong psychological and ideological barrier. Some initiatives by former exile K. Gawlikowski are particularly noteworthy in this respect. In the late 1990s Gawlikowski created a strong Asia and Pacific Research Centre within the Institute of Political Science of the Polish Academy of Sciences.[30] At almost the same time he also created the Centre for East Asian Civilization at the private University of Social Sciences and Humanities in Warsaw,[31] and in 1998 he initiated publication of the *Azja Pacyfik* yearbook,[32] the first and for a long time the only academic publication focusing on contemporary East and Southeast Asia, especially China (the University of Gdańsk has recently been trying to follow suit in this respect, but so far its efforts have not been noteworthy).

Almost simultaneously, another center of contemporary Asian studies was established at Jagiellonian University in Cracow, where a new Faculty of East Asia and the Middle East, separate from the Faculty on Japanese and Chinese Studies, was created (its long-time director is Adam Jelonek, former Polish Ambassador to Malaysia).[33] Recently, another Center for East Asia, specializing especially on contemporary economic issues, was created at the University of Gdańsk (by Ewa Oziewicz and Marceli Burdelski, and under the directorship Kamil Zajdler). Finally, it is possible to study contemporary China, an area of study that did not exist during the Communist era. It should be noted that another center for East Asian studies was established at the University of Łódź (under Małgorzata Pietrasiak and Dominik Mierzejewski, among others).

In the early 1990s, immediately after the change in the political system, a new window of opportunity for China studies was opened, one that, due to political reasons, had previously been completely shut, that is, Taiwan as a viable partner. The official line of the new democratic Polish governments was to follow the "democratic system" on Taiwan. President Lech Wałęsa (1990–1995), famous former Solidarity leader, was tempted to visit the island, but for geostrategic reasons he could do so only as a private person, which he did several times during the presidency of Chen Shui-bian in Taiwan.

This warm political climate allowed for the expansion of trade and economic relations with Taiwan and provided an opportunity to engage in China studies on the island. According to data provided by the Taipei Economic and Cultural Office in Poland, official student and scholar exchanges were first initiated in the early 1990s and have since been growing substantially, from 51 people at the end of 2005 to 128 people at the end of 2012.[34]

The scientific exchange agreement signed between Poland and the PRC during the visit of President Hu Jintao to Poland on June 8, 2004 openly stipulated—for the first time—that mutual, intergovernmental, annual exchanges of all kinds (students, PhD students, scholars, lecturers, and interns), composed of some thirty-five people, should be initiated in both directions (in 1987 the number was raised to forty, as the agreement had been signed for only two or three years).[35] However, it is impossible to assess how many Polish students have gone to China to study in recent years, as a great wave of exchanges is taking place outside of official channels, with private schools and private institutions playing a special positive role. According to one study, in 2006 as many as 386 Polish students visited China.[36]

2.6. A "Strategic Partnership" (2011–Present)

At the end of 2011, another high-level official visit by the Polish President was organized, the first visit since the visit of A. Kwaśniewski. During his stay, President Bronisław Komorowski, mainly in response to Chinese initiatives, signed a special strategic cooperation agreement. In an attempt to make the agreement a reality Chinese Prime Minister Wen Jiabao, the first person to hold the position of premier since the systemic change in Poland, visited Warsaw. In April 2012 Wen proposed several bilateral, mainly economic, projects, to be paid for with Chinese funding and with help from Chinese sources.[37] However, the Polish response to these new initiatives so far has been rather moderate and limited. There is still no pro-China lobby of any kind in Poland (the only politician with a substantial interest in the Middle Kingdom so far is Waldemar Pawlak, the former deputy prime minister and leader of the Polish People's Party).

Notwithstanding the new initiatives, two phenomena that are rooted in the past are still strongly visible in official Polish behavior: 1) Polish elites are somewhat prejudiced toward China, maintaining a distance from Chinese initiatives; 2) China is still treated as a developing Third World country on the other side of the world, rather than as a potential global power. The rapidly growing Chinese role in the international arena, especially after the global economic crisis of 2008, has finally brought China into Polish public discourse. But even now the Chinese role is limited and less important, both politically and in the mainstream media.

To some extent, political constraints still exist. However, simultaneously, one can also note some creativity when dealing with China; probably for the first time since the Communist era when it was by definition impossible, and after the democratic change it has been limited due to differing strategic choices in the two countries. Only now, in the first years of the second decade of the twenty-first century can a real and growing interest in China be observed in Poland, especially in the economic arena and in publishing. Fortunately, there have been more impressive results in other fields, as will be presented in further detail in the next section.

3. Sinology as Destiny

Encounters with China can take many different forms. Some people may choose China as a narrow, academic specialization, whereas others may choose the Middle Kingdom as a way of life, remaining devoted to it for a lifetime. If it is not rejected at an early stage, something that occurs quite frequently, China can be a serious choice in every aspect of an individual's life. Of course, in the case of countries that are so distant in all respects (including language, culture, civilization, etc.), and when there are no ethnic or local similarities, the individual choice must be especially strategic or long term. Let us examine some Polish cases.

3.1 Sinology in the Narrow Sense

This choice means nothing more than taking up oriental and sinological studies, followed by an academic or professional career.

3.1.1. Sinology as an Academic Career

As noted above, the first Sinology Faculty was created at Warsaw University prior to World War II in 1933. Its reestablishment after the war, and the political and diplomatic incentives after the proclamation of the PRC, provided an opportunity to promote sinology as an academic career. Some of those who went to China in the 1950s (and the early 1960s) took advantage of this opportunity, for instance, M. Künstler, R. Sławiński, and T. Żbikowski, who later became well-known names in the field of Polish sinology.[38]

During this era of political alliance, the first institutionalized academic exchanges and growing public interest led to the publication of two masterpieces in Polish sinology, written by its most important representatives: Witold Jab o ski (the first director of the faculty, until his premature death in Beijing in July 1957), Janusz Chmielewski (the long-time second director of the faculty), and Aleksy Dębnicki and Olgierd Wojtasiewicz (educated in France). The first publication is *Antologia literatury chińskiej* (An Anthology of Chinese Literature), covering the period from ancient times to Mao, published in 1956, and the second publication (by the same authors, with the exception of A. Dębnicki) is a 1953 Polish version of Zhuang Zi's classic, entitled *Prawdziwa księga południowego kwiatu*. Both volumes have been, quite rightly, obligatory texts for many generations of young Polish sinologists.

For a long time the Sinology Faculty at the University of Warsaw was the only place to engage in sinology as an academic career. A second faculty, at Jagiellonian University in Cracow, was not established until 1987. A year later, a similar faculty was established at the University of Adam Mickiewicz in Poznań. Finally, in 2011, Catholic University in Lublin (under director R. Sławiński, who previously had been first in Warsaw and then in Cracow; he passed away in late 2014) was established. Thus, opportunities to engage in sinology gradually, but constantly, began to grow.

It is too early to determine what kind of academic impact the creation of the Confucius Institutes will have. Until now, all four in Poland (in Cracow, Poznań, Opole, and Wroc aw) are affiliated with Polish academic institutions or universities. The two most active, in Opole and Cracow, have chosen slightly different approaches. Opole specializes in language and business courses, whereas Cracow produces scientific volumes of some merit.[39] It is too early to judge what can really be expected from such symbiotic actions on both sides. However, it will be useful to observe how they progress.

3.1.2. China-Watchers

During the Communist era only a small number of Poles, due to political circumstances, chose to be constant observers of China. The most prolific and visible case is that of J. Rowiński (a member of the fourth group that was sent to the PRC in 1954), who, like many of the others, immediately upon his return to Poland in 1960 joined the Polish Foreign Ministry and soon thereafter returned to China (not leaving Beijing until December 1968).[40] After his return to Poland he joined the Polish Institute of International Affairs and—mainly using the pseudonym A. Halimarski—became a commentator on Chinese affairs in the media, including in *Polityka*, the most influential official weekly at the time.

Of course, during the Communist era there was no other choice but to remain close to the official line. It was only later, after the Solidarity Movement spring of 1980–81, when Poland experienced large and impressive underground political and publishing activity (*samizdat*), supported by the strong Polish political community abroad, that some new opportunities were opened. One of them, the most important intellectual force in Polish émigré intellectual life, was Jerzy Giedroyc's Paris-based monthly, Kultura, in which K. Gawlikowski published studies on contemporary China. Because he lived abroad after the imposition of martial law he also, although less frequently, published political commentaries.

The democratic changes in 1989 affected every aspect of life. Finally, there was a chance to become a truly independent commentator. However, China did not occupy mainstream interest for two major reasons: 1) Poland "veered to the West" and wanted to become anchored in the Western institutional framework (NATO, the EU, OECD, the Council of Europe, etc.) and it basically neglected the so-called Third World; 2) The aftermath of the Tiananmen massacre, as described above.

In the mainstream Polish media the image of China remained unchanged until another fault-line appeared in global affairs, i.e., the economic crisis of 2008. By that time, a new generation in Poland had come to the fore with respect to China studies. Most representatives of this new generation have been educated in either China or Taiwan and they have deep personal knowledge of the country. Thus there have been some completely new, previously unknown, initiatives. In 2009 Radosław Pyffel inaugurated a private think-tank, called the

Poland-Asia Study Centre, that has become more and more visible in the Polish media.[41] Another initiative, by a circle of former Polish students in China, was introduced in early 2012. It is located both in Mainland China and in Poland (among its driving forces are Wojciech Jakóbiec, now in Beijing, Konrad Godlewski in Shanghai, and D. Mierzejewski in Łódź).[42] They have also created the Web site: "Na temat Chin" (On China).[43] For the first time, we now have some objective commentaries on contemporary China written by China specialists, some of whom are actually based in China. This represents completely new progress in Polish public discourse.

3.2. Sinology as a Way of Life

In a broader sense, sinology may also be chosen as a way of life by certain individuals. In this respect, knowledge of the Chinese language can be used as a tool to further one's career, whether it is in the bureaucracy, business, or even, in unique cases, politics.

3.2.1. Bureaucratic/Diplomatic Careers

During the Communist era almost all graduates of Chinese universities were tempted to enter the central bureaucracy or to become career diplomats. The only exceptions were those who studied art in China (Stanisław Tworzydło) or those who remained in the academy and chose a different way of life. Graduates of the Sinology Faculty at Warsaw University, the only sinology faculty during most of the history of the Polish People's Republic (1944–89), did not have language skills, therefore their choices were limited. However, there were several exceptions, e.g., Jerzy Bayer, a former Polish ambassador to Thailand and Burma/Myanmar, or Stanisław Leśniewski, who for a long time worked in Polish economic diplomacy as a translator.

The situation changed almost completely after the systemic change when the number of graduates studying in China (or Taiwan) began to grow dramatically. Diplomacy and the state bureaucracy were no longer their only options. They could also choose to become directly involved in economic life.

3.2.2. Sinology as a Business Opportunity

Business opportunities were completely non-existent during the Communist era. This choice emerged relatively recently, especially after 2008, when it became obvious that China also represented a great business opportunity.

After Tiananmen, unlike Hungary, Poland did not liberalize the visa regime for PRC citizens. Thus, it has been only recently that Chinese, still in limited numbers, have begun to offer their business skills in Poland. (There are some 3,000 PRC nationals in Poland, whereas there are some 30,000 PRC nationals in Hungary, a country with one-third the population of Poland.) Additionally, there were no possibilities to work in Chinese companies in Poland, but this situation began to change after President Komorowski's visit to China and implementation of the "strategic partnership," when two Chinese banks opened branch offices in Poland and many Chinese companies began to invest in the country.[44]

However, Polish individuals, as opposed to institutions, began to see China as a viable business opportunity. Many of these individuals, whose number is constantly growing, are graduates of Chinese colleges and universities. Among them are K. Godlewski, who exchanged a career in journalism in Poland for a stay in Shanghai, Łukasz Sarek (whose wife, Katarzyna, a PhD student in the Sinology Faculty of the University of Warsaw, is emerging as one of the important columnists dealing with Chinese affairs, publishing mainly on the Web site *Kultura Liberalna* [Liberal Culture]),[45] or W. Jakóbiec.

We should also note a spectacular ongoing initiative on Polish, not Chinese, territory. Adam Marszałek, who has a large private publishing house in the town of Toruń, probably the largest scientific publisher other than the official Polish Scientific Publisher (PWN), with support of the Chinese Embassy in Warsaw, has in recent years signed a number agreements with Chinese publishing houses, providing many books and publications directly from the Chinese market. Unfortunately, practically all of these publications, of varying value in both their original and final versions,[46] are translated from English and not directly from Chinese. Still, this is the first time since the early 1960s that Polish audiences have had access to renowned Chinese authors.[47]

3.2.3. Sinology as a Political Choice?

A world apart from each other, both in terms of geography and politics (and ideology), Poland cannot offer any "Chinese solution" for a political career. It was only in the early 1950s when bilateral relations were in alignment that official friendship was supported by the higher authorities. This is no longer the case, even as the global position of China continues to grow.

Poland does not have any pro-China political lobby in terms of a political party, including among the post-Communist social-democratic party (SLD). Since the Tiananmen events, there cannot be a real friendship, or even a political solution with political gains. What we have instead are verbal declarations of "friendship" and many official delegations, always ready to visit this "exotic" country, something that has been described as "sight-seeing diplomacy."[48] The only Polish high-level politician interested in Chinese affairs is—as already noted—W. Pawlak, whose political influence has declined in recent years. Politically, China does not represent an opportunity in Poland, even though it is slowly becoming an option to build a fruitful economic or business career.

4. Sinology: Individual Choices

It is here that the dividing line between the Communist and the democratic eras is the sharpest. The realities of the two political systems were so different that individual choices made during these two periods were incomparable.

4.1 Prior to 1989: The Communist Era

4.1.1. The China-born Generation

Since the nineteenth century a small Polish community existed in China. According to a meticulous study by Marian Kałuski, a Polish journalist in Australia, this Polish community in the Northeast (Dongbei) town of Harbin was created as a result of the involvement of Polish engineers and workers in the construction of the Trans-Siberian Railway. After completion of the project, some of them decided not to return to Poland, which—due to the partition—was to a large extent part of the Russian Empire. At its peak in 1903, there were some 7,000 Poles residing in China; 2,000 in Harbin and 500–600 in Tianjin and Shanghai when Poland again became an independent state after World War I. A major evacuation of this community was arranged in July 1949, and then again partially in 1958, despite the officially proclaimed "friendship" in Sino-Polish bilateral relations. The final blow to this community came with the Cultural Revolution, after which only a single Pole, Edward Stokalski, remained. At 95 years old, he left Harbin for Poland in December 1993 and died shortly thereafter. Thus ended the chapter of the only Polish community in China.[49]

One member of the Harbin community, Edward Kajdański, graduated in 1951 from the Harbin Institute of Technology and left the country the following year, to later become a Polish diplomat focusing on economics. After his retirement from the Foreign Service, he became a prolific writer on Polish-Chinese affairs. Among his works there is also an important study of the first Polish sinologist, Jesuit clergymen Michał Boym (1612?–59).[50] He also left some interesting and unique memoirs about life in the Polish community of Harbin.[51]

E. Kajdański's life experiences are basically incomparable. The only other well-known case, important from the perspective of Polish sinology, is that of Jerzy Sie-Grabowski, also Harbin-born and a product of a mixed marriage, who was a long-time lecturer of Chinese in the Sinology Faculty at the University of Warsaw. In the 1960s he translated a number of works of Chinese literature (especially in the monthly *Chiny*). while later, especially in the 1970s and 1980s, he became a translator for official Polish delegations and bilateral talks, mainly focusing on economics.

As of the present, there is no one who can compare to these two individuals. We will probably have to await a new generation before there will be any comparable replacements.

4.1.2. In-comers

This option can be observed in many countries, but in Poland during the Communist era it was almost completely unique, that is, to go to a Communist country from the West. The only case, important for Polish sinology, is that of Witold Rodziński, the son of the world-famous Polish musician and conductor, Artur Rodziński. A graduate of Columbia University in New York, in the late 1940s he first joined the UN service and later the Polish Foreign Service. He was ambassador in London and later, at an early stage of the Cultural Revolution (1966–69), he served in the PRC. In 1974 he published his monumental *History of China,*[52] an achievement that remains unmatched (the volumes by R. Sławiński noted earlier are less comprehensive). Later, as a constant commuter between East and West, he also published an English version of his history.[53] He died in Poland in December 1997.

Another "in-comer" of a different sort, a Chinese who settled in Poland, is the first wife of R. Sławiński—Irena Sławińska/Hu Peifeng—who became a relatively well-known journalist during the Communist era and was not only an important translator of literature, but also the author of a popular 2004 volume entitled *Things Chinese*.[54] A similar case is that of the German sinologist, Professor Karin Tomala, who went to Poland from the former German Democratic Republic in 1970s after she married one of the most renowned Polish experts on German issues, Professor Mieczysław Tomala (both passed away in 2014).

The democratic era is still too young to make judgments about the contributions of these various personalities. Of course, W. Rodziński's choice cannot be replicated, for obvious reasons. For now, we do not see anyone from China (or any other country) ready to build his or her career in Poland or emerging on the Polish scene. However, the unique case of the relatively young (in his early 30s) Nicolas Levi, of French origin, who lives in Poland, has started to emerge as a leading expert on North Korea. This seems to confirm that such an option still remains open.

4.1.3. Refugees and Commuters

Among the more than forty young people who were sent to China prior to 1956, and some additional persons in the following decade, a surprisingly small percentage left Poland after studying in China. The only case of seeking political asylum is that of René Goldman, who left Poland for Canada after 1956 and became a professor of Chinese studies at the University of British Columbia in Vancouver and a scholar specializing in Maoist studies.[55]

The unique experience of a Polish youth of Jewish origin, among so many, seems to confirm an observation made by Professor J. Rowiński: "My views were leftist and I thought that big things were going on in China."[56] Rowiński seemed not to be isolated in his convictions, then or later, as there were no real political dissidents in the group during the Communist era, maybe with the sole exception of M. Künstler, who was anti-ideological and anti-political by definition (and by personal choice). K. Gawlikowski left Poland after declaration of martial law. When he returned to Poland more than a decade later, his political views were generally pro-PRC. It is unlikely that everyone in Poland shares his view that "China today no longer represents a strange, exotic country with a mysterious system of writing, but rather it is an important political and economic partner of Europe."[57] Considering the level of knowledge about China in Polish public discourse, these words still sound more like wishful thinking rather than an expression of hard facts or reality.

Currently, during the democratic era, a dramatic political choice is no longer necessary. What can be observed more frequently, but it is still too early to make any final judgment, is a possibility to easily travel between countries, societies, and civilizations, as we have already observed during this period of globalization. During the previous Communist period, such a choice was either dramatic—to seek asylum—or coincidental, for instance those who were sent to China between 1950 and 1966. For example, Jadwiga Jankowska (a member of the first group) when in China married one of the most important China scholars in Hungary, Barna Tálas and then went to Budapest. Stanisław Kuczera (a member of the third group) went to the USRR where he became a renowned Chinese scholar.[58] Barbara Szelewa, a graduate of the Sinology Faculty in Warsaw, went to Bulgaria for many years after she married. But these cases were for personal reasons. All of the others remained in Poland.

Another interesting case of a commuter is that of Professor Zbigniew Słupski, a renowned translator of ancient Chinese literature, who was educated in Prague in the former Czechoslovakia and stayed there for a long period. However, he eventually moved to the Sinology Faculty of Warsaw University. Nevertheless, he is still treated as one of "our own" by Czech sinologists.[59]

4.2. After 1989: The Democratic Era

4.2.1. Taiwan as a Choice

Only after the collapse of the Communist system did Taiwan become a real counterproposal for both experienced and novice scholars of sinology in Poland. Among those who studied in the PRC before the Cultural Revolution only R. Sławiński openly selected this option, keeping his distance from the PRC and publishing on Taiwan-related issues.[60]

Among the younger generation of Polish sinologists Bogdan Zemanek from Jagiellonian University in Cracow is also following this route. He has already published several important scholarly studies on a wide range of Taiwanese issues (nationalism, Taiwan's image, its legal status, and so forth)[61] and is emerging as a leading "authority on all things Taiwanese" in Poland. There are indications that he will not be the last one to follow in this direction, but it is still too early to make a judgment.

4.2.2. China Bound: The New Generation—PRC or Taiwan–Educated?

The democratic era has brought about a new generation of Polish sinologists who are either China- (or Taiwan-) educated. They go to China, usually by their own choice, unlike their predecessors who were not randomly selected or who were selected for their political affiliations or convictions. Their number, political difficulties (see above, Children of Tiananmen) notwithstanding, greatly exceeds the number that was sent to China during the previous era. This is a group that is much more diverse, and one that has more choices and opportunities at their disposal in terms of where and what to study.

A preliminary assessment of their achievements reveals the tremendous potential of this group. With the exception of those who have chosen business or diplomatic careers, many have remained in the world of academia and research. Here, two great achievements, one individual and one collective, should be noted. Individually, M. Jacoby, a graduate of the Taiwanese tertiary education system, has produced a new Polish translation of Zhuang Zi's classic, completely different from the aforementioned classic that was translated in the 1950s.[62] Unfortunately, the author is dividing his time between the Sinology Faculty at the University of Warsaw and the Adam Mickiewicz Institute, the Polish counterpart of the Confucius, Goethe, or Cervantes Institutes. Thus, he is also involved in the direct management of cultural affairs (exhibitions, visits, etc.) and, in addition to his research, plays a prominent role in cultural life. Regardless, his research up to this point is indicative of his great potential.

One collective achievement, in all respects a pioneering work in Poland, is noteworthy. It is a volume entitled *To Understand the Chinese: Cultural Codes of Chinese Communities*.[63] With the exception of J. Rowiński, it was prepared by the younger generation of scholars, all educated in China or Taiwan, representing an entirely new situation on the Polish publishing scene.

Another example of this new, unprecedented situation is the volume *Ancient Chinese Wisdom in Short Sentences*, edited by Taiwan-based Piotr Plebaniak.[64] This is an effort to introduce to a wide Polish audience, in a very attractive editorial form, the rich world of Chinese proverbs and traditional sayings known as *chengyu*.

5. Conclusions

In its relations with China, democratic Poland, as it emerged from the Cold War world order, is a unique country in the post-Communist world. By mere coincidence one date, that of June 4, 1989, completely affected, mainly due to the Polish situation, political relations between the two sides.

It was not until the 2008 crisis in global markets and the rapid change in China's international role that there was a change in Poland as well, especially in the recent two or three years after the establishment of the "strategic relationship" between the two countries. However, it is still more of a declaration than a reality overflowing with content. The image of the PRC in Poland, deeply distorted during the 1989–2008 period, has still not been completely normalized. Although China is beginning to be regarded as a major power, in Poland it is still regarded as highly non-transparent and unpredictable. It is treated as a distant, exotic country that is difficult to comprehend.

The change in the political system had a tremendous effect on the small world of Polish sinology as well. Due to the fact that almost no one in sinological circles was an open supporter of Solidarity, all diplomats dealing with China survived the transition to democracy, and some have now reached the pinnacles of their careers, at ambassadorial levels, in democratic Poland. Of course, there are no longer any academic obstacles to studying China. The geographical distance, accompanied by the ideological and psychological barriers after Tiananmen, were the only obstacles to engaging with contemporary China. This situation changed to a certain extent after 2008, when the paramount role of the PRC as a global power became obvious. Since then, the climate for Polish contacts with China has changed to some extent, as confirmed by the "strategic cooperation" agreement of December 2011, but its final results remain unknown.

Only during the last decade did Polish sinology, as understood in academic terms, finally diversify. There are no longer two separate worlds of diplomats and state bureaucrats dealing directly with China on the one side, and academic sinologists keeping their distance from PRC realities on the other. These changes can be summarized by the following:

- Those who go to China are not politically selected nor are they sent by coincidence, as was the case for their counterparts in the 1950s and the early 1960s. People now can make individual choices about whether or not they want to study China. This represents a positive development.
- New centers to study contemporary China have been created (in Warsaw, Cracow, Gdańsk, and Łódź). However, the study of China is not institutionalized, and there is no official China-related think-tank. Thus it is a primarily a story of individual efforts.
- New initiatives to create think-tanks, blogs, and Web sites are blossoming, mostly as private initiatives, whereas any coordinated support from above (by the central authorities) is lacking, especially with respect to academic studies on contemporary China (the sinology faculties at some universities focus primarily on language, linguistics, culture, or literature).
- The number of publications on China is growing rapidly, both in terms of the number of translations of important Western scholars, as well as the results of efforts by the growing number of Polish sinologists, many of whom are members of the younger generation who have been educated either in China or in Taiwan.

Since 1990 new windows of opportunity have opened and have been fruitfully exploited in terms of scientific and academic exchanges, allowing individuals to go to China or Taiwan on their own without any official support.

Despite the great efforts by the constantly growing number of Polish sinologists, the image of China in Poland was brutalized, biased, and ideologically manipulated for so long due to the completely different strategic and political choices of the two countries on June 4, 1989 that any return to normalcy will probably take some time, especially since the countries are no longer political allies as they were for a short time in the 1950s.

Sinologists seem to act contrary to this official line, while their political choices are of a different nature, usually one of involvement rather than negation. Thus, one can expect some positive results from the study of China in Poland due to the growing number of individual efforts rather than due to coordinated cooperation at the highest levels where political will and intent are not necessarily compatible.

Notes

1. The author would like to express his deep gratitude to Marcin Jacoby, University of Warsaw, for sharing his experience, knowledge, and especially for allowing his interviews with some of the major individuals in Polish Sinology in recent decades to be used in this research effort. Hopefully, these have contributed to a further enrichment of the study.
2. Simon Leys, *The Burning Forest. Essays on Chinese Culture and Politics* (New York: Owl Book, 1987), p. 95.
3. Simon Leys, *The Hall of Uselessness: Collected Essays* (New York: New York Review Books, 2013), p. 361.
4. On the role of China and Mao Zedong in the Polish Autumn, see Jan Rowiński, "ChRL a wydarzenia październikowe w Polsce: Czy Chińczycy uchronili nasz kraj przed radziecką interwencją?" (The PRC and the Polish October of 1956: Did the Chinese Save our Country from Soviet Intervention?), in *Polska-Chiny: Wczoraj, dziś, jutro* (Poland-China: Yesterday-Today-Tomorrow), edited by Bogdan Góralczyk (Toruń: Wydawnictwo Adam Marszałek, 2009), pp. 239–289. This volume was published on the occasion of the sixtieth anniversary of the establishment of Sino-Polish bilateral diplomatic relations and includes research by the best Polish scholars on China. English version was published in 2014, Chinese — under preparation.
5. Milan Kundera, "The Tragedy of Central Europe," *New York Review of Books*, Vol. 31, No. 7 (April 26, 1984), pp. 109–123.
6. For more, see Góralczyk, ed., *Polska-Chiny*.
7. As was openly stated in the first mutual agreement on cultural exchanges, signed in Warsaw on April 3, 1951.
8. Interview with B. Dąbrowski by M. Jacoby.
9. Interview with Z. Góralczyk by M. Jacoby.
10. Paweł Jasienica, *Kraj nad Jangcy* (A Country on the Yangtze) (Warsaw: Prószyński i S-ka, 2008).
11. All these "products" are now regarded as outdated. However, one should note at least two volumes of some value. Both were produced by the Soviet Academy of Sciences: *Najnowsza Historia Chin 1917–1976* (The Newest

History of China 1917–1976) (Warsaw: Książka i Wiedza, 1976) and *Historia nowożytna Chin* (A Modern History of China) (Warsaw: Książka i Wiedza, 1979). The latter volume covers the era from the Opium Wars to the May 4 Movement of 1919.

12. An interesting phenomenon has been observed: Chinese Communist realities were treated harshly, partly to condemn the domestic situation or to reveal the similarities. See Stanisław Głąbiński, *Mao i inni* (Mao and Others) (Warsaw: Książka i Wiedza, 1974). Another author, B. Góralczyk, fruitfully used this approach in the Cracow intellectual monthly *Zdanie* (The Opinion) throughout the 1980s.

13. It is a great achievement of Polish sinology that a group of people under Rowiński's guidance published four volumes of "for internal use only" documents from the Cultural Revolution era (a final, additional volume was published during the political thaw of the Solidarity Movement in 1980).

14. According to K. Gawlikowski, a political refugee then in Italy after the declaration of martial law in December 1981 and close to the cradle of the Solidarity Movement Bureau abroad in Brussels, there was an initiative by the Chinese authorities to make contact with the Solidarity Movement abroad. Unfortunately, this initiative was not taken seriously by the Polish side. K. Gawlikowski, "ChRL a ruch 'Solidarności'..." (The PRC and the Solidarity Movement...), in *Polska-Chiny*, edited by Góralczyk, pp. 305–306.

15. Two students in the Sinology Faculty of the University of Warsaw went to China in 1979 as members of the first group since 1966 within the framework of an agreement of the faculty with the Polish Foreign Ministry. For a number of years, some students in the faculty were sent to the Polish Embassy in Beijing for half-year or academic-year internships to study Chinese and to learn about China.

16. Interview with A. Łobacz.

17. Wei Jingsheng, "The Fifth Modernization: Democracy," December 1978, in *The Courage to Stand Alone: Letters from Prison and Other Writings* (London: Penguin Books, 1998), pp. 199–212.

18. The official translator on the Polish side was K Burski, a graduate of Chinese universities and then chancellor in the embassy (and later ambassador). See *Zhongguo he Bolan jianjiao 60 zhounian/60 rocznica nawiązania stosunków dyplomatycznych między Chinami a Polską* (A Special Album Prepared by Department of Europe [Waijiaobu Ouzhou Si] of the Chinese Foreign Ministry) (Beijing: Shijie zhishi chubanshe, 2009), p. 51.

19. The best and most comprehensive (874 pages) Polish study on Sino-Soviet relations during the Gorbachev period is *Tadeusz Dmochowski, Radziecko-chińskie stosunki po śmierci Mao Zedonga* (Sino-Soviet Relations after the

Death of Mao Zedong) (Gdańsk: Wydawnictwo Uniwersytetu Gdańskiego, 2009).

20. During the many visits in both directions, including by the prime minister, other ministers, and parliamentarians, the old "China hands" from the 1950s emerged again—as translators or experts. Z. Góralczyk, then deputy chief of mission in Beijing, replaced K. Burski as official government translator, whereas Jerzy Sie-Grabowski, a long-time lecturer on Chinese in the Sinology Faculty at the University of Warsaw, played the same role for economic delegations (in the late 1980s he was always in Beijing).

21. M. Jacoby, "Zarys historii wymiany kulturalnej pomiędzy Polska a Chinami w latach 1949–2009" (An Outline of Cultural Exchanges between Poland and China 1949–2009), in *Polska-Chiny*, edited by Góralczyk, p. 340.

22. Furthermore, academically, contemporary China was virtually ignored, with the exception of the work by J. Rowiński at the Polish Institute of International Affairs. Among the most fruitful attempts to describe China during this period are two books by a former Beijing correspondent for the Polish Press Agency. Ludwik Mysak, *Sześć lat w Chinach* (Six Years in China) (Warsaw: Iskry, 1988) and *Chiński process stulecia* (The Chinese Trial of the Century) (Warsaw: Książka I Wiedza, 1990), on the Gang of four trial.

23. It produced some good results; among its graduates are already prominent personalities, such as Paweł Milewski (born in 1975) and since 2013 Polish ambassador to Australia (earlier serving as chancellor in the Polish Embassy in Beijing and as a translator for official Polish delegations), and Maciej Gaca, former cultural chancellor in the Polish Embassy in Beijing, now in Polish mission in Taipei (formerly specializing in Naxi language at the university).

24. Only recently, under Małgorzata Religa's leadership of the faculty, can one observe some positive changes in this respect.

25. For one of the best Polish studies of the first chapter during this process, see Tadeusz Kowalik, at www.polskatransformacja.l (www.polishtransformation.pl) (Warsaw: MUZA S.A., 2009).

26. Crucial documentation is included in *The Tiananmen Papers*, edited by Zhang Liang (New York: Public Affairs, 2001). On the crucial, fateful decision to clear the square, see pp. 355–362. For the Polish perspective, see B. Góralczyk (an eyewitness to the events), *Pekińska Wiosna 1989: Narodziny ruchu demokratycznego w Chinach* (Beijing Spring 1989: The Birth of the Democratic Movement in China), (Warsaw: Familia, 1999).

27. The very first and highly emotional report was written by the famous journalist and globetrotter, Wojciech Giełżyński, *Mord na Placu Tianamen* (Slaughter on Tiananmen Square) (Warsaw: Wojciech Pogonowski Ed., 1990).

28. A phrase from Ma Jian, *Beijing Coma* (New York: Farrar, Straus and

Giroux, 2008). A Polish version of this 2008 novel has been available since 2010.

29. M. Jacoby, "Polish Sinology in the 1950s and 1960s: Individual Stories and General Conditions for Development." Paper presented at the International Symposium on Evolving Sinology, Taipei, October 2011.

30. Of the many publications under its guidance, at least three collective volumes are of special value: *Chiny: Przemiany państwa i społeczeństwa w okresie reform 1978–2000* (China: Country and Social Change in the Era of Reform 1978–2000), edited by Karin Tomala (Warsaw: 2001), and a second volume, edited by K. Tomala and K. Gawlikowski (Warsaw: 2002). For a more recent publication, see W. Dziak, K. Gawlikowski, and M Ławacz, eds., *Chiny w XXI wieku: Perspektywy rozwoju* (China in the XXI Century: The Development of Perspectives) (Warsaw: 2012). Individual efforts include B. Góralczyk, *Chiński Feniks: Paradoksy wschodzącego mocarstwa* (Chinese Phoenix: Paradoxes of an Emerging Power) (Warsaw: Wydawnictwo Sprawy Polityczne, 2010), and *Przebudzenie smoka: Powrót Chin na scenę globalną* (A Dragon Awakening: The Return of China to the Global Scene) (Warsaw: Rambler, 2012).

31. Its great scholarly achievement is K. Gawlikowski and M. Ławacz, eds., *Wielkie przemiany w Chinach: Próba bilansu reform Deng Xiaopinga* (Great Change in China: Balancing Deng Xiaoping's Reforms) (Warsaw, 2012).

32. Almost all of its content, with the exception of the last two issues, is available at www.azja-pacyfik.pl

33. At least one sinologist of the younger generation who spent a longer period in China, from this faculty should be mentioned—Łukasz Gacek. He published three volumes: L. Gacek, *Chińskie elity polityczne w XX wieku* (Chinese Political Elites in the 20th Century) (Cracow: Księgarnia Akademicka, 2009); *Bezpieczeństwo energetyczne Chin* (Energy Security in China) (Cracow: Księgarnia Akademicka, 2012), and *Zielona energia w Chinach. Zrównoważony rozwój–ochrona środowiska–gospodarka niskoemisyjna* (Green Energy in China. Sustainable Development-Environmental Protection-Low-emission Economy), (Cracow: Wydawnictwo Uniwersytetu Jagiellońskiego, 2015).

34. The author is grateful to Mr. Yen-shin Chu from the Taipei Office in Warsaw for providing this data.

35. Marceli Burdelski, "60 lat stosunków Polski z ChRL: Rys historyczny" (60 Years of Polish Relations with the PRC: A Historical Sketch), in *Chiny w oczach Polaków* (China in Polish Eyes) (Gdańsk: 2010), p. 145. This is a special anniversary volume on the occasion of the establishment of diplomatic relations produced by the University of Gdańsk.

36. Józef Pawłowski, "Z dziejów badań nad Chinami w Polsce, studiów polonistycznych w Chinach oraz polsko-chińskich kontaktów naukowych" (On

the History of China Studies in Poland: Polish Studies in China and Sino-Polish Scientific Contacts), in *Polska-Chiny*, edited by Góralczyk, pp. 368–390.

37. B. Góralczyk, "Miejsce Polski w strategii gospodarczej i polityce zagranicznej Chin po przekazaniu władzy na XVIII zjeździe KPCh" (The Place of Poland in Chinese Strategy and Foreign Policy After the Transition of Power at the Eighteenth Party Congress in China), at http://www.gochina. gov.pl/ekspertyzy_gochina, accessed October 1, 2013.

38. M. Künstler was long-time director of the faculty and at the same time a prolific translator (mainly from French and English), as well as a writer of academic or—more frequently—popular works, spreading knowledge about China. T. Żbikowski was a translator of, among others, *Xi You Ji* (Journey to the West) (Warsaw: Czytelnik, pt. 1, 1976; Warsaw: Czytelnik, pt. 2, 1982). Specializing in modern Chinese history, Maria Roman Sławiński finalized, two volumes, in both English and Polish editions: *Historia Chin i Tajwanu* (History of China and Taiwan) (Warsaw: Wydawnictwo Naukowe ASKON, 2002) and *The Modern History of China* (Cracow: Ksiegarnia Akademicka, 2006).

39. One of the most important is Adam W. Jelonek and Bogdan S. Zemanek, eds., *Confucian Tradition: Towards the New Century* (Cracow: Wydawnictwo Uniwersytetu Jagiellońskiego, 2008).

40. Interviewed by M. Jacoby.

41. www.azja-pacyfik.pl, accessed on January 5, 2014.

42. Mierzejewski recently published an important volume on the foreign policy of PRC. See D. Mierzejewski, *Między pragmatyką a konfucjańska moralnością: Dezideologizacja retooryki chińskiej polityki zagranicznej w okresie reform* (Between Pragmatism and Confucian Morality: The Removal of Ideology in Chinese Foreign Policy during the Reform Era) (Łódź: Wydawnictwo Uniwersytetu Łódzkiego, 2013).

43. www.natematchin.pl, accessed January 5, 2014.

44. The first attempt occurred when a company named COVEC built a small part of the highway between Warsaw and Łódź. But because of the completely different business mentalities the venture ended in a bitter retreat.

45. www.kulturaliberalna.pl, accessed January 5, 2014.

46. See details at http://www.marszalek.com.pl/. This is a matter worthy of an independent study.

47. Adam Marszałek Publishing House focuses primarily on scientific books, mainly in the humanities (economics, sociology, etc.), but only partially dealing with literature. However, Chinese literature, including Nobel Prize Winner Mo Yan, has recently been well represented and is visible on the

Polish market from many other publishers. This is another issue worthy of a special case study.

48. B. Góralczyk, "Skończmy z wycieczkową polityką wobec Chin" (Let's Finish with Sight-Seeing Diplomacy Toward China), at http://kulturaliberalna.pl/2012/07/17/koniec-polskiej-sinofobii/, accessed October 1, 2013.

49. Marian Kałuski, *Polacy w Chinach* (Poles in China) (Warsaw: Instytut Wydawniczy PAX, 2001), pp. 31, 68.

50. Boym is known in some circles as the Polish Marco Polo. He left many important studies, especially on Chinese medicine and geography. E. Kajdański, *Michał Boym: Ambasador Państwa Środka* (M. Boym: The Ambassador of the Middle Kingdom) (Warszawa: Książka i Wiedza, 1999) (a revised and enlarged edition of an earlier edition).

51. Góralczyk, ed., *Polska-Chiny*, pp. 197–236; Gdańsk, ed., *Chiny w oczach Polaków*, pp. 73–103. Recently E. Kajdański finalized his efforts to describe the Harbin Polish community in a large volume of his memoirs: E. Kajdański, *Wspomnienia z mojej Atlantydy* (Memoirs from My Atlantis) (Cracow: Wydawnictwo Literackie, 2013).

52. Witold Rodziński, *Historia Chin* (A History of China) (Wrocław: Ossolineum, 1974).

53. W. Rodziński, *Walled Kingdom: The History of China from Antiquity to the Present* (New York: Free Press, 1984).

54. Irena Sławińska and Hu Pei-fang, *Chińszczyzna* (Things Chinese) (Toruń: Wydawnictwo Adam Marszałek, 2004).

55. His profile can be found at http://www.zoominfo.com/p/Rene-Goldman/298080145, accessed October 2, 2013.

56. Interviewed by M. Jacoby.

57. Interviewed by M. Jacoby.

58. On his role, see the volume published on the occasion of his eighty-fifth birthday, *Sinologi mira k jubileju Stanislawa Kuczery* (Sinologists of the World on Stanislaw Kuczera's Birthday) (Moscow: Institute Wostkowiedenia RAN, 2013). Especially important is the interview with Kuczera by the younger Russian sinologist S.W. Dimitrew, pp. 17–74.

59. His profile can be found at http://www.sinologia.uw.edu.pl/pods/436_zbigniew-slupski-ph-d-professor, accessed January 5, 2014.

60. For instance, his translation from Chinese of Juan Ch'ang-rue, *Taiwan Mijian Xinyang: Tradycyjne wierzenia ludowe Tajwanu* (Kraków: Księgarnia Akademicka, 2007), and his *Historia Tajwanu* (History of Taiwan) (Warsaw: Elipsa, 2001).

61. His profile can be found at http://www.orient.uj.edu.pl/instytut/pracownicy/zemanek-bogdan, accessed October 2, 2013. Seealso B. Zemanek, *Tajwańska tożsamość narodowa w publicystyce politycznej* (Taiwanese

National Identity in Political Journalism) (Cracow: Księgarnia Akademicka, 2009).

62. Jacoby's translation is more "scholarly," whereas the predecessor is more "artistic." *Zhuangzi: Nanhua zhenjing—Zhuangzi: Prawdziwa księga południowego kwiatu*, translated by M. Jacoby (Warsaw: Iskry, 2009).

63. Ewa Zajdel, ed., *Zrozumieć Chińczyków: Kulturowe kody społeczności chińskich* (To Understand the Chinese: Cultural Codes of Chinese Communities) (Warsaw: Wydawnictwo Akademickie Dialog, 2011). The authors include K. Sarek, Józef Pawłowski (currently in the Polish Embassy in Beijing) from the same faculty, as well as two people based in Taiwan, Leszek Niewdana and Zbigniew Wesołowski. J. Pawłowski recently published the important volume, Przeszłość *w ideologii Komunistycznej Partii Chin* (The Past in the Ideology of the Chinese Communist Party) (Warsaw, 2013).

64. P. Plebaniak, *Starożytna mądrość chińska w sentencjach* (Ancient Chinese Wisdom in Short Sentences) (Warsaw: Wydawnictwo Naukowe PWN, 2010).

Chapter 9

"The Songs of Ancient China" : The Myth of "The Other" Appropriated by an Emerging Sinology

Olga Lomová and Anna Zádrapová

1. Chinese Poetry in Czech Translation

In our interviews with former students of Jaroslav Průšek (1906–80), all of whom can be regarded as belonging to the "Prague School," we repeatedly encountered the same reply to our question about what had motivated them to study Chinese: it was the Chinese poetry translated by Bohumil Mathesius (1888–1952). It turns out that for the generation of Czech scholars who began to show an interest in China either during World War II or shortly thereafter, being a sinologist meant being an enthusiast for classical Chinese poetry as presented by a non-specialist.

Mathesius discovered Chinese poetry on his own shortly after World War I, based on French, German, Russian, and even Latin translations. His interest in Chinese poetry to some extent was related to the second wave of chinoiserie fashion in the early twentieth century. Unlike the translations of Chinese poetry in other European countries, Mathesius's adaptations of Chinese poetry were more than a literary experiment and they had a lasting impact on the general Czech public.[1]

Reading prefaces, postscripts, translators' remarks, and other explicit comments on the translations by Mathesius, an image of Chinese poetry (representing ancient China) among Czech readers during the formative period of Czechoslovak sinology can be reconstructed. This reconstruction reveals some interesting results for current and future deliberations on sinology as a Western discipline shaped also by concerns unique to the European experience. It demonstrates the existence of an ideological network that combines traditional topoi about the Orient with a genuine and serious study of Chinese civilization.[2] As a result, we may ask a more general question: How much was the creation of sinology in postwar Czechoslovakia part of a romantic enchantment and an unreflected search for "The Other" as a solution to the feeling of domestic crisis, and also to what degree was scholarship on China shaped by a romantic idealization of the object of study?

2. Bohumil Mathesius

It is indicative that the person who inspired future Czech sinologists was not a specialist on China. In the 1920s Bohumil Mathesius was an established literary critic and translator of poetry from German, French, and Russian (he was also a poet, not particularly successful, who authored several poetry collections). During the 1920s and 30s, and with considerable success, he introduced Czech readers to important European poets, such as Schiller, Blok, Jesenin, and others. He also made an important contribution to the theory of translation, as expressed in his essays on the topic. His approach to the translation of Western poetry contributed to a broader understanding of the poetry translation tradition that had been developed by Czech scholars and translators since the late nineteenth century. This means that he carefully studied the language and form of the original in comparison to the potential of the Czech language to express not only the meaning of the original poem, but also its formal and stylistic qualities in the most natural and aesthetically satisfying ways. Working exclusively with the original language was a prerequisite for such an approach.[3] However, in the case of Chinese poetry Mathesius suddenly cast aside his belief in poetry translation based on an intimate knowledge and reproduction of the original language and style and instead created free adaptations when working with translations from third languages.

We can note here that Mathesius exercised in his translations certain criteria of topicality: "We should translate what the receiving cultural organism needs to be translated."[4] Mathesius's interest in

Chinese poetry represented a very concrete fulfillment of this statement. Naturally, this idea allows the individual translator to be free in terms of both responsibility and choice—and Mathesius made very avant-garde choices during his entire life.

Mathesius published his first book-length translation of Chinese poems—most of them by Li Bai—in 1925, but at that time it did not attract much interest among readers. It was not until 1938, shortly before the Nazi occupation of Czechoslovakia, that Mathesius returned to the publication of Chinese poetry—and this time with great success. First, he translated poems for the Czech translation of the book *My Country and My People* by Lin Yutang (Prague, 1938; with the introduction by Pearl S. Buck). This book, originally written in the English language by a Chinese author introducing Chinese culture to Western readers, immediately became popular in Czechoslovakia and contributed in a substantial way to the development of a widespread image of China as a country with rich humanistic traditions. One year later, Mathesius published his second anthology of Chinese poetry—*Zpěvy staré Číny* (Songs of Ancient China). On this occasion the response of Czech readers was enthusiastic and the publication initiated a general interest in Chinese poetry throughout the country. Here, Mathesius's understanding of topicality finally and definitely met the needs of the public.

Like other European translators of the time Mathesius approached Chinese poetry in a haphazard way, bringing together without distinction poems from the *Shijing* to the Ming dynasty drama arias; the majority of the poems in his anthology, however, present Tang poetry, and mainly Li Bai, Wang Wei, and Du Fu, who since the Song dynasty had been extolled in China as the three greatest poets of the golden age of Chinese poetry.[5] This anthology was so successful that in 1940 Mathesius published a continuation, entitled *Nové zpěvy staré Číny* (New Songs of Ancient China) (a second printing appeared in 1942, followed by several reprints after the war, in 1946, 1947, and 1949). During the war, a private and limited circulation printing of Chinese wine drinking poems appeared, also translated by Mathesius. In the following year, a bibliophile edition of Li Bai's poems was published, the result of newly initiated cooperation between Mathesius and Jaroslav Průšek, at that time a young scholar teaching Chinese language and culture in an evening school attached to the Oriental Institute in Prague.[6] In 1949, in close collaboration with Průšek, Mathesius published *Třetí zpěvy staré Číny* (Third Songs of Ancient China).[7]

Mathesius made a number of comments on his translations of Chinese poetry, making explicit what attracted him to Chinese poetry and what he hoped to achieve. First, Mathesius was aware of the difference between his other poetry translations, which were based on a careful study of the language and the style of the original, and his "Chinese" translations, which he referred to as "variations on a literary theme."[8] Despite his self-restraint, from the very beginning translations of Chinese poetry were of essential importance for Mathesius, who viewed them as more than mere playful exercises. In a 1940 essay, he explicitly distanced himself from the vogue of chinoiserie ("these are fake objects covered with Chinese lacquer with falsely applied Chinese motifs"[9]). Unlike such Orientalist fantasies he regarded the Chinese poems that he was rewriting in Czech as truthful expressions of an alien culture that introduced important lessons about humanity to Europeans.

Mathesius expressed a belief in a substantial philosophical difference in the Chinese tradition and it was this difference that interested him. Through poetry he hoped to achieve a true understanding of Chinese culture and to identify with it. His understanding of this cultural difference was based on a peculiar notion of several keywords through which the uniqueness of China might be grasped. In the above-noted essay, he further states:

> "To get inside the other culture means to acquire good knowledge about it, which means to explore thoroughly five or six keywords and to emotionally identify with them; those keywords are the most different from us, and through them they [the Chinese] perceive the world in a unique way, different from others."[10]

Later, he explains how he achieved such an identification in relation to Chinese poetry: through a careful reading of *Daodejing* and *Zhuangzi*,[11] after which "half of everything was in front of me as an open book." Mathesius also briefly mentions his studies regarding Chinese poetics,[12] which created conditions for poets "to be concise and earnest." (In his first 1925 translation he did indeed show some interest in the formal structure and style of the original, and made observations on some of the more formal aspects of Chinese, that is Tang poetry, but in his later works he no longer elaborated on this issue.[13]) After acquiring this knowledge, Mathesius started to translate, or rather to rewrite, Chinese poems. In his own words, he "transformed them into a primordial language of emotions, into a human mother tongue of lyricism."[14]

In other words, when confronting Chinese poetry, Mathesius abandons the approach to translation based on an intimate knowledge of the language of the original that he had adopted in the case of European poetry, and he no longer regards the language of the original of any importance. This is because the core of the poetic message is, according to him, hidden "behind the words." Mathesius believed that this core message could be studied in a rational way (through the study of Chinese philosophy, literary history, and poetics), but it could also be acquired in an irrational way, through a subconscious identification with the lyrical message of the poem, a course that Mathesius was convinced he was following. It should be pointed out that behind the idea of an irrational identification with The Other was Mathesius's firm belief in a universal humanity inherent in the deeper layers of all different traditions and cultures. This is based on a conviction that people in China may think differently, but deep inside they share the same primordial emotions with us; they are first and foremost, despite all cultural differences, the same human beings as human beings in the West.

Mathesius ignored the original language of Chinese poems and relied on translations into other languages, without questioning the relationship between his sources and the Chinese originals. On the other hand, the language of the Czech translation was for him of utmost importance. He carefully deliberated every single Czech word in all its shades of meaning and, as he later confessed, it sometimes took him many weeks before he could finally decide upon a single expression. It is difficult to explain how a translator so meticulous about every detail of the language in which he worked could believe in a truthful recognition of the original via randomly collected translations in different languages of varying quality, yet this was exactly how it was.

What did Mathesius discover that was so unique about China as revealed in Chinese poetry? In an afterword to the 1950 edition of *New Songs from Ancient China*, he uses metaphorical language to write about "a gurgling stream of clear water" that he can hear in Chinese poetry.[15] This pronouncement, later also borrowed by Průšek, summarizes the

idea of Chinese poetry as a source of purification and vitality. After his
first encounter with Chinese poems in the early 1920s, Mathesius was
fascinated by the difference he believed he had discovered in Chinese
poetry. At that time Europe had been shattered by World War I and was
experiencing a deep spiritual crisis. Under these circumstances Mathesius perceived Chinese poetry as an expression of a culture which could
be an antidote to a "corrupt" Europe. According to Mathesius, Western
civilization was "endowed with a contradiction of mind and heart that
was irreconcilable" and this had led Europe to "eternal grief, endless
worries, and fatigue."[16] In his view, this failure of Western civilization
could only be remedied by the "simplicity and purity"[17] expressed in
Chinese poetry. Fourteen years later, on the eve of World War II,
Mathesius, when praising Chinese poetry, again speaks about the crisis
of Europe:

> "It seems to me that now, when so many things have broken down, we have
> found ourselves in a situation in which we have to look at ourselves and at
> human life in general from a distance, and we have to knock on the pillars,
> buttresses, and beams of our humanity (in order to examine their current
> validity)."[18]

In other words, Mathesius viewed ancient Chinese poetry as a
mirror by which Europe would be able to recognize its failure to offer a
viable alternative to war. His earlier negative view about Western civilization achieved deeper meaning and clearer contours with the approach
of World War II. In Mathesius's view, Europe had become a victim of
its own ambitions, capriciousness, expansionism, and pursuit of individ-
ualism and originality. As a result, individuals were suffering and were
unable to achieve real happiness, and society as a whole was deterio-
rating as a result of social inequality, disharmony, and the threat of a
destructive war. Unlike Europe, Mathesius believed that in China there
existed "unity and harmony—unity of heart and mind in the sense that
Confucius had already spoken about—permanence, stability, non-
violence, and the absence of a wish to conquer, as well as the art of
discovering happiness in the smallest things in this world."[19] (We realize
the naivety of his belief given the war situation in China at that time,
but for some reason Mathesius, not unlike many of his contemporaries
in Central Europe, was blind to the contemporary situation in China.)
   Mathesius does not mention the Nazi threat and approaching war,
but at first sight it is clear that he is targeting the political situation in

Central Europe: the Munich Agreement in which the French and British allies sacrificed Czechoslovakia to Hitler; and the Nazi expansionism that Mathesius—as well as others—perceived as representing a total failure of European civilization.

3. Jaroslav Průšek

We do not have any evidence of Jaroslav Průšek's early interest in Chinese poetry. According to his testimony in *My Sister China*,[20] when he entered the University in Prague in 1925, he was attracted to ancient history from the perspective of Europe. It was only during his study of the campaigns of Alexander the Great in the Orient that he began to be interested in Eastern civilizations, and soon thereafter he decided to explore ancient China. Because there was no way at that time to receive such an education in Prague, he travelled to Germany, Sweden, and later to China and Japan to study the Chinese language and Chinese civilization. While in China, Průšek was in contact with the May Fourth generation of intellectuals who inspired efforts to re-evaluate the domestic cultural heritage and to create a modern (i.e. westernized) literature. He returned to Czechoslovakia at about the same time as Mathesius, with stunning success, published his *Songs of Ancient China*, and the two soon began to collaborate on further translations of Chinese poetry (during World War II, they would prepare together privately published translations of Li Bai).[21] Interestingly, the translations produced in collaboration with a sinologist do not essentially differ from the "variations on Chinese themes" produced earlier by Mathesius alone, when working without access to the Chinese sources. We have to assume that the sinologist resonated with the interpretations of the poet.

In 1946 Jaroslav Průšek joined Mathesius to write introductions and postscripts to his translations, making general comments on Chinese poetry. In these sometimes rather long texts, we can find expressions of Průšek's explicit embrace of the translator and, using his authority as a sinologist, he basically confirms those ideas earlier expressed by the translator himself. A certain process of adapting to Mathesius's opinion is visible in terms of the way this occurred. In his first essay on Chinese poetry (written in April 1946, published next year), Průšek still maintains a certain distance. He confesses, even with a touch of sarcasm, that vis-à-vis Mathesius's translations, he is putting aside his own opinions as an academic:

"I, as a professional sinologist tempered by academic experience, should write on other topics: I should compare the translations with their Chinese originals, discover and criticize the differences, seek the origins of each poem and trace the way it became part of the collection, demonstrate my erudition and heuristic intelligence. But I give up. ... I recite these verses in silence and I do not care whether the origin was a careful Russian translation by Alekeseev, or a free adaptation from German or French; I do not care whether the original really compares melancholy to the aroma of resin from a pine tree. Perhaps at other times I am uncompromising, even irritable, in academic matters, but I do not want to be like that when it comes to poetry. I am content that Mathesius uses his own poetic language to express the same voice that I hear in Chinese poetry, the poetry that is the most beautiful eternal tomb of the human race."[22]

Here Průšek is indirectly admitting that the translations, in terms of their philology, are far removed from the Chinese originals. But, at the same time, when he says that he "recites silently" the verses of melancholy and hears voices from the "most beautiful eternal tomb of the human race," he is also confessing to being under the spell of the topoi of the Western imagination about the Orient that was prevalent in intellectual circles in Europe during the early part of the twentieth century. This obvious retreat from Průšek's position as a critical scholar is even more noteworthy in the light of his reputation as a conscientious academician and his own emphasis on academic integrity.[23]

Průšek in fact confirms Mathesius's original understanding of Chinese poetry as expressed in the metaphor of a "gurgling stream of clear water," that is a distant and soothing voice of an alien culture which promises salvation to a Europe which had proved to be self-destructive in the great wars. Průšek's statement is even more surprising given the fact that in his research on Chinese literature he was inspired by the Prague Linguistic Circle's linguistically based understanding of literature. But suddenly, when confronted with Chinese poetry, it seemed to him unimportant that the translator did not read the poems in the original language; the sources of the translation became irrelevant and even the original metaphors could be changed. After all, what was important? What made this poetry distinctly Chinese in the eyes of the translator and the enchanted readers, including the one who had read the originals and must have seen the difference? Why was it so appealing to Czech readers that it even inspired some of them to become sinologists?

In the same essay in which he confesses that he cast aside his academic erudition when reading Chinese poetry in Czech translation,

Průšek also mentions his personal experience during a visit to China in the early 1930s. He remembers how he experienced a revelation of eternity after he climbed a tower in a "medieval Chinese town" and saw the Yellow River below. And it is this eternity, according to Průšek, who is here perhaps borrowing and subverting Hegel's view of the absence of historical change in China shared by many since the 19th Century, that represents China's contribution to humanity. This eternity "finds expression in Chinese poetry. This feeling was captured by Mathesius, as he gave the feeling a word and a rhyme, and let it flow like a river in eternal melancholy."[24] In other words, Průšek is stating that Chinese poetry is predestined to capture eternity, whatever he may mean by that word, as a quality and value present especially in China. Some of his other writings also reveal a similar opinion, i.e. in relation to China's contribution to mankind. Eternity is for Průšek of universal and positive value. Perhaps a distant echo of Herder's famous description of China as an "embalmed mummy," this timeless China becomes in his view the "beautiful eternal tomb of the human race" from which future resurrection will come. We hear from Průšek that the reason why Chinese culture is eternal and thus worthy of emulation in the West is that it teaches humility, the most important virtue needed in order to attain harmony, stability, and eternal peace. Apparently, due to the impact of the war that had just ended, Průšek further writes:

> "There is no eternity in the high and mighty of the world. … Only culture based on humility, life which does not brawl against the Grand Smelter when smelting and transforming everything into new forms, is eternal."[25]

Reading Průšek's travelogue *My Sister China,* we find more evidence of such feelings and they are not only limited to poetry. For example, when observing and experiencing the Chinese landscape, Průšek gets carried away by ideas of eternity, the passage of time, and the worthlessness of individual ambitions vis-à-vis history:

> "Diving into this labyrinth of bare rock faces, clay incisions, steep-banked beds of rivers and brooks that contain no water but are filled with sun-scorched gray red boulders. … I invariably succumb to the same overwhelming, intoxicating feeling of abandon, escape, and dissolution. Here among these hills I am no longer an entity of much value. … Here one is just a lump of earth temporarily vegetating where the rains have not yet carried away all the topsoil wedged in between the rocks and, after a while, is destined to return again to its origins."[26]

Thinking about Průšek's strategy in reading Chinese poetry in Czech translation, one is reminded of his wartime writing about the Tang poet Li Bai. In 1942, when introducing the life of the poet, Průšek relies on popular legend rather than historical fact.[27] The following statement about his decision to give preference to legend over fact signals his conscious romantic idealization of Chinese poetry:

> "We do not care that the legend has probably nothing in common with the reality, that in fact Li Bai during his young years must have been a sort of buster, later serving for a short time at the court of the emperor Minghuang, and eventually dying in his bed at home as an old inebriate, his liver and kidneys destroyed by alcohol. How much more truthful to poetry is the legend than the sober facts of history!"[28]

Let us return to Průšek's postscript to the anthology of Chinese poetry prepared by Mathesius that was published shortly after World War II, in 1946. In complete accordance with, and as a supplement to Mathesius, Průšek claims that Europeans had lost their former self-confidence, their "belief that they are exclusive, stronger, more powerful, more beautiful, more interesting, and more attractive than others."[29] Průšek expresses the opinion that a lesson must be taken from Chinese poetry (and hence also from Chinese culture in general, though this is not explicitly stated here) about humility and subordination to the larger community. According to Průšek, eternity never rests in the individual, but it can be achieved in the totality of human beings.

Generally positive feelings among people in Czechoslovakia toward China after World War II, together with the political interest of the Czechoslovak government, found expression in the establishment of the Czechoslovak-China Society in December 1945. Jaroslav Průšek was elected its first president (and Mathesius vice president). In his inaugural lecture,[30] entitled "Hodnoty čínské kultury" (The Values of Chinese Culture), Průšek explicitly formulates his ideas about China as an example for Europe.[31] His words are just as emotional and passionate as those earlier used by Mathesius. Průšek summarizes the basic values of Chinese culture as he saw them and as he had already expressed in *My Sister China*: the permanence of an ancient civilization, tolerance of thought, and harmony among people and with nature as it found its expression in marvelous poetry as well as in painting and philosophy (the *Tao*). These are presented in opposition to the self-assertion and violence of the West that had resulted in the horrors of war. He also mentions the disillusionment of the Europeans with a belief in progress and the power of modern technologies, and the need for a renovation of humanistic moral values.

Furthermore, in his speech Průšek paints an idealized picture of Chinese (Confucian) political ideology, juxtaposing it with "Machiavellian ideas about government ruling over Europe for at least the last 400 years." He states:

> "Especially today, when also we in Europe seek a way to replace the blind play of free economic and political forces without any restrictions and conflicts with each other, we definitely can find great inspiration in Chinese concepts of political philosophy, or, in other words, those fashionable today in Chinese ideology. The reason is that [the Chinese system] is the only one in the history of mankind that is not based on religion, but rather is based on philosophy and a world view, and this order in principle views all people as equal, and—most importantly—its entire way of ruling strived to employ moral criteria. The Chinese system of governance never follows any rule that applies different criteria to the behavior of a politician and to the behavior of a private person."[32]

In his inaugural speech Průšek also discusses the "values for a sophisticated and cultured spirit" that are inherent in Chinese culture and literature. He also mentions art as complementary to literature and expresses admiration for "the perfect balance inherent in Chinese painting, architecture, and literature," comparing it to the *sophrosyné* of the art of ancient Greece. While praising the qualities of Chinese art, which, according to Průšek, have been "pursued, but so far have not been achieved by today's [Western] artists," he uses epithets such as "monumentality, yet simplicity," "timeless beauty," "perfect aesthetic balance," and "refined taste rooted in thousands of years of totally uninterrupted tradition."

Admiration for Chinese art went side by side with poetry as another important aspect of Chinese culture that had attracted the Czech public since the prewar period. This continued after the war, inspiring future sinologists in tandem with the translations of Chinese poetry.[33] In 1946, on the occasion of an exhibition of modern Chinese ink paintings organized under the auspices of the ambassador of the Republic of China to Czechoslovakia, Wunsz King (Jin Wensi [金問泗], 1892–1968), as well as the Czechoslovak minister of foreign affairs, Jan Masaryk (1886–1948), Průšek again elaborates on the aesthetic appeal of Chinese art and its relevance for postwar European art.[34]

We may assume that the huge task of improving Western civilization could be assigned to ancient Chinese poetry and art because these were distant enough in space and time from postwar Czechoslovakia, and seemed totally different, alien, and, as such, could be thought of as offering solutions for a society that had been shattered by war.[35] As a result, not only the translator without any academic background in sinology, but also Průšek, a rigorous scholar with broad knowledge of Chinese language and history and also someone who had personal experience resulting from a visit to China, could perpetuate the Orientalist myth. After the horrifying experience of World War II, Průšek and Mathesius searched for a "touch of eternity" in what they both imagined was an ancient, harmonious, collectivistic society, where every man and woman knew his/her place and could prosper as a small part of a larger unity, not differentiated from the others. Behind these ideas we can see the old European topos of China as "lifelessly frozen in ... vast, timeless immobility"[36] reinterpreted in a positive way.

This belief in the lessons from the otherness of China is reflected in yet another feature that Průšek admires in Chinese poetry—the reputed positive lack of originality. As much as eternity means belonging to the totality, the ambition to become unique in artistic creation turns out to be foolish. As Průšek says: "Why not have one thousand exquisite variations of one perfect theme?" He further adds: "Perfection excludes originality; once something truly perfect is made, it can only be repeated, otherwise we will abandon the previously achieved quality."[37]

4. The Impact of the New Ideology

Průšek's postwar essays on Chinese poetry and the values of ancient Chinese culture also reveal a smooth transformation from the earlier romantic idealization of Chinese poetry and Chinese culture to the ideology of New China in the context of the revolutionary change that was occurring in both postwar Czechoslovakia (where the Communist victory is dated to February 1948), and in China. This is best illustrated by a November 1949 special issue of the popular journal *Nový Orient* that was dedicated to the establishment of the People's Republic of China. The cover of the issue is embellished with a reproduction of Qi Baishi's (齊白石) (1864–1957) painting of a blooming red plum. The issue includes a long speech by Průšek, delivered on the occasion of a

Prague meeting celebrating the establishment of the PRC. In his speech Průšek interprets recent Chinese history as a process of the emancipation of the masses, culminating in the establishment of the PRC. This is followed by articles dealing with Chinese agriculture and land reform, biographies of the leaders of communist revolution, Mao Zedong, Zhu De, and Zhou Enlai, and an overview of the civil war that took place ahead of the victory of the Chinese Red Army. These articles, dealing with politics and utilizing official rhetoric, are framed by Chinese poems translated by Mathesius. The selection is most revealing; Tang masters (Du Fu and Li Bai) are quoted side by side with twentieth-century authors writing in *baihua*, mostly minor authors of revolutionary poems. All of them are translated in the same beautiful modernist idiom Mathesius had originally developed for translations of ancient masters.[38] Among them, only Du Yunxie (杜運燮) (born 1918) can be identified as a modernist, someone whose style would be distantly similar to Czech modernist poetry.

Literary dogma in both post-1948 Czechoslovakia and post-1949 China shared the same basic values that were derived from the Soviet concept of socialist realism: admiration for "the people," the concept of class struggle, a critical distance from the "decadent, false, and artificial Western (imperialist) culture," and an accentuation of simple "realism," easy to understand and carrying a didactic message. Průšek partially adopted the language of the official ideology in his popular essays on Chinese poetry published in the 1950s, but he also retained his earlier admiration for values of simplicity and eternity. In so doing, he could not avoid highly problematic claims; at times, he even contradicted himself. At the beginning of his postscript to the new 1950 edition of *Zpěvy staré Číny ve třech knihách: parafráze staré čínské poesie* (Songs of Ancient China in Three Books: Paraphrases of Ancient Chinese Poetry), Průšek first attacks what he calls "Orientalist thinking and its mythology," referring to it as "the most infamous legacy from the period of imperialism." He presents "Orientalist thinking" as an expression of colonial dominance and contempt for Asian cultures. "It is high time," writes Průšek, "to learn about the facts and to do away with previous rash judgments and overbearing preconceptions. There is no reason to approach the nations of Europe and Asia differently."[39]

Despite his authentic commitment to universal humanity, at the same time Průšek still preserved the stereotypical understanding of

Chinese poetry as the antipode of a "decadent" West. In a postscript to the 1950 edition of Mathesius's Chinese poetry in Czech translation, Průšek generalizes about Chinese culture. According to his thinking, it had always been more natural and of a higher quality than Western culture. As an analogy to prove his claim he mentions the sophistication of traditional Chinese crafts. He compares the art of ancient Chinese poets who, he claims, embody the ideal of simplicity inspired directly by nature, to the perfection achieved by Chinese working men— craftsmen and farmers—using very simple tools.[40] Furthermore, Průšek elaborates on Chinese poetry as an example of art interested in real nature, unlike the depictions of nature in early Western literature, where plain nature "as it is" was suppressed by religious symbolism.

Shortly after Mathesius's death in 1952, at the height of the impact of Stalinism in Czechoslovakia, his collected translations of Chinese poetry were published under the title *Zpěvy staré a nové Číny* (Songs of Ancient and New China). As the title suggests, traditional (mostly Tang) poetry, is placed side by side with contemporary political poetry. Průšek wrote an extensive postscript for the book, in which he uses the concept of "people's literature,"[41] borrowed from the theory of socialist realism, to praise all Chinese poetry. According to this interpretation, partially echoing publications in the People's Republic of China at the time, tradi- tional Chinese poetry embodies the ideals of "people's literature" because it is believed that the sentiments of its greatest authors, Li Bai and Du Fu, were always with the common people rather than with the ruling class. Průšek's argument is that Chinese poetry allegedly "in the absolute majority of cases, and especially in its best works, expresses the feelings of the people, not the feelings and caprices of the minority ruling class."[42] The close relationship between the ancient poets and the common people can be seen, according to Průšek, in popular legends about the poets that had circulated among the people for hundreds of years. Průšek also mentions the continuing general popularity of ancient Chinese poetry among Chinese people, and contrasts this with the liter- ature of the modern "decadent, capitalist West" that is limited to only a handful of readers.[43] As a result, Průšek concludes, the people of China can draw strength and inspiration for their fight for a better future from their intimacy with Chinese poetry rather than from the West. Průšek adds that during all human history, both Chinese and Western, humanity was oppressed by the exploiting classes and had to be "cured by the medicine of true art"—that is, Chinese poetry. We can see here the continuity with the idea expressed in his wartime essay on Li Bai, in which he prefers legend over facts; this time "the poetic" serves the demands of the new Communist ideology understood as the ultimate expression of humanism.

The 1953 anthology is interesting also as an attempt to bridge Chinese tradition with the revolutionary changes in contemporary China. Průšek, in his Epilogue, finds continuity in the position of the poets in traditional China, who, he states, "have always been on the side of the people." Thus, contemporary poets writing on political topics can be understood as continuing the efforts of their ancient predecessors— the differences of language, form, styles, and imagination are again irrelevant, as were the Chinese originals irrelevant for Mathesius's translations of classical poetry—with one big difference that gives the poets of New China an advantage over their ancient precursors: in New China, according to Průšek's words, the poets can put their ideals into practice; they not only express the feelings of the common people, but they also know how to help the common people, how to bring them freedom and a bright future.

In sum, in the 1953 Epilogue Průšek reinterpreted his earlier romantic ideas about simplicity, universal values, and the power of Chinese poetic tradition to be in accord with the dogmas of socialist realism, including the adoption of language imbued with the rhetoric of the official ideology. We can only guess as to the extent to which this was due to a sincere belief in the new dogma, or whether he rather adopted the official stance in order to protect and promote the universal values in which he believed and which, under the conditions of Stalinist Czechoslovakia, he could not easily promote, unless referring to the people of China, the ally in the Socialist Camp. The second option seems plausible in particular with regard to his denials of Western-inspired modern Chinese literature. Such an opinion appears suspicious as Průšek was an enthusiastic reader of both Chinese and Western modernist authors. He was also a personal friend to many of the protagonists of pre-revolutionary modern Chinese literature, and his published research on Chinese modernist literature expressed a high opinion of its achievements. In addition, Průšek's former students claim that his writings that conformed to the Stalinist ideology of the early 1950s— mostly addressing wider audiences—were motivated by his wish to avoid possible censorship and to enable the publication of ancient Chinese poetry that he believed carried a message to Czech readers, of particular importance during that period.[44]

Given that Průšek initially embraced the romantic vision of Chinese poetry, and later reformulated it to be consistent with the rhetoric of Soviet socialist realism, does this mean that he failed as a scholar? Was his academic knowledge insufficient? We do not believe that this is the case, and there is much evidence in Průšek's other publications indicating that he himself was aware of the complex nature of traditional Chinese poetry. We have already referred to Průšek's explanation as to why he used romantic legends rather than sober facts to introduce Li Bai to Czech readers, thus revealing his awareness about the differences between myth and reality. In the same essay Průšek elaborates in some detail on language and the style of the poet, concluding with words that reflect the ideas and rhetoric of the Prague Linguistic Circle: "All this makes a Chinese poem an original aesthetic structure, hard to imitate in the material of other languages."[45] Similarly, in his 1964 endnote to a translation of a poem by Mathesius, included in a selection of *huaben* stories, Průšek reminds his readers that this is not a true translation. In a detailed commentary he makes corrections to the poem as rendered by Mathesius, providing his own word-for-word "unpoetic" yet "exact" version and explicitly pointing out what the translator omitted and what he added to the original in order to achieve a poetic effect.[46]

In the mid-1950s Průšek wrote a preface to the *Songs of Ancient China*, which was later included in the 1957 edition. He opens the preface with a polemic against some of his own earlier romantic views. He criticizes the concept of "Chinese poetry" as reflected in anthologies consisting of poems from different periods and written in different styles, but translated in the same manner without any formal and stylistic distinctions and believed to be expressions of the same "spirit of Chinese poetry." He also writes: "It is time to publish books on various periods of Chinese poetry, even on individual poets," and he goes on to enumerate the most urgent tasks for Czech sinologists in the near future.[47]

However, in the very same edition Průšek again, both directly and indirectly, advances the idea that Mathesius's translations are truthful to the Chinese original. Unlike in previous editions, Průšek arranges the translated poems in chronological order, implying that the translations reflect the progression of the history of Chinese literature. He also claims that the poems, for which he provided Mathesius with prosaic translations, "are not free adaptations, but exact translations—as far as we can speak about exact translations of poetry from Chinese where we have to leave out all considerations of the original form." [48] Contrary to what he had written earlier about the translations, in this essay Průšek asserts that even the earlier translations based on versions of Chinese poetry in Western languages are to a large extent truthful to the Chinese originals. His main argument is that Mathesius studied articles about Chinese poetry and translations by the renowned Russian sinologist V. Alekseev and thus achieved a profound knowledge of Chinese literature.

5. Conclusion

The fact that Průšek supported the Orientalist myth, even though he was aware of its romantic idealization of Chinese poetry, indirectly reflects the depth of his attachment to the ideal world created by Mathesius. As noted in the writings and oral testimonies by senior sinologists, the power of these translations had universal appeal among Czech readers, inspiring an interest in sinology. The poet Mathesius, and later the sinologist Průšek, with his authority as a scholar and teacher, used Chinese poetry to establish the idea of China as a world that would be an alternative to their own imperfect reality. This vision was transmitted to Průšek's pupils and through the power of popularization, which according to Průšek was an integral part of the academic duty of every scholar, to the general public in the former Czechoslovakia. This alternative imaginary world enabled them to immerse themselves in a beautiful fairytale, yet at the same time it was a fairytale in which familiar things could be recognized and desired, a world for which it was worth living, despite all the tragedies and desperation of the actual reality. In general, people need this kind of imaginary world, especially during times of crisis and the horrors brought about by war or the actions of a totalitarian regime. At such moments in history assurance is needed in relation to the possibility of harmony and eternity, an assurance that can be found in a persuasive way only in an uncompromised source—most probably a source not well known and seemingly alien—that is, The Other, unconsciously created of topoi inherent in the culture of the recipient. Chinese poetry interpreted as an expression of the desired harmony, simplicity, purity, and noble humanism thus became a reflection of everything contemporary that European society lacked and longed for in its own—and known only too well—world. This image could be manipulated in such a way that it would become incorporated into a new political ideology, and live on even after the takeover of the totalitarian regime, eventually being incorporated within the image of New China perpetuated by the new political ideology in Czechoslovakia. It is only natural that Průšek, as we know for example from his travelogue *My Sister China*, was fully aware of the serious problems with which China would have to deal, but he saw them as more or less transitional phenomena, typical of a society in change. His main position was one of hope and a vision of a great Chinese future rooted in its idealized past.

We will never know to what extent Průšek was sincere in his efforts to interpret classical Chinese poetry in terms of socialist realism, and to what degree this interpretation was a clever strategy aiming at subverting official dogma. But, as confirmed by the widespread popularity of Mathesius's translations, it was a successful attempt within the boundaries of the totalitarian ideology to negotiate a space for humanistic as well as aesthetic values that in principle rejected this very same ideology.

Deliberating upon Průšek's ambivalent interpretations of Chinese poetry, we are reminded of the conclusions outlined in a comparative study of the image of China in twentieth century travel literature (represented by Julius Dittmar's 1952 travel book *In neuen China*) and in some stories by Franz Kafka. Goebel, in referring to Edward Said's *Orientalism*, writes: "Dittmar's travel book and Kafka's self-reflective response show that the West's experience of Asian cultures in the twentieth century, despite a commitment to empirical observation and realistic description, is necessarily implicated in the same ideological network that has characterized the history of European writings on the Orient, a network that combines stereotypical topoi with genuine interest in non-Western civilizations."[49]

The question is whether the ideological network to which Goebel is referring is impenetrable and to which degree it can be changed by those, who have a "genuine interest" in the study of China. We can argue for the possibility of change and the overcoming of the Orientalist ideology by pointing out that in their academic research Průšek and his students eventually passed over the cultural construct of Chinese poetry as an expression of the eternal and absolute Other, and they transformed their romantic imagination into opening up new pathways to understanding China. Thus, in the end they contributed to the acquisition of genuine knowledge about the cultural differences (and similarities) between Chinese and European traditions. Borrowing the expression of Zhang Longxi, they were moving in the direction of the "fusion of horizons," and eventually expanded the horizons of knowledge in the West.[50]

Notes

1. Fascination with Chinese poetry in the early twentieth century avant-garde poets and critics in Europe were not exclusive to Czechoslovakia. Another example is Miloš Crnanski and the beginnings of Serbian modernism. See Tatjana Micic, "Anthology of Chinese Lyrical Poetry by Miloš Crnjanski: The Similarities of Spiritual and Poetic Aspirations as a Reason for Translating Chinese Lyrical Poetry into the Serbian Language," *Azijske in Afriške Študije*, Vol. 8, No. 2 (2004), pp. 3–22. The Czechoslovak example is extraordinary in terms of the widespread popularity of Chinese poetry, extending beyond intellectual circles.

2. The interplay of stereotypical topoi with genuine attempts to overcome them has so far been discussed mainly in studies about the impact of China on Western literature, such as Rolf J. Goebel, "Constructing Chinese History: Kafka's and Dittmar's Orientalist Discourse," *PMLA*, Vol. 108, No. 1 (1993), pp. 59–71.

3. On Mathesius, see Jiří F. Franěk, *Bohumil Mathesius* (Praha: SNKLU, 1963) and Anna Zádrapová, "Čínská poezie česky: Otázka interpretace a překladu čínské básně v českém prostředí ve 20. Století" (Chinese Poetry in the Czech Language: On the Interpretation and Translation of Chinese Poetry in the Twentieth Century), M.A. thesis, Charles University, Prague, 2009. Mathesius was also the author of original poetry, but his contribution in this respect is less visible. See also Anna Zádrapová, "Bohumil Mathesius, Jaroslav Průšek a Zpěvy staré Číny," SOS, Vol. 11, No. 2 (2012), pp. 239–271.

4. Bohumil Mathesius, *Básníci a buřiči* (Poets and Rebels) (Praha: Lidové nakladatelství, 1975), p. 206.

5. Mathesius does not identify his sources, but they can be at least partially reconstructed. The impact of German translations by Klabund (a pseudonym for the expressionist writer Alfred Henschke, 1890–1928) is evident, as well as Russian translations by the sinologist V. Alekseev (1881–1951). The impact of Judith Gauthier (1845–1917) is also visible, either directly or

through Russian re-translations by Gumiliev. On Gauthier and Gumiliev, see Maria Rubins, "Dialog across Cultures: Adaptations of Chinese Verse by Judith Gautier and Nikolai Gumiliev," *Comparative Literature*, Vol. 54, No. 2 (Spring 2002), pp. 145–164. On the translations of J. Gauthier and their impact in other European countries see Pauline Yu, "Travels of a Culture: Chinese Poetry and the European Imagination," *Proceedings of the American Philosophical Society*, Vol. 151, No. 2 (Jun., 2007), pp. 218–229.

6. Bohumil Mathesius, *Krásná slova o víně* (Beautiful Words about Wine) (Praha: Private printing, 1943); Bohumil Mathesius, *Li Po: Dvacet tři parafráze starého čínského básníka* (Li Bai: Twenty-three Paraphrases of the Ancient Chinese Poet) (Praha: R. Kmoch, 1942).

7. After World War II, whenever there were poems to be adapted into beautiful Czech verse, Mathesius was invited by Jaroslav Průšek to participate, especially in translations of classical novels and stories from the Chinese (e.g., Liu E, *Lao Can youji*, selections of *huaben* stories, and others).

8. Bohumil Mathesius, *Zpěvy staré Číny* (Songs of Ancient China) (Praha: Melantrich, 1939), p. 83.

9. Bohumil Mathesius, *Nové zpěvy staré Číny* (New Songs of Ancient China) (Praha: Melantrich, 1940), p. 50.

10. Ibid.

11. *Daodejing* was available to Mathesius in a careful Czech translation by Rudolf Dvořák, *Lao-tsiova kniha o Tau a ctnosti* (Laozi on Dao and Virtue) (Kladno: Jaroslav Šnajdr, 1920); on this and other Czech translations of Daodejing see Olga Lomová, "Tao-te-ťing v proměnách času (1878–1971)" (Daodejing in Historical Perspective [1878–1971]), *Fragmenta Ioannea Collecta Supplementum*, No. 3 (2010), pp. 203–216; with respect to Zhuangzi, he most probably read the book in German translation by Richard Wilhelm, though a Czech version of this translation also existed.

12. He does not mention his sources, but most probably he had read articles by the Russian scholar V. Alekseev. He could have easily become acquainted with them as he was reading and translating a substantial amount of Russian literature.

13. He refers to a well-formed structure, perfect control of the subject, a sense for detail and concise evocative expression, dynamism, and perfect coincidence of the theme and imagery. See Bohumil Mathesius, *Černá věž a zelený džbán* (Black Tower and Green Jug) (Praha: Otakar Štorch-Marien, 1925), p. 44.

14. Mathesius, *Nové zpěvy staré Číny*, p. 51.

15. Mathesius, *Nové zpěvy staré Číny*, p. 50.

16. Mathesius, *Černá věž a zelený džbán*, p.44.

17. Ibid.

18. Mathesius, *Zpěvy staré Číny*, p. 83.

19. Ibid., p. 80.

20. *My Sister China* (*Sestra moje Čína*, first edition, 1940; English translation, Prague, 2003) is a volume of Průšek's memoirs about his visit to China in 1932–34. He also writes about his personal contacts with Chinese intellectuals as well as his impressions of Beijing and Xi'an. There is also a Chinese translation available (*Zhongguo, Wo de jiemei* 中國我的姐妹. Beijing: Waiyu jiaoxue yu yanjiu chubanshe, 2005.).

21. Mathesius, *Li Po: Dvacet tři parafráze starého čínského básníka.*

22. Jaroslav Průšek, "Několik slov k Mathesiovým zpěvům" (A Few Words on Mathesius's Songs), in *Zpěvy staré Číny*, edited by Bohumil Mathesius (Praha: Melantrich, 1947A), pp. 87–88.

23. In the introduction to an early collection of his papers on Chinese culture, in which his essay on Li Bai is also included, Průšek writes: "Most of the essays collected in this volume are based on my own study of the original sources. Although it is possible to pretend to be an authority in an area without being a competent critic and without anyone noticing them, I would despise such work and I would have no respect for myself if I pursued that direction." Průšek, *O čínském písemnictví a vzdělanosti* (On Chinese Literature and Scholarship), (Praha: Družstevní práce, 1947, p. 9).

24. Průšek, "Několik slov k Mathesiovým Zpěvům," p. 87.

25. Ibid., p. 88.

26. Jaroslav Průšek, *My Sister China* (Prague: Charles University, 2003), p. 306.

27. Originally the essay was published in *Dvacet tři parafráze starého čínského básníka* (Twenty-Three Paraphrases of an Ancient Chinese Poet) (Praha: 1943). It was later republished in the volume *O čínském písemnictví a vzdělanosti.*

28. Průšek, *O čínském písemnictví a vzdělanosti*, p. 138.

29. Průšek, "Několik slov k Mathesiovým Zpěvům," p. 88.

30. Held at the Oriental Institute in Prague on December 19, 1945. On these events, see Ivana Bakešová, *Legionáři v roli diplomatů: Československo-čínské vztahy 1918–1949* (Legionaries and Diplomats: Czechoslovak-Chinese Relations 1918–1949) (Praha: Univerzita Karlova, Filozofická fakulta, 2013), p. 190.

31. Jaroslav Průšek, "Hodnoty čínské kultury" (Values of Chinese Culture), *Nový Orient*, Vol. 1, No. 5–6 (1945–1946), pp. 14–16. The journal was established shortly after the end of World War II based on an initiative by Zdeněk Hrdlička (1919–1999); participants included students and scholars of various Asian languages and cultures.

32. Ibid., p. 16.

33. Personal communication with Zlata Černá. The interest among the Czech general public, but also among artists and critics, in Chinese painting during

the 1920s and 1930s requires a separate study. Several Czech painters had already begun to collect Chinese art before World War II, and one of the most influential avant-guard Czech painters, Emil Filla (1882–1953), even wrote a theoretical essay on landscape painting inspired, among others, by traditional Chinese landscape painting. After World War II Filla created two series of large experimental paintings in which he combines in an original manner a theoretical knowledge of Chinese art with his own modernist vision. See also Michaela Pejčochová, "The Formation of the Collection of 20th-Century Chinese Painting in the National Gallery in Prague: Friendly Relations with Faraway China in the 1950s and Early 1960s," *Arts Asiatiques*, No. 67 (2012), pp. 98–106.

34. Jaroslav Průšek, "Ideál čínské krásy a moudrosti" (The Ideal of Chinese Beauty and Wisdom), *Nový Orient*, Vol. 3, No. 2–3 (1947–1948), pp. 28–33.

35. As China and Czechoslovakia both embraced the Soviet model of socialism at more or less the same time, Mathesius began to translate and Průšek began to study the poetry of New China, hardly describable by such epithets as humble or reflecting eternity. This period, however, is not the focus of the present study.

36. Zhang Longxi, "The Myth of the Other: China in the Eyes of the West," *Critical Inquiry*, Vol. 15, No. 1 (Autumn 1988), p. 116. On the image of eternal immobility as created in the nineteenth century, see also pp. 123–124. The topos of China "frozen in timeless immobility" and images of China in the West are discussed by many scholars of Orientalism.

37. Průšek, "Několik slov k Mathesiovým Zpěvům," p. 89.

38. *Nový Orient*, Vol. 5, No. 2–3 (November 1949).

39. *Zpěvy staré Číny ve třech knihách: parafráze staré čínské poesie* (Praha: Melantrich, 1950), p. 202.

40. Ibid., p. 203.

41. "People's literature" is our translation of "lidovost," which is the Czech translation of the Soviet concept of "narodnost'" (i.e. *renminxing* 人民性 in Chinese).

42. Jaroslav Průšek, "Doslov" (Epilogue), *Zpěvy staré a nové Číny* (Songs of Ancient and New China) (Praha: Mladá fronta, 1953), p. 99.

43. Ibid., p. 98.

44. Zlata Černá referred to this during a panel discussion at the Conference of Czech and Slovak Sinologists, Brno, November 2011.

45. *O čínském písemnictví a vzdělanosti*, s. 149.

46. Jaroslav Průšek, *Podivuhodné příběhy z čínských tržišť a bazarů* (Strange Stories from Chinese Bazaars and Marketplaces) (Praha: SNKLU, 1964), pp. 301–303.

47. *Zpěvy staré a nové Číny* (*Songs of Ancient and New China*) (Praha:

SNKLHU, 1957, p. 235). This edition borrowed its title from an earlier edition published in 1953, but reorganized and enlarged the original selection of translations. The tasks for Czech sinologists that Průšek mentions here were partially fulfilled by his students who published five book-sized translations of individual Chinese poets between 1958 and 1987 (Bai Juyi, Tao Yuanming, Pu Songling, Li Bai and Han Shan), and also two anthologies of traditional poetry (of Song *ci*, and three Tang nature poets: Wang Wei, Meng Haoran, and Bai Juyi).

48. Ibid., p. 237.
49. Goebel, "Constructing Chinese History," p. 68.
50. Zhang Longxi, "The Myth of the Other: China in the Eyes of the West," p. 131.

Chapter 10

Between Sinology and Socialism: The Collective Memory of Czech Sinologists in the 1950s

Ter-Hsing Cheng

Beginning in the 1950s the development of Czech sinology became possible, first of all because "socialism" had built a bridge between China and Czechoslovakia, and, second, because of active promotion by Czech sinologist Jaroslav Průšek. As for senior Czech sinologists, their common memories of studying sinology include New China of the 1950s and the role of Průšek. This chapter explores how senior Czech sinologists construct their memories of the 1950s based on Maurice Halbwachs's theoretical discussion on "collective memory." Halbwachs's memory theory suggests that the construction of collective memory must have a "social framework," in which the present perspective is used to reconstruct the past, so that the memory is a construction, not a recovery. Among the Czech sinologists of the 1950s, their sinological knowledge was inspired by Průšek and the feasibility of having direct contacts with socialist China. However, this chapter examines how the senior sinologists reconstruct the link of the "social framework" between sinology and socialism during the most important period in the foundation of their ideas in the 1950s, after "normalization" in the 1970s and the 1980s, and during the period of "democratization" in the 1990s.

The chapter will construct the collective memory of the Prague School of Sinology in the 1950s based mainly on autobiographical memories rather than historical memories. The development of Czech sinology in the 1950s was primarily due to the contribution of Průšek and the socialist transformation of New China. Socialist China offered two possibilities for the development of sinology: first, it provided an opportunity for friendly relations among the socialist countries, including among overseas students; second, it provided an opportunity to study contemporary Chinese literature. New China's socialist transformation provided the best external conditions for Průšek, whose acquaintance with a number of contemporary Chinese writers in the 1930s and the 1940s had resulted in his focus on Chinese literature in the 1950s. The developmental framework for Czech sinology in the 1950s, or the social framework of the collective memory of Czech sinologists, must be understood against the backdrop of the mutual penetration of sinology and socialist China. This chapter discusses the background framework for the construction of Czech sinology in the 1950s—the link between New China and the other socialist countries as well as relations between Průšek and socialist China. The chapter then analyzes the Czech sinological experience in the 1950s based on Halbwachs's theory of collective memory.

1. Jaroslav Průšek and the Socialist Framework

The first time that the founder of the Prague School of Sinology, Jaroslav Průšek (1906–80), visited China was in 1932 and the main purpose of his trip at that time was academic study. He had planned to study Chinese economic history, but after exposure to Chinese society, his research interests shifted to social life, customs, and the folk arts. Průšek remained in China until 1937. During his stay, the Japanese government invited him to visit Japan, but Průšek was relatively sympathetic to China and he condemned Japanese aggression. While in China, he traveled throughout the country. He met the writers Mao Dun, Bing Xin, Ding Ling, Guo Moruo, Shen Congwen, Zheng Zhenduo, and others, and he corresponded with Lu Xun. In 1937, after his return to Czechoslovakia, he translated and published "The Scream." Also, while in China he wrote *My Sister China*, based on his impressions from his research. This book, which was published in 1940, "evoked interest in China and Chinese culture among a number of Czech young people, leading to their future dedication to Chinese studies."[1]

In September 1956, a delegation from the *People's Daily*, led by Li Yanning, visited the Oriental Institute in Prague to interview Průšek.

The interview, published in the *People's Daily* on October 4, 1956, praised Průšek for his rich writings, especially those related to sinology, for example, "On Chinese Literature and Culture," "Chinese People's Literature," "Chinese Literature and Education," "New Chinese Literature," "Chairman Mao Zedong and Chinese Literature," and "Literature and Tradition After Liberation." In addition, the *People's Daily* noted that Průšek "celebrated the Chinese revolution with great enthusiasm, and introduced New China to the Czech public." Beginning in 1932, he used the pen name Batac, to edit and write many newsletters and articles on the Chinese revolution and the Chinese workers and peasant movements that were published in the Czech Communist Party journal *Creators*. In 1935, he wrote about the Chinese Red Army's advance, and after the founding of the People's Republic, he introduced and praised New China with even greater passion. In 1949, he published *The Chinese People's Fight for Freedom*, and thereafter translated it into Slovak. These books have now also been translated into Polish and Hungarian.[2]

Průšek graduated from Charles University in Prague in 1928 during the period of the first Czechoslovak democratic republic. His stay in China between 1932 and 1937 was part of the ten-year period of the golden construction of the Chinese National Government. Although Průšek's political ideology seemed to be less important to him than his sinological research, according to the people he met in China and the political articles that he wrote, he appeared to have a certain degree of affinity with socialist China as well as the Communist regime in Czechoslovakia in the 1950s and even the 1960s. Seemingly due to Průšek's political attitudes and political ideology, he received support from the Czechoslovak and Chinese Communist regimes which became external influential factors behind his establishment of the Prague School of Sinology.

Průšek visited China more than three times. In addition to his academic visit from 1932 to 1937, he also served as the head of a delegation of Czech cultural representatives from December 10, 1950 to February 23, 1951. The delegation spent more than two months in China, visiting Beijing, Shanghai, Hangzhou, Guangzhou, and Wuhan, and meeting with many prominent politicians, academics, and people from all walks of life. They visited factories, schools, libraries, museums, and nurseries, as well as enjoying performances of both the new opera and Peking opera. Chinese newspapers reported on Průšek's trip in the *People's Daily* of December 12, December 14, December 18, and December 22, 1950, and January 3, February 16, and March 29, 1951, among others. These articles, reporting at some length about Průšek's mission, were indicative of the importance that the Chinese government attached to the trip.

During this visit, the group also purchased a number of books for the "Lu Xun Library" (with an inscription by Guo Moruo) that had been established at the Czech Institute of Oriental Studies in 1952. This was to become the largest Chinese-language library in Central Europe. The establishment of the Lu Xun Library was related to the fact that when Průšek returned to Prague in 1937, he brought back a number of Chinese books for the Oriental Institute. However, a real Chinese library could not be established in Czechoslovakia during the capitalist period. It was only after the establishment of the Czechoslovakia workers and peasants Government that the aspirations of the sinologists for a library could be realized. The Chinese Government provided them with many Chinese books as gifts from the Chinese people. In order to meet the growing interest in China among the Czech people, Czech sinologists made great efforts to receive full support from the Czech Government to establish the Chinese library in Prague.[3] The *People's Daily* (March 11, 1952 and March 12, 1957) and *Wen Wei Po* (March 29, 1959) both published reports on the new Czech Lu Xun Library.

This chapter, based on official Chinese newspapers tracking Průšek's relationship with China, attempts to understand the external socialist ideology in the 1950s that contributed to the founding of the Prague School of Sinology. The author suggests that the establishment of the Prague School was contingent on the socialism of Communist China in the 1950s. In a section of a May 19, 1959, *Wen Wei Po* article, entitled "Czech Sinological Research to Flourish; A Large Number of Books and Works to Introduce China," there is a section on Czech sinologists' careful study of China's Great Leap Forward. Their activities included various workshops on political and economic developments during China's socialist construction period and invitations to people who had visited China to report on the communes, the steel movement, and the Cultural Revolution. They were particularly interested in the poetry created by the working classes during the Great Leap, and some sinologists offered to translate these poems.[4] Naturally, the official Chinese newspapers were full of ideological language.

However, in addition to the political ideology that provided the Prague School of Sinology with external support, how did the Czech sinologists become involved in the social ideology of the 1950s? One important factor contributing to Chinese modernity was the exploration of modern Chinese literature, based in particular on the social concerns of the early leftist writers in the 1930s and the 1940s.

On September 28, 1956, Průšek served as head of a delegation of the Czechoslovak Academy of Sciences that visited China for more than one month (September 28–November 8, 1956) and signed a cooperation agreement with the Chinese Academy of Sciences. This was the third time that Průšek visited China.[5]

Thereafter, from the 1960s, he had few opportunities to return to China until the 1980s due to his own health issues, the changes in the political environments in China and Czechoslovakia such as growing Sino-Soviet hostility, the Chinese Cultural Revolution, and the Czech Prague Spring. Young Czech sinologists, who had studied in China in the 1950s, attained an international reputation in sinology in the 1960s. However, the experience of studying in China in the 1950s remained an important legacy that their Western counterparts did not enjoy. The establishment of the Prague School of Sinology was mainly due to Průšek's personal contributions as well as to the external political factors. The research question addressed in this chapter focuses on where the line fell between sinology and socialist ideology.

2. Empirical Research and the Political Framework for Sinology

Empirical data collected for this chapter include official Chinese data and media reports and transcripts of interviews with sinologists at the Prague School. There are obvious differences between these two types of materials. The official data from the 1950s are ideologically-based and are intended to provide academic sources for the other socialist countries as part of the International Communist Movement against the backdrop of the Cold War structure. Foreign students studying in China during the 1950s were primarily from other socialist countries (see Tables 1 and 2). The Czech sinologists who were interviewed adopted a distinctive perspective because they had also experienced the political purge of the Prague Spring and the end of the Communist regime in 1989. This chapter uses Halbwachs's theory regarding collective memory to explain the content of the interviews and to test the research hypothesis that "socialism" was the social framework for their collective memory.

Due to the influence of Průšek's research focusing on modern Chinese literature on the Prague School, many of the sinologists were familiar with famous Chinese writers and based their research on their work. This chapter examines those sinologists of the Prague School who lived and studied in China in the 1950s. Their interactions with Chinese society affected their ways of thinking about China, producing a great deal of passion for the object of their studies. However, how did the subsequent political purges and the political ideology affect their sinological studies? This does not mean to imply that their socialist concerns negatively affected their sinological achievements. Socialism represented the political and social mainstream in the 1950s, but the boundaries between socialism and sinology were not necessarily blurred.

By collecting data from the official Chinese media and transcripts of interviews with sinologists of the Prague School, the chapter will attempt to reconstruct the sinologists' memories of living in China in the 1950s and to determine how they were able to acquire knowledge and emotional support in China during the early stages of their sinological studies. The following tables present records on the number of foreign students in institutions of higher learning in Beijing in 1959 (Table 1) and 1964 (Table 2), both based on collections by the author. By the end of the 1950s Sino-Soviet hostility was growing and the Soviet Union and the Eastern European countries were gradually reducing the number of students they sent to China, resulting in a dramatic decline in the number of foreign students in China by the early 1960s. As indicated in Table 1, in the late 1950s most of the foreign students in China were from the socialist countries. Vietnam sent the most students, followed by the Soviet Union. Czechoslovakia was represented by the relatively modest number of nine students. In 1964 (Table 2), due to the serious deterioration in Sino-Soviet relations, almost all of the Soviet bloc students had departed China. Therefore, the 1950s can be regarded as a key period for Soviet and Eastern European students to study in China, and by the 1960s they had generally left the country due to political reasons.

Table 1. Foreign Students in Institutions of Higher Learning in Beijing (1959)

Country	N	Country	N	Country	N
Soviet Union	71	Bulgaria	4	Italy	2
Vietnam	358	11 socialist countries, 601 students		Nepal	2
N. Korea	45	Indonesia	36	Australia	2
E. Germany	36	United Arab Emirates	14	France	2
Mongolia	36	Spain	4	Yugoslavia	2
Poland	14	India	3	Iceland	1
Hungary	12	Thailand	3	Norway	1
Romania	12	Sri Lanka	2	Denmark	1
Czechoslovakia	9	U.S.	2	Iran	1
Albania	7	Burma	2	17 capitalist countries, 80 students	

Source: References on Higher Education, Archive Office, Beijing

Table 2. Foreign Students in Institutions of Higher Learning in Beijing (December 1964)

Country	N	Country	N	Country	N
N. Korea	58	Cambodia	4	Chad	1
N. Vietnam	320	Burma	17	Uganda	1
Albania	47	Laos	4	Nigeria	1
Cuba	17	Thailand	6	Great Britain	1
Mongolia	24	Sri Lanka	10	France	20
Poland	2	Afghanistan	3	Belgium	1
E. Germany	1	Pakistan	7	Italy	1
Romania	5	Japan	7	Sweden	2
Bulgaria	2	S. Vietnam	5	Switzerland	2
9 socialist countries, 476 students		Syria	1	U.S.	2
Indonesia	38	Cameroon	14	25 capitalist countries, 194 students	
Nepal	36	Tanzania	10		

Source: References on Higher Education, Archive Office, Beijing.

In addition to validation of the data through official Chinese reports on foreign students in the 1950s to explore China's exchanges with other socialist countries, Table 3 presents a content analysis of the *Wen Wei Po* newspaper to examine Chinese coverage of overseas sinology. Data was also collected from *Xinmin wanbao*, but the sample was too small so it is not reported here. Most newspapers ended publication in the 1970s due to the Cultural Revolution, but from the *Wen Wei Po* sample for the 1950s it can be seen that reporting on overseas sinology mainly focused on the Soviet Union. In the 1950s and the 1960s there were few reports on Western sinology, but by the 1980s the number of such reports increased. This was due in part to the political situation; with the return of capitalism and market forces, there was much more interest in the field of Western sinology

The official data collected for this chapter are fairly limited, but reveals the initial development of sinology in the 1950s against the background of China's political framework. The author intends to continue to collect material about the study and living conditions of Czech sinologists in China during the 1950s. Beginning in the 1950s, there were a number of Chinese national policies and regulations related to foreign students studying in China, such as the 1963 university instructions on "Several Points for Organizing Foreign Students for Travel." The second point in these instructions states that school personnel who take students for travel should obtain letters of introduction indicating their political affiliations in order to arrange for their reception, and the school personnel shall be responsible for reporting on the students to the reception units. In addition, an official 1964 notice,"On Foreign Students' Purchase of Recreational and Sports Tickets," in which the first point states: "Tickets for Beijing's major theaters, cinemas, and sports stadiums are available for foreign students. The Principal's Office or the International Student Office shall provide letters of introduction to the theaters, cinemas, and sports stadiums, and they are permitted to contact the ticket offices." Some of these links may have been of considerable importance for foreign students in China, such as the "letters of introductions," the students' "political affiliations," and so on, ultimately affecting the students' knowledge about contemporary Chinese society.

Table 3. Reports on Sinology in *Wen Wei Po*

	Soviet Union	Czech Republic	France	U.S.	Japan	Germany	Switzerland
1950s	9	1	0	0	0	0	0
1960s	1	0	0	0	0	0	0
1970s	0	0	0	0	0	0	0
1980s	2	0	2	1	1	1	0
1990s	5	0	0	1	0	0	1

3. The Theory of Collective Memory

For the structural analysis, this section will be based on Maurice Halbwachs's theory of "collective memory."[6] The first study of "collective memory" was carried out by French scholar Maurice Halbwachs (1877–1945), who argued that discussions of memory must be distinguishable from traditional psychology; in his view, a psychologist limits memory to the personal level, but memory, just like people, can belong to many different groups, and thus people's memories will change depending on the different groups. Halbwachs first used dreams to justify his "social framework." He pointed out that our dreams tend to be fragmented pieces, lacking in structure, continuity, and rules, and they are not rooted in the social context or the social structure. Dreamers are not able to reminisce about their past in a coherent way. The fragmented images in dreams decipher the coherence and structure of real-life memories.[7] Halbwachs compares real-life memories and dreams to prove that memories are conditioned by society. Each memory has its own social connections and social context, and memories are triggered by the society.

Halbwachs believes that a carrier of memory can be an individual, a society, or a group, but the system itself cannot be recalled by memory. The individual must be linked with the multiple groups to which he belongs in order to make sense of the relative strength of his memories. In short, to understand collective memory it must be analyzed from the group context to which the individual belongs, because each memory must be retained by a real body. In Halbwachs's analysis of family memories, kinship is the social framework of family memories and family memories attain meaning through introspection of this social framework. Memory can also be continued by the social framework, but the social framework may change with the social situation, thus indicating the instability of the social framework. The social framework does not consist of carefree memories of the past; rather it consists of the carrying out of the memories of the past under the existing framework, especially for those who did not visit the past. Halbwachs notes that only by positioning memory in the corresponding group can we understand each section of a memory in individual thought. Moreover, unless we correlate the individual to the multiple groups to which he/she belongs, we will not be able to properly understand the relative strength of these memories or their unification in individual thought.[8]

Halbwachs divides memories into two types, historical memories and personal memories, in the course of one's life experiences. The social framework will change because of the social situation, and the formation of a collective memory is easily affected by the power of discourse in a text, or even by a purposive construction. A man with power can control the collective memory of intangible abstractions by controlling the cultural media and the relevant material objects. Halbwachs, based on the legends in the *Book of Gospels of the Holy Land*, studies the different memories of the pilgrims to the Holy Land, and verifies that memory is fictional and discontinuous in nature. He shows that "in every period in order to meet the urgent needs of Christianity and to adapt to its needs and aspirations, the Christian collective memory reformed all of the details on the life of Christ, as well as memory about the locations of the appearance of these details."[9] This illustrates that the truth of Christianity has been invented, and churches rewrote the fictional Holy Land into the Gospels in order to make these fictional facts seemingly more authentic. Therefore, in collective memory, historical details are no longer necessary, and present beliefs and common experiences are sufficient conditions for constructing a collective memory.

In his chapter on "The Collective Memory of Religion" Halbwachs explains that religious memory is not saved in the past, but it reconstructs the past by virtue of material relics, rituals, scriptures and traditions, and recent psychological and social materials; in other words, the "now" is used to reconstruct the past.[10] In addition, religious memory attempts to link the past and present together through repeated rituals and traditions of the past, and religious memory can be anchored in the historical context to strengthen the legitimacy of the religion. Similarly, the forgetting of memory is also the outcome of the operation of power. When a strong memory is accessed, the original memory may be replaced or even excluded.

In sum, the characteristics of collective memory include, first, that the memory must be able to continue when anchored in the social framework; second, the social framework is constructed in the present moment; third, there is a fictional and utilitarian nature of the collective memory. Based on these characteristics of collective memory, the present social framework constructs the collective memory of the experience of Czech sinologists living and studying in China between sinology and socialism in the 1950s. The social framework of the 1950s' collective memory is different from that of the following periods, i.e., the Sino-Soviet split, the Cultural Revolution, Czech normalization in the 1970s and the 1980s, and Czech democratization in the 1990s. The development of Czech sinology was obviously affected by politics, especially the Prague Spring. The collective memory of Czech sinology in the 1950s has gradually become a legend about Czech sinology.

This chapter first analyzes the situation for students from the socialist countries who studied in China in the 1950s and then looks at the official reports to examine the government emphasis on the development of sinology during the socialist period. Nine in-depth interview transcripts were provided by Professor Olga Lomová and her colleagues to explore Czech sinological experiences in the 1950s through the social framework of collective memory.

4. Results of the Analysis

Most Czech sinologists were introduced to sinology through the influence of Průšek and the establishment of New China. Průšek's *China, My Sister*, which became important reading to introduce Czech readers to contemporary China, relates his adventures in China in the 1930s. Milena Velingerova first began her sinological career by reading Průšek's book. In her interview, she stated: "I came to the faculty in 1950 after many difficulties due to my family background. My motivation had nothing to do with the political situation in China, which we heard about all the time. But I received Professor Průšek's book as a birthday present when I was 18 years old. I did not know Professor Průšek at all and I wasn't interested in him, but as soon as I read the book, I knew this was the right thing for me to do." In another case, Venceslava Hrdlickova also mentioned the importance of Průšek's book and the founding of New China: "For my husband, history provided a larger view of world events. We were going out together, exchanging books, engaging in discussions, and he frequently mentioned Průšek's *My Sister China*, which was translated as *Vsichni lide jsou bratri*. ... So we were taken, or he was taken, by China; he expected that it was a country that would have a great future."

In addition to the inspiration of Průšek's works and of Průšek himself, the establishment of New China also attracted interest in sinology among Czech youth. Zdenka Hermanova recalled his first encounter with sinology: "I didn't want to study English, I wanted something special. The PRC had been established in 1949. I was taken by that and when I went to university, I wanted to study Chinese and Japanese. But Japanese wasn't offered that year. We took Far Eastern History as our second subject. I wasn't satisfied with it, so I went to Prague to protest. This was the first time that I spoke with Professor Průšek." Josef Kolmas also referred to New China: "Of course! I had to first go to Průšek with my request. … Thanks to certain circumstances—the establishment of the PRC, the Chinese delegation, the textbook by Bartusek and Palát, and, of course, the interactions between Olomouc and Prague—I started to study Chinese." Venceslava Hrdlickova mentioned her husband as an example of someone who was influenced by Průšek and New China: "No, I think he was not interested in sociology at the time we visited Průšek, that means before we went to university. He was interested in China's future and thus he was interested in the possibility of learning about such a distant society."

In short, the combination of two factors, Průšek and New China, created an environment for the development of Czech sinology; if either of these two factors had not existed, the later brilliant development of Czech sinology would not have occurred. Therefore, Zbygniew Slupski stated:

> "I would call them China specialists. I was not the founder; Průšek was the founder. Průšek indeed was an exceptional person. He was like that even earlier, in the 1930s when he traveled to China. He had distinctive opinions at that time. He belonged to the leftist intelligentsia, and when he went to China, his worldview changed. Read *My Sister China*. The man speaking there is a man who knows what he wants, where he is heading, and what the future will bring him. After World War II, and especially after February, Průšek understood there was an opportunity to establish sinology in Czechoslovakia. He used the occasion, and he also became involved in the growing political party. Due to these circumstances, he was able to establish the field of sinology."

China and the Eastern European countries had had few interactions and connections in the past. However, the international system during the Cold War narrowed the distance among them. Under the Nazi occupation between 1939 and 1945, Czech universities were forced to close. After the end of World War II, Průšek began to actively promote sinology in Czechoslovakia. When New China was established, the Czech government urgently needed experts on China. Therefore, the study of China assumed an important position in Czechoslovakia in the 1950s. Augustin Palát described this situation: "When Průšek tried to build something for the existence of the discipline in 1947 or 1948, he got always the same stereotypical answer: 'We are in the middle of building a two-year plan; we have no time now.' Then, after the PRC was established, things changed overnight. The authorities needed many people able to learn to speak Chinese, in the shortest time possible." Even Czech companies began to consider the huge China market and sent employees to study Chinese. Vladislav Drinek was one of them: "I was a worker at the Bata Company. It was there that I first heard about the potential of the Chinese market. I was generally interested in history. That was all, my interest wasn't very deep. As a trainee at Bata Industrial High School I had received a basic education about China."

The combination of Průšek and the establishment of New China played a vital role in the construction of collective memory among the Czech sinologists of the 1950s. Průšek's legacy, including his writings and the works by those contemporary Chinese writers whom he met in the 1930s, offered cultural capital to the younger generation of Czech sinologists, for example Zbygniew Slupski's research on Lao She, Marian Galik's research on Mao Dun, and Milena Velingerova's research on Guo Moruo. Průšek's writings on Chinese contemporary literature happened to be in line with mainstream ideas about China's socialist transformation, and Průšek's political, academic, and cultural resources were a main factor contributing to the development of Czech sinology. Milena Velingerova described these Czech characteristics as the following:

> "We knew nothing about classical Chinese literature. Professor Průšek said: 'I know the modern Chinese writers, so we'll talk about them. Our discipline will deal with modern Chinese literature.' From today's point of view, there is something special about Czech sinology. We did not follow the Western model. There was no one who studied modern Chinese literature, but Professor Průšek had his own reasons for it. I mean he didn't know any classical Chinese literature. But he knew the writers, and he had a great influence on us because he knew those people and he had seen China. So Czech sinology was a pioneer due to a totally different approach to sinology. I think this made a strong impression on us, at least on me."

As Oldrich Svarny suggested, "Průšek founded Czech sinology, with the aim, of course, of covering every field of China studies. I was chosen to be a Chinese phonetician." Venceslava Hrdlickova stated that even though Průšek emphasized contemporary studies, he never neglected the importance of history. She said: "We were astonished and charmed. He [Průšek] had a talk with us about plans for the future; his foresight and instinct were evident from very early on. He was interested in modern China, in the China that was about to be, and not. … Well of course, he also stressed the importance of studying history, but he expected us to think about the future. This was very important." Zbygniew Slupski judged Průšek from yet another perspective:

> "He definitely was an extraordinary person. It is hard to judge the quality of his founding act, since there was nothing to start from: there were no books, no materials, no money, no nothing. So Průšek started from scratch. Due to the fact that Průšek was a significant political figure in the world of academics, he stressed a number of different things—the library, money for employees, and so forth—so sinology could somehow begin. What were the teaching standards? Well, of course, they weren't very good from today's standards, but how could you maintain any standards when there were no basic reference books?"

Marian Galik and Josef Kolmas offered differing judgments about Průšek. Marian Galik: "I remember one thing that was quite typical for Průšek. I told him I would work on Mao Dun's short stories. He reacted strongly in front of my classmates: "Other than Lu Xun's short stories, modern Chinese short stories are worth nothing." After two years, he began to work on modern short stories—on the basis of my paper. … That was Průšek." In addition, Josef Kolmas stated: "Průšek was … a streamlining person. He had an idea, but he wasn't able to elaborate on it. This he left to others, and they appreciated him: Thank God someone had an idea! Those who caught the idea were grateful for receiving the motivation that lasted until their deaths. He had insight—that was his greatest virtue. Gálik says Průšek had many ideas, but he didn't carry them out. That is Gálik's theory. Gálik needed to finalize Průšek's ideas."

Most of the interviewees, with the exception of Vladislav Drinek, had either studied with or were affected by Průšek. During their sinological studies, they also attempted to follow Průšek's experiences of the 1930s to a certain extent. With respect to the development of Czech sinology, Průšek is a legendary figure. Due to his personal influence, Czech sinology primarily focuses on contemporary Chinese literature. In a comparison with Polish sinology, Zbygniew Slupski believes that this development was also due to Czech cultural traditions. As he stated, "It seems to me that the development of Czech sinology followed Czech cultural traditions: first poetry and the arts, and then, to a lesser degree, history and philosophy. In contrast, in Poland, with the exception of one academic sinologist, there were very few sinologists who were interested in Chinese literature and Chinese art. But there were a number of people who were devoted to the problems of politics, ideology, and the economy. There was also interest in political developments and political institutions." Průšek is representative of the collective memory of Czech sinologists, and despite their varying evaluations, his contributions to Czech sinology are indisputable.

Another collective memory among the Czech sinologists of the 1950s is their experiences in China, including their schooling, work, and travels. Milena Velingerova's first impression of the Chinese Communist Party was quite strange: "The Chinese Communist Party is a democratic party, so it used democratic methods to achieve power. Based on what I had read, I knew something about the peasants and their better living conditions under the Communist Party. But that was all I knew." Vladislav Drinek described his first knowledge about China: "It was all something new. Five thousand years of history and what China represented in world history. In this light, the backward situation in contemporary China somehow seemed weird." Marian Galik also regarded China as a strange country: "I had read various things in books: the Chinese are selfish and arrogant; they offer you something but they expect you to refuse it. So my image of China was not at all very positive."

Unlike the sinologists in the non-socialist countries, the young sinologists in Eastern Europe could travel to China to study, and they could actually have contact with social development in socialist China. Young Czech sinologists could study in China for four years, or even more, and receive degrees in China. Zdenka Hermanova spent a long time in China and received an academic diploma: "I was nominated to receive a scholarship to go to China in 1953. ... The first year I attended language courses with Korean students. ... After that year, we entered the Chinese Language Department. Vochala and I both wanted to have our diplomas recognized, so we spent one more semester to fulfill the requirements for a degree. Thus we did not return [to Czechoslovakia] until the spring of 1958." However, Milena Velingerova stayed in China for only one year: "It was by pure accident that I went to China. For some unknown reason, Professor Průšek had chosen me to be a guide for Zheng Zhenduo. So I went to China and immediately became involved with a group of outstanding people at the Institute for Chinese Language and Literature. ... I was in China in 1958–59, during the most terrible year of the Great Leap Forward. ... I traveled throughout China with two students from Poland, but I only found out about the Great Leap Forward after I returned to Czechoslovakia."

Venceslava Hrdlickova accompanied her husband China, who worked as a cultural attaché in 1951 and 1954. However, they had already visited China as part of a delegation led by Průšek in 1950. She reported: "I wasn't a member of the delegation. I simply traveled as a wife since my husband was expected to stay on as cultural attaché. So I traveled as a family member. ... Our delegation traveled throughout the country. Of course, we were watched and we couldn't go wherever we wanted, but we went to Nanking, Canton, and to Lu Xun's hometown. The friendship between Průšek and Lu Xun played a significant role because he was honored by the government at the time. However, when we worked in China, we could not travel too much." Augustin Palát worked as successor to Hrdlickova's husband as cultural attaché from 1954 to 1959. He appeared to maintain good social relations with Chinese and he traveled a bit, and he even established a friendship with the Dalai Lama in Tibet.

Marian Galik received help from Průšek and spent more than a year in China in 1958. He said: "Professor Průšek gave me a letter of introduction addressed to Mao Dun. ... When I pulled the letter of introduction out of my pocket at the office for foreign students, the staff immediately contacted the Ministry of Culture and within one month I met Mao Dun. ... I was the first foreign scholar to go to Wu Zheng. ... I would often go to the library, travel, or buy books. I was buying two types of books: those about Mao Dun and those about Yu Dafu. Mrs. Doležalová could never have written her book without me. How did I do it? It was simple. I learned that guanxi was very important. Mao Dun told me I should meet Mr. Yue Yiqin who was then chairman of the Shanghai Chinese Writers Union. This man gave me a letter of introduction to visit the retail sales department of the largest bookstore."

Young Czech Sinologists had the opportunity to study, work, and travel in China in the 1950s, but the most important factor was that they were able to maintain a close relationship with Průšek. Galik took the letter of introduction from Průšek to visit Mao Dun. Velingerova was introduced to Zheng Zhenduo during the latter's stay in Czechoslovakia, and then Zheng provided her with warm assistance in China. When Hrdlickova and her husband joined the Czech cultural delegation in China, Průšek introduced them to many people in Chinese cultural circles. Palát also maintained a close working relationship with Průšek. The personal experiences of the younger Czech sinologists followed in the footsteps of Průšek's experiences in the 1930s, making social visits and getting to know cultural figures in order to become more familiar with contemporary literature. Therefore, to a certain extent, the experience of Czech sinology in the 1950s can be considered as an extension of Průšek's earlier experiences. Although visitors were not free to travel in Communist China of the 1950s, they still had an opportunity to experience contemporary Chinese society. These real-life experiences in China were very valuable, and because Westerners still could not enter the country, the works by Czech sinologists and their participation in international symposia provided firsthand information to the outside world about contemporary China.

Olga Lomová referred to her own learning experience in the 1980s and raised the following question to Slupski: "Now I will ask my last question. What were the political demands on the students during that time? As far as the humanities were concerned, the university students of my generation were subject to a serious selection process. Politically reliable persons enjoyed priority when it came to selection. This is what Kubešová told me: 'Don't think you are clever; we always prefer loyal people. ... Did political pressure affect your personal involvement in sinology at the time?' Slupski replied: 'Well, pressures did exist; there was a basic cell of the Communist Party, and it controlled all those things.'"

The collective memory of Czech sinologists regarding the 1950s is mainly related to Průšek and New China. However, the social framework of their collective memory was mainly a mix of the development of sinology and the effects of the political ideology. Although most of the interviewees did not refer directly to the political ideology of the 1950s, its existence was obvious.

5. Conclusion

Průšek's experience in China in the 1930s had a significant impact not only on his own sinological achievements, but also on the establishment of the Prague School of Sinology. After Nazi Germany occupied the Czech Republic in 1939, Czech universities were forced to close down. After the end of World War II, Průšek taught at Charles University. The Czechoslovak Communist regime was established in 1948, and the Chinese Communist Party seized control of China in 1949. Průšek began to select Czechoslovak students to study in China in the early 1950s, and this lasted for about ten years, until the 1960s, because of the Sino-Soviet hostility, the Chinese Cultural Revolution, and the Prague Spring. In addition to his personal academic abilities, Průšek made significant contributions to the development of sinology in the Czech Republic and to the promotion of Sino-Czech cultural and academic exchanges. In the 1930s Průšek was immersed in Chinese society and he became familiar with left-wing writers. Thus he developed closer links with socialist China than he had with the ruling Guomindang government. After 1949, on several occasions Průšek served as the head of Czech delegations to China due to his good relationship with the new Chinese government. Due to his familiarity with Chinese society, he was able to promote Sino-Czech cultural and academic exchanges. However, because Průšek and other Czech sinologists refused to criticize China in the wake of the Prague Spring movement, they were purged. Actually, the experiences of Czech sinologists in China in the 1950s were important factors in their life histories. Their emotional attachments to Chinese social life based on their actual experiences of studying in China in the 1950s became an important part of their collective memories.

However, due to the Chinese Cultural Revolution, the Prague Spring movement, and the collapse of the Czech Communist regime, few Czech sinologists whom we interviewed discussed their passions and ideals about socialist China in the 1950s. According to Halbwachs's theory of collective memory, the present social framework is the key point to reconstruct the past. Socialism is no longer part of the contemporary mainstream ideology, thus the social framework of their collective memory of the 1950s may be considered anti-socialist. This is something that warrants further research. I was deeply moved by the devotion of the Czech sinologists, as revealed in their interviews. They wrote 600–700 academic works, and by the 1960s they had acquired international reputations, due, in no small part, to their experiences in the 1950s. It is hoped that the present study will represent a first step in filling the gap in the literature about the significance of the experience of Czech sinologists in the 1950s.

The construction of collective memory about the 1950s among Czech sinologists is mainly based on the political mix between sinology and socialism. First, relations between China and Czechoslovakia were friendly, thus enabling the growth of student exchange programs. Second, Průšek played a prominent role in the development of Czech sinology and in the collective achievements of the Prague School. Nevertheless, in the 1950s political censorship existed in both China and in Czechoslovakia, though to a lesser extent than in the following decade due to the Chinese Cultural Revolution, which had a negative effect on the free development of Czech sinology. Průšek is a legendary figure in Czech sinology. That is, without Průšek's contribution, the achievements of the group of young Czech sinologists in the 1950s would never have been realized.

Notes

1. Jaroslav Průšek, *Zhongguo, Wo de jiemei* (My Sister China) (Beijing: Waiyu jiaoxue yu yanjiu chubanshe, 2005).
2. Yanning Li, *People's Daily*, October 4, 1956.
3. Ibid., December 3, 1957.
4. *Wen Wei Po*, March 29, 1959.
5. *People's Daily*, September 29, October 19, and October 22, 1956.
6. Maurice Halbwachs, *Lun jiti jiyi* (On Collective Memory) (Shanghai: Renmin chubanshe, 2002).
7. Suzanne Vromen, "Maurice Halbwachs on Collective Memory," *American Journal of Sociology*, Vol. 99, No. 2 (September 1993), pp. 510–512.
8. Halbwachs, *Lun jiti jiyi*, pp. 93–94.
9. Ibid., p. 407.
10. Ibid., p. 200.

Chapter 11

Tangut (Xi Xia) Studies in the Soviet Union: The Quinta Essentia of Russian Oriental Studies

Sergey Dmitriev

The history of Tangut studies is not very well known, including among Orientalists. This is a pity because it is an area that has preserved fairly well specific features of the so-called Classical Orientalism that has been lost in other areas of Oriental studies. Even now, Tangut studies are very much like the Orientalism of one hundred years ago: it is populated by several dozen researchers, most of whom are well acquainted. A general bibliography of Tangut studies consists of four to five hundred items; so, unlike in other fields, researchers can easily follow all the new publications on the subject. Despite the relatively small number of researchers, Russian Tangutology is distinguished by its rich and even dramatic history.

Tangut was first mentioned on a runic funerary inscription of Bilge Khagan, ruler of the East Turkic Khaganate, dated AD 735. It is clear that at that time people who spoke one of the languages of Qiangic subgroup of the Tibeto-Burmese group lived in the northwest of the Tibetan plateau and on the territory of modern Gansu province. In the second part of the seventh century the Tangut leaders were strong enough to be considered among the most dangerous vassals of the Chinese empire; from the Tang and Song dynasties respectively they received the prestigious right to bear the family name of Chinese emperors. At the end of the tenth century the Tanguts, semi-dependent from the Song empire, established a completely independent state, mentioned in Chinese sources as the Western Xia (Xi Xia 西夏). Tangut name was most likely the "State of High Whiteness" (or the State of White and Lofty) (羏尾熵 *Phôn mbɪn lhiə*).[1] Successful campaigns against their neighbors (Kitans, Uighurs, Chinese, and Tibetans) allowed the Tanguts an opportunity to create a relatively large and self-sufficient state. In 1038 the Tangut ruler, known by his Chinese name Yuanhao (元昊), proclaimed himself emperor.[2] An important indication of the independence of the states of the *Pax Sinica* at that time was the invention of a new writing system, and the Kitans and the Jurchens also invented their own writing systems.

As far as we know, this was a purely political decision. It seems that many Tanguts spoke and read Chinese, and many others used the Tibetan alphabet. After the introduction of the new writing system, they very likely continued to use Chinese or Tibetan in their everyday life. The intellectual elite of the Tangut state was almost certainly bilingual (or even trilingual, including Tibetan),[3] and all parts of Tangut life and culture were strongly influenced by Chinese culture. So, according to an order issued by Yuanhao, Tangut writing was developed in 1036–38 by philologists under the guidance of a counsellor and relative of the emperor, Yeli Renrong (野利仁榮), who is mentioned in Tangut sources as the Great Tutor I-riẹ (荔腝).[4] It is clear that the philologists were deeply influenced by Chinese science and traditions, and some of them may even have been Chinese. In spite of this, Tangut writing was created not as an unobjectionable follower of Chinese writing, but rather as a strong rival. Using all of the finely elaborate instruments of Chinese philology and lexicology at that time, Tangut scientists were capable of creating a very elaborate logograph writing system based on an original and very non-Chinese fundamental idea.[5] Of course, this was not mandatory, but a degree of originality in the national writing was a symbol of the real independence of the Tangut state.

In 1227 the Tangut state was destroyed by the Mongol hordes of Genghis-khan. However, the Tanguts survived and managed to contribute to the formation of the greatest empire in the Old World, that is, the Mongol empire. Among the dignitaries of the Yuan dynasty (1260–1368),[6] whose biographies can be found in the official annals of the *Yuan shi* (The History of the Yuan 元史), we can easily identify many officials of Tangut origin. It seems that the vanquished Tanguts were successful intermediaries between the Mongols and the Tibetans and greatly helped to spread Buddhism among the Mongol nobles. An interesting model of interactions between an emperor and a state teacher—the head of the Buddhist sangha of the empire—was very likely borrowed by the Mongols from the Tangut state.[7] When Mongol rule was defeated, the situation for the Tanguts deteriorated. After some cruel campaigns, the land of the Tanguts became part of China under the Chinese Ming dynasty (1368–1644). The Ming emperors tried to do their best to prevent a new invasion into China by the Mongols. One of their policies was to suppress ethnic and religious groups that had been allies of the Mongols during the period of Yuan rule. The Tangut regions were considered suspect, hence the border with the steppe was closed and the Tanguts were clearly considered among the "collaborators." Thus the Ming armies devastated the Tangut cities and the Tanguts were decimated. The Tangut language and writings were maintained only in some monasteries for several generations (possibly up to the sixteenth century), but their extinction was inevitable. This marked the end of the Tangut civilization, as the people were dispersed and assimilated by the Chinese, Mongols, or Tibetans,[8] and the cities were burned and either repopulated by Chinese or became deserts.

But that was not the end: *habent sua fata libelli.*

As already noted, from a very early period, possibly as early as the eighth century, these people were known as Tanguts. But this was not their proper name. They called themselves *Mi-ndzịwo* (𗼋𗟲), where the second character is "man" and the first character "Mi" is a logogram to indicate both the Tangut language and the Tangut people.[9] So "Tangut" is a Turkic word that was adopted very early by the Mongols, who continued to use it even after the destruction of the Tangut state and the disappearance of the Tangut people and their culture. We know that up until the nineteenth century Mongols called the tribes of warlike nomads in northeastern Tibet (the region of Kukunor, north of the historical region of Amdo) and a part of Gansu "Tangut." Some of these nomads were Tibetans (the Goloks, for example), but many were Mongols, assimilated by the Tibetans.

The word "Tangut" was also accepted by the Russians relatively early. During the first period of their penetration through Siberia the Russians acquired information about China and its neighbors mainly via the Mongols. In the seventeenth to eighteenth centuries, the word

"Tangut" in Russian (and in the scientific Latin of Russian scholars) referred to "Tibet."[10] At the same time, this word became relatively popular among Western botanists who used it as the scientific names of some plants (for example, *Rheum tanguticum*, *Aconitum tanguticum*, *Clemats tangutica*, and many others). We strongly suspect that in most cases these scientists were confused by their Russian colleagues and were referring rather to Tibet.

However, this mistake was later corrected. In an important book by the famous Russian investigator Nikolaj Przhevalsky (Николай Михайлович Пржевальский) (1839–88), *Mongolia and the Land of the Tanguts*,[11] as in Mongolian, the "Tangut" referred to a nomad population at the Mongol-Tibetan frontier. But, of course, this did not refer to the "real" historical Tanguts, who by that time seemed to have been completely forgotten.

But by the end of the nineteenth century some of the Tangut texts were discovered and examined by Western scholars. In 1870, an English missionary and colleague of James Legge, Alexander Wylie, published an article about an inscription in six languages found on the gates of a fortress called Jüyongguan (居庸關) located near Beijing.[12] The inscription dated back to 1345 and consisted of six practically identical texts in Sanskrit, Tibetan, Mongolian (in the so-called square script), Uighur, Tangut, and Chinese. Wylie was absolutely correct in his suggestion that in all the texts there was one same part: it was the transcription of the Sanskrit dhāraṇī, but he was incorrect about the Tangut part. He had decided that it was Jurchen. In 1882, the French diplomat, historian, and linguist Gabriel Devéria published an article about a Jurchen inscription on a stele from Yantai (宴臺).[13] In this article Gabriel Devéria noted that the inscription on the gates of Jüyongguan was definitely not Jurchen. He suggested that possibly it was Xi Xia (Tangut) writings. In 1895, under the supervision of Prince Roland Bonaparte, all of the texts on the Jüyongguan gates were published.[14] The dhāraṇī part of the Tangut text was analyzed by the great French sinologist Edouard Chavannes. Even at this time, the Tangut origins of the text were based on only a very uncertain assumption. It was not until 1898 that the problem was finally resolved. Devéria published a bilingual inscription from the Dayunsi temple (大雲寺) in Liangzhou,[15] and one part of that inscription was in the same writing as the unrecognized Jüyongguan text. The text of the Chinese part said that the inscription had been completed in 1094 and the writing was that of the Xi Xia state. The question was thus resolved, but the text remained undecoded and unread, and the available inscriptions were too small to become a "Rosetta stone."

In 1904 a translator in the French Embassy in Beijing, M. G. Morisse, published a study on the Tangut text of the Lotus sutra (*Saddharma Puṇḍarīka Sūtra*).[16] M. G. Morisse had bought this text near the White Pagoda Temple (白塔寺) that had been ravaged by the Boxers. This was one of the few buildings from the Yuan dynasty that remained in Beijing. The text had been previously studied by an unknown Chinese scholar, and many of the Tangut characters were provided with handwritten notes and Chinese translations. Thanks to this unknown Tangutologist, Morisse could make many important discoveries about the structure of Tangut phrases; he decoded some of the characters and revealed the pronunciation of others (mainly the special characters that were used for phonetic transcriptions of Sanskrit and Chinese words). He also very reasonably assumed that Tangut must be part of the Tibetan group of languages. This was a big achievement, but further progress seemed to be impossible. The Buddhist texts did not provide many relevant materials for decoding a language, and, unfortunately, the entire corpus of texts in the Tangut language seemed to be limited to these few texts. In short, scientists did not have an instrument to do the decoding and there was almost nothing to decode.

But Providence was benevolent to the Tanguts. In 1907 Piotr K. Kozlov (Пётр Кузьмич Козлов) (1863–1935), an apprentice and follower of Prjevalskij, organized a Mongol-Sichuanese expedition to explore the western border of China. One of the targets was the ruins of the abandoned city of Khara-Khoto.[17] During excavation of this city in 1908 and 1909 Kozlov found hundreds of paintings, statues (which are now in the Hermitage Museum in Saint-Petersburg),[18] and, above all, hundreds of various kinds of Tangut texts.[19] The Tanguts were once again allowed to speak, and the desert had saved their words from the destructive forces of time.

These findings were extremely valuable not only for Tangut culture, but also for Russian Tangut studies, which prior to that time did not exist. The main corpus of the Tangut texts was transferred to the Asiatic Museum in Saint-Petersburg.[20] Thus Russian scholars had the first possibility to study this new and extremely challenging material. Not only did Kozlov's luck determine a boom in Tangutology (especially in Russia), but it also created a new area for research in Oriental studies. Before the findings in Khara-Khoto, the term "Tangut" was rarely used by Western scholars. They preferred to call the newly discovered language and writings by the Chinese term "Xi Xia." The reason for this is very clear; before Kozlov's findings, an overwhelming number of the sources about the Tanguts were in Chinese. The Mongolo-Turcic term "Tangut" was relatively popular only among Russian intellectuals and it is quite probable that it was due to Kozlov's findings that the Russian scholars gave Tangutology its name.[21]

The results of the Khara-Khoto discoveries appeared rapidly. A young sinologist and professor at Saint-Petersburg University, Aleksej I. Ivanov (Алексей Иванович Иванов) (1878–1937), found in the newly arrived Tangut xilographs a Tangut-Chinese dictionary *Mi źạ ngwu ndzẹe mbu pịạ ngu nịe* (𘋊𗏁𗐱𗟲𗆍𗖨𘋤𗪛) (Timely Pearl in the Palm of the Tangut and Chinese Languages 番漢合時掌中珠), compiled in 1190 by the Tangut scholar Kwəlde-rịephu (𗋒𘝦𗱕𘉋).[22] Finally, this was a real Rosetta stone (the characters were not only translated, but they were also transcribed phonetically into Chinese characters). In 1909 Ivanov published some of the results of his study.[23] This short article (full of mistakes due to the haste of the author who hurried to inform the world about the new possibilities for decoding the Tangut language) was an important impetus for the development of Tangut studies throughout the world. In 1916 the publication of important research by Berthold Laufer (1874–1934), a famous American anthropologist of German origin,[24] provided many correct conclusions about the Tangut language. It was during these years that the first research was published by Chinese Tangutologists, including Luo Fucheng (羅福成) (1885–1960), Luo Fuchang (羅福萇) (1895–1921), and his father, the famous philologist Luo Zhenyu (羅振玉) (1866–1940).[25] At the same time, Władyłsaw Kotwicz (Владислав Людвигович Котвич) (1872–1944), the Russian and Polish Mongolist and Turcologist,[26] also began to work with the Tangut texts.

In 1925 Ivanov was the chief translator in the Soviet Embassy in Beijing, but he also attempted to continue his studies of Tangut. In that year he was visited by a Japanologist, Nikolaj A. Nevskij (Николай Александрович Невский) (1892–1937),[27] who had been one of Ivanov's students in the early 1910s. After his graduation from Saint-Petersburg

University (where he primarily was a student of the sinologist Vasilij M. Alekseev [1881–1951]), in 1915 Nevskij was sent to Japan for further studies. After the Russian Revolution of 1917 he decided to remain in Japan and to work in the field of the language, religion, folklore, and customs of the Japanese, Ainu, and Ryukuans. In 1927 he traveled in Taiwan to study a language of the Zou (鄒), one of indigenous people on the island.[28] But beginning in 1923–24 (may be even before) he began to study the Tangut texts, which was extremely difficult because they were so far away in Russia.[29] In 1925 Ivanov gave him some copies of the Tangut texts and dictionaries that he had brought to Beijing. This was probably the defining moment when Nevskij decided to turn to Tangut studies. In Osaka in 1926 he published his research about Tibetan transcriptions of Tangut words (handwritten Tibetan notes can be found on many of the Tangut texts and it seems that some Tanguts used the Tibetan alphabet in their everyday life).[30] But it was becoming clearer that in order to undertake a profound study he needed to be in Leningrad and to work with the Tangut texts directly. So in the autumn of 1929 Nevskij returned to Leningrad. His wife Mantani Isoko (萬谷 磯子) (1901–37) and their daughter Elena joined him in 1933.

During his first years in Leningrad it seems that Nevskij's dreams were coming true. He worked at the Institute of Orientalism of the Academy of Sciences of the USSR (which in 1930 had replaced the Asiatic Museum), in the university, and at the Hermitage. He finally had an unlimited possibility to study Tangut manuscripts and xylographs.[31] He published many papers on Tangut issues in the Soviet Union and China.[32] In 1935 he became a doctor of sciences. In the famous illustrated book *Den' mira* (One Day of the World),[33] promoted by Maxim Gorky as a momentary snapshot of the life of the entire world on the same one day (September 27, 1935), we can find some brief information about Professor Nikolay Nevskij who was working on decoding the Tangut language. Who could ask for more?

But suddenly things began to change. In the summer of 1937 the Soviet Union became engulfed in the terrible period of the Great Purge, when at least one million people were executed or died in concentration camps, condemned to high treason against the Soviet state. Investigators of the People's Commissariat for Internal Affairs tried to impress their bosses, including Stalin, by revealing huge plots of spies and traitors. The Institute of Oriental Studies, full of researchers who had traveled abroad and who had knowledge of many strange languages, was too tempting a target. The investigations revealed an underground group of Japanese spies, organized and coordinated by Nikolay Nevskij. Even a director of the institute, a famous Turcologist, academician Alexandr Samojlovich (Александр Николаевич Самойлович) (1880–1938), was arrested as a member of "Nevskij's group."[34] Nevskij was arrested in the night of October 3–4, 1937,[35] and several days later his wife was arrested as well. They were condemned and executed on November 24, 1937. Alexey I. Ivanov had been executed earlier, on October 8, also as a Japanese spy. Their places of burial remain unknown.[36]

Russian Tangutology was thus physically exterminated.[37] Only after the death of Stalin in 1953 did the situation begin to change, but the line had already been broken. In 1955 the young sinologist Evgenij I. Kychanov (Евгений Иванович Кычанов) (1932–2013), a recent graduate from the Oriental Faculty of Leningrad University, became a graduate student in the Oriental Manuscripts Section of the Institute of Oriental Studies (beginning in 1956 the Leningrad filial of the institute) and he intended to work on Tangut studies. But he did not have a proper scientific adviser because among the specialists at the institute there were no Tangutologists. At the time, there were many rumors that Nevskij was still alive and that he would soon return, like the many who returned from prisons in the 1950s. "Don't worry, Nevskij will be your adviser," some colleagues told Kychanov. But Kychanov and others had to become Tangutologists on their own. This was no easy task.

Before 1960, the Tangut find was closed to everyone except Zoia I. Gorbacheva (Зоя Ивановна Горбачёва) (1907–79), who was its keeper after Nevskij's death.[38] It was mainly because of a fear that someone might steal Nevskij's drafts and misappropriate his results, but also because of an absence of specialists who could work with the texts.[39] In 1960 strong support by academician Nikolay I. Konrad (Николай Иосифович Конрад) (1891–1970), a friend and a classmate of Nevskij—who had also been a victim of the Great Purge, but he had survived—had a huge impact on Tangut studies. Konrad did everything possible to publish a two-volume facsimile of the Tangut dictionary that had been prepared by Nevskij.[40] It had only been a draft that Nevskij had put together for personal use, and it was incomplete and unpolished. Regardless, it was the first such dictionary in the world,[41] containing almost all known Tangut characters and including translations, examples, and sometimes phonetics.[42] At last, the Tangut texts could be read. In 1962, for his work on these two volumes Nevskij was posthumously awarded the Lenin Prize.[43]

This publication, just like Ivanov's article about, "Timely Pearl in the Palm" in 1909, provided a strong impetus for Tangut studies throughout the world, and especially in the Soviet Union. A Tangut work group was formed at the Leningrad branch of the Institute of Oriental Studies. Except for the famous sinologist Vsevolod S. Kolokolov (Всеволод Сергеевич Колоколов) (1896–1979), all other members of the work group were young—Evgenij Kychanov, Mikhail V. Sofronov (Михаил Викторович Софронов) (b. 1929), Ksenia B. Kepping (Ксения Борисовна Кеппинг) (1937–2002), and Anatolij P. Terent'ev-Katanskij (Анатолий Павлович Терентьев-Катанский) (1934–1998).[44] The quantity and quality of the members allowed important explorations during a very limited period of time.

In 1963 M. V. Sofronov and E. I. Kychanov published *Studies on the Phonetics of the Tangut Language*,[45] in which they make a first attempt to reconstruct Tangut phonetics. In 1968 Evgenij I. Kychanov edited the *Sketch of the History of the Tangut State*,[46] the world's first detailed account of Tangut history. In the same year there appeared a two-volume Tangut grammar by M. V. Sofronov,[47] the first scientific grammar of the language and a very important study on its phonetics. In 1969 Vsevolod S. Kolokolov, Ksenia B. Kepping, Evgenij I. Kychanov, and Anatolij P. Terent'ev-Katanskij, based on the results of very complicated work, published a translation of the *Sea of Characters*, an etymological dictionary of fundamental importance for understanding the principles of Tangut writings.[48]

This was the largest work group in the history of Russian Tangut studies. Its impact, both as a team and as individuals, was abundant and important. Due to the work of the members of this group, Tangut writing was finally well decoded and sources in Tangut studies achieved a new level of analysis.[49]

After the 1960s the members of the group generally worked individually, but they still produced very good results.[50] Ksenia Kepping studied many important Chinese texts translated into Tangut but she mainly focused on linguistic issues.[51] Anatolij P. Terent'ev-Katanskij published some pioneering books about Tangut civilization[52] and translated the very important Tangut glossary, *Mixed Characters* (completed by Mihail V. Sofronov).[53] Evgenij I. Kychanov became a recognized elder among the Soviet Tangutologists, not only because of his impressive career[54] but also because of his enormous impact on Tangut studies. Among his nearly 350 publications,[55] arguably the most notable is a brilliant translation and study of a Tangut code of the twelfth century[56] and an impressive Tangut-Russian-English dictionary,[57] which in many respects even exceeds the work by Nevskij.

Unfortunately, all of these wonderful scholars of this fantastic generation had almost no students, mainly because of the political and economic turmoil in the former Soviet Union that began in the 1980s, which obviously was not propitious for research in the fundamental sciences, especially the humanities. Unfortunately, the field of Russian Tangutology today is inactive and there is almost no one to resume the splendid work of the earlier generations.[58]

Russian Tangutology passed through all the important stages that constitute so-called Classical Orientalism. First, Russian Tangutologists were rather brave travelers and adventurers, more actors in the great game than armchair scientists. We can easily put Piotr Kozlov in the same category as Sir Marc Aurel Stein and Sven Hedin. During the next stage, they represented some of the finest and most brilliant minds, equal to Paul Pelliot or Wang Guowei, keen geniuses who were capable of providing an impetus to move their science forward, despite very difficult pressures.

During the years of Great Purge, Russian Tangutology was part of Russian Oriental studies, a part of Russian history, and the brilliant minds became martyrs. Progress ended for many years with the bullets of the executioners. In Tangut studies this terrible situation was even more obvious due to the very small number and the extreme value of each person involved. The next generation, just like those in Russian sinology, was numerous and talented, but the gap between generations was more clear than the gap in sinological studies. The previous generation had been physically destroyed. Young scholars had to teach themselves to become good successors. We can only imagine their achievements had their predecessors remained alive to train them.

Today, as in the other Oriental sciences in Russia, we again find a gap between generations and so far there is no solution to this problem. What will be the future of Tangut studies in Russia? Will it be able to preserve its old-fashioned and familiar features that are so rare in modern science? Such a charming archaism may be a great risk for this science. Will Tangut writings again be silenced? We shall see.

As a conclusion, we would like to explain why this paper was written. Of course, any history is interesting and somehow useful, but why would anyone other than Russian Tangutologists care about Russian Tangutology? Is this topic too narrow? Maybe, but we believe that this is not the case. First, as already noted, Tangutology is a very good and demonstrative case to understand the basic fluctuations in the history of all Russian Orientology during the twentieth century. Second, every scientific tradition, especially in the field of the humanities, is absolutely crucial for the next generation of researchers; we cannot make any progress without knowledge about our scientific ancestors. Finally, when scholars are focused on low salaries and obtaining grants, it is important to remember those in the past who literally gave their lives to continue their research. We owe them a great debt.

Notes

1. For the pronunciation of Tangut characters, we use the system devised by Mihail V. Sofronov; see Mihail V. Sofronov, *Grammatika tangutskogo jazyka* (A Tangut Language Grammar) (Moscow: Nauka, Glavnoe izdatel'stvo vostochnoj literatury, 1968), Vol. 1, pp. 69–144.
2. For more details, see Evgenij I. Kychanov, *Ocherk istorii tangutskogo gosudarstva* (Sketch of the History of the Tangut State) (Moscow: Nauka, Glavnoe izdatel'stvo vostochnoj literatury, 1968); Li Fanwen, ed., *Xi Xia tongshi* (A General History of the Western Xia) (Yinchuan: Ningxia renmin chubanshe, 2005).
3. According to the texts, a large proportion of the population in the Tangut state was Chinese; the Chinese also held important posts in all ranks of the bureaucracy.
4. To picture the multicultural and polyethnic nature of the Tangut state, it should be noted that I-ṛiẹ (Yeli) was very probably a Tangut transcription of Yelü (耶律)—a family name of the ruling Liao (遼) dynasty (915–1125) of the Kitan empire. We do not know whether the creator of Tangut writing was Kitan by culture or by language, or whether he already been assimilated by the Tanguts. For more on Tangut writing, see Nikolaj. A. Nevskij, "Tangutskaja pismennost' i ejo fondy" (The Corpus of Tangut Writing), in *Tangutskaja filologia*, edited by Nikolaj A. Nevskij (Moscow: Izd-vo vostochnoǔ lit-ry, 1960), Vol. 1, pp. 74–94.

5. Fortunately, we have Tangut dictionaries (especially the etymological *Sea of Characters* (·iwə ngôn 𗼇𗊏); for the Chinese edition, see Shi Jinbo et al., eds., *Wenhai yanjiu* (Study of the *Sea of Characters*) (Beijing: Zhongguo shehui kexue chubanshe, 1983); about Russian translations, see *Tangutskaja filologia*, edited by Nevskij, which possesses a very detailed explanation of the basic methodology of Tangut writing as proposed by the creators of the writing themselves. It is very clear that Tangut script is one of the most interesting and charming writing systems—a logographic writing—that was not transformed over the centuries (even after thousands of years), unlike the constantly changing systems of transitional rules (and most of these rules were never explained or even written down). In contrast, the Tangut system of writing was invented by several intellectuals within a very short period of time. That work was based on a clear logic and a strong ambition to make it not *à la chinois*.

6. A state ruled by Mongol rulers, descendants of Genghis-khan. The emperor of the Yuan was the formal head of all the Chingisid states, formed from the Russian princedoms, in the vast areas the Balkans and Syria, to South Siberia, Korea, and Burma in the second half of the thirteenth century. The Yuan emperor mainly ruled in China and some neighboring lands, including the territory of the former Tangut state.

7. See Ruth W. Dunnell, "The Hsia Origins of the Yüan Institution of Imperial Preceptor," *Asia Major, 3rd Series*, Vol. 5, No. 1 (1992), pp. 85–111.

8. In the border areas of Sichuan, Yunnan, and the Tibetan Autonomous Region there still exist some Qiangic languages; many of them (especially those of the rGyalrongic branch) seem to be very close to Tangut. See James A. Matisoff, "'Brightening' and the Place of Xixia (Tangut) in the Qianqic Branch of Tibeto-Burman," in *Studies in Sino-Tibetan Languages: Papers in Honor of Professor Hwang-cherng Gong on His Seventieth Birthday*, Language and Linguistics Monograph Series W-4, edited by Lin Yin-chin et al. (Taipei: Institute of Linguistics, Academia Sinica, 2004), pp. 327–352; Xiang Bolin (Jacques Guillaume), *Jiarong yu yanjiu* (Study of rGyalron Languages) (Beijing: Minzu chubanshe, 2008).

9. See Nevskij, ed., *Tangutskaja filologia*, Vol. 2, p. 133.

10. That is why, unfortunately, we cannot begin the history of Russian Tangut studies with the brilliant work of Gerard Friedrich Müller, the great Russian historian of German origin, the "father" of Siberian history (1705–83), known in Russia as Fiodor Ivanovich Miller (Фёдор Иванович Миллер), *De scriptis tanguticus in Sibiria repertis commentatio*. See Gerard F. Müller, *De scriptis tanguticus in Sibiria repertis commentatio Gerardi Friderici Mülleri, Commentarii Academiae scientiarum imperialis petropolitanae, X (ad annum MDCCXXXVIII)* (Petropoli, Saint-Petersburg: Typis

Academiae, 1766), pp. 420–468. This work contains some Tibetan texts, among other things, found by Müller during his travels in South Siberia.

11. Nikolaj M. Prjevalskiy, *Mongoliya i strana tangutov: Trehletnee puteshestvie v vostochnoj nagornoj Azii* (Mongolia and the Land of the Tanguts: Three Years of Travel in Eastern Upland Asia) (Saint-Petersburg: Tipografija V. S. Balasheva, 1875–76), Vols. 1–2.

12. Alexander Wylie, "On an Ancient Buddhist Inscription at Keu-yung kwan," in *North China: Journal of the Royal Asiatic Society of Great Britain and Ireland, New Series*, Vol. 5, Part 1 (1870), pp. 14–44.

13. Gabriel Devéria, "'Examen de la stèle de Yen-t'aï': Dissertation sur les caractères d'écriture employés par les Tartares Jou-tchen. Extraite du Houng-hue-in-yuan, traduite et annotée," *Revue de l'Extrême-Orient*, publiée sous la direction de M. Henri Cordier, première année, 1882, Vol 1. No. 2 (Paris, 1883), pp. 173–186

14. Prince Roland Bonaparte, ed., *Documents de l'époque mongole des XIIIe et XIVe siècles: Inscriptions en six langues de la porte de Kiu-Yong Koan, près Pékin; lettres, stèles et monnaies en écritures Ouïgoure et 'Phags-Pa dont les originaux ou les estampages existent en France* (Paris: Gravé et imprimé pour l'auteur, 1895).

15. Gabriel Devéria, *L'écriture du royaume de Si-Hia ou Tangout : Extrait des Mémoires présentés par divers savants à l'Académie des inscriptions et belles-lettres, Ire série, tome XI, Ire partie* (Paris, 1898); Gabriel Devéria, «Stèle Si-Hia de Leang-tcheou», *Journal Asiatique ou Recueil de mémoires d'extraits et de notices relatifs à l'histoire, à la philosophie, aux langues et à la littérature des peuples orientaux, IXe série*, Paris, Vol.11, No. 1 (January–February 1898), pp. 53–74, 1 pl.

16. M. G. Morisse, *Contribution préliminaire a l'étude de l'écriture et de la langue Si-Hia, par* M. G. Morisse, *Interprète de la Légation de France à Pékin, Extrait des Mémoires présentés par divers savants à l'Académie des inscriptions et belles-lettres, Ire Série*, Vol. 11, No. 2 (Paris, 1904).

17. Khara-Khoto (𗗽 𗼩), in Mongolian "Black City," was located in western Inner Mongolia. It was founded in 1032 and was a center of the northern provinces of the Tangut state, one of the fortresses on the frontier with the nomads. In Tangut times, the city had the name Źįęnįa (㴑阤 , "Black Water") due to the nearest river. Mongols still called this river Ejin Gol, so the Tangut name remained. In 1372 the city was besieged, taken and ravaged by Ming Chinese forces. During the siege, Chinese forces barraged a river and forced its waters to change course. That was fatal for the city. Within a very short time, it was swept away by the desert and abandoned by all the inhabitants who had survived the seizure. For more details see Piotr K. Kozlov, *Mongolia i Amdo i mertvyj gorod Khara-Khoto* (Mongolia,

Amdo, and the Dead City of Khara-Khoto) (2nd ed.; Moscow: Gosudarst-vennoe izdanie geograficheskoj literatury, 1947), pp. 80–82; Nikolaj A. Nevskij, "O naimenovanii tangutskogo gosudarstva" (About the Name of a Tangut State), in *Tangutskaja filologia*, edited by Nevskij, Vol. I, p. 40.

18. See, for example, Kira F. Samosiuk, *Buddijskaja jivopis iz Khara-Khoto XII-XIV vv. Mejdu Kitaem i Tibetom: Kollekcija P. K. Kozlova* (Buddhist Painting from Khara-Khoto, XII-XIVth Centuries, Between China and Tibet: P. K. Kozlov's collection) (Saint-Petersburg: Gosudarstvennyj Ermitag, 2006).

19. On the excavations, see Kozlov, *Mongolia i Amdo*, pp. 75–87. A Tangut collection at the Institute of Oriental Manuscripts of the Russian Academy of Sciences, which mainly consists of texts brought by P. Kozlov, numbers more than 8,000 items; see Zinaida I. Gorbacheva and Evgenij I. Kychanov, comps., *Tangutskie rukopisi i ksilografy* (Tangut Manuscripts and Xylographs) (Moscow: Izdatel'stvo vostochnoj literatury, 1963), p. 17.

20. After Kozlov's findings, a number of Tangut texts were obtained by scientific institutions in other countries, and this process continues today. But the Saint-Petersburg collection is still unrivaled in terms of both quantity and especially quality.

21. Indeed, "Tangutology" as a term is no better than "Xi Xia studies": both use foreign names for this people. We suggest that something like Mi studies or Milogy would be much more precise. But science is not always about logic.

22. In many books he is mentioned under a Chinese variant of his name, Gulemaocai (骨勒茂才), which, of course, is rather strange.

23. Aleksej I. Ivanov, "Zur Kenntnis der Hsi-Hsia Sprache," *Bulletin de l'Académie Impériale des Sciences de St.-Pétersbourg* (Saint-Petersbourg, 1909), Vol. 3, Series 6, pp. 1221–1233.

24. Berthold Laufer, "The Si-hia Language: A Study in Indo-Chinese Philology," *T'oung Pao, Series 2*, Vol. 17, No. 1 (1916), pp. 1–126.

25. See, for example, Luo Fucheng, *Xi-Xia yi Lianhua-jing kaoshi* (A Study of a Tangut Translation of the Lotus Sutra) (S.l., 1919); Luo Fuchang, *Xi-Xia guoshu lüeshuo* (A Brief Talk on the Tangut National Script) (Kyoto: Higashiyama gakusha shirushi, 1914); Gulemaocai, *Fan-Han heshi zhang-zhong zhu* (Timely Pearl in the Palm of the Tangut and Chinese Languages by Gulemaocai), edited by Luo Zhenyu (Tianjin: Yiantang, 1924).

26. Kotwicz arrived in Saint-Petersburg in 1891 to study in the university's Oriental Faculty. From 1900 he headed the Department of Mongol Philology, and he participated in many scientific expeditions to Kalmykia (1894, 1896, 1910, and 1917) and Northern Mongolia (1912), where, among other things, he studied the Turcic runic texts. After graduation he

stayed in the capital and worked in the Ministry of Finance. Up to 1917 he combined work in the ministry with research at the university. After 1917, Kotwicz organized an Institute of Living Oriental Languages in Petrograd and from 1920 to 1922 he was its director. In 1923 he was elected professor and corresponding member of the Academy of Sciences. But in 1923 he decided to return to Poland, and in 1924 he became head of the Department of Far Eastern Philology at Lvov University, one of the finest intellectual centers in prewar Poland. He became president of the newly established Polish Oriental Society (Polskie Towarzystwo Orientalistyczne) in 1927 and chief editor of *Rocznik Orientalistyczny* (Orientalist's Annual). See M. Lewicki, "Władysław Kotwicz (20.III 1872–3.X 1944)," *Rocznik Orientalistyczny*, Vol. 16 (1953), pp. 11–29.

27. On his life, see Lidiia I. Gromkovskaya and Evgenij I. Kychanov, *Nikolaj Aleksandrovich Nevskij* (Moscow: Nauka, Glavnoe izdatel'stvo vostochnoj literatury, 1978).

28. See Nikolaj A. Nevskij, "Materialy po govoram cou" (Materials on the Dialects of the Zou Language), *Trudy Instituta vostokovedenia Akademii nauk SSSR* (Papers of the Institute of Orientology of the Academy of Sciences of the USSR), t. XI (Moscow-Leningrad: Izdatel'stvo Akademii nauk, 1935); more detailed publications were edited many years after his death. See Nikolaj A. Nevskij, *Ajnskij folklor: Issledovaniia i teksty* (Folklore of the Ainu: Research and Texts) (Moscow: Nauka, 1972); Nikolaj A. Nevskij, *Folklor ostrovov Mijako* (Folklore of the Miyako Islands) (Moscow: Nauka, 1978); Nikolaj A. Nevskij, *Materialy po govoram jazyka cou: Slovar dialekta severnykh cou* (Materials on the Dialects of the Zou Language: A Dictionary of the Northern Zou Dialect) (Moscow: Nauka, Glavnoe izdatel'stvo vostochnoj literatury, 1981). Some posthumous œuvres by Nevskij were collected in "Na steklah vechnosti ... Nikolaj Nevskij. Perevody, issledovanija, materialy k biografii" (On Eternity Glasses ... Nikolay Nevskij: Translations, Research, Biographical Data), *Peterburgskoe vostokovedenie* (St. Petersburg Journal of Oriental Studies) (Saint-Petersburg: Peterburgskoe vostokovedenie, 1996), No. 8, pp. 255–485. (The full publication about Nevskij is pp. 243–561, pp. 255–485 are pages of Nevskij's own works.)

29. Vasilij M. Titianov, who was with Nikolaj A. Nevskij in a prison ward in 1937, remembered that Nevskij told him that his interest in the Tangut language began much earlier, just after Kozlov's expedition; he said that one of the objectives of his journey to Japan in 1915 was to find a specialist who could help him with the decoding of Tangut writing. See "Na steklah vechnosti," p. 516.

30. Nikolay Nevsky, "A Brief Manual of the Si-hia Characters with Tibetan

Transcription," *Research Review of the Osaka Asiatic Society* (Osaka: Osaka Asiatic Society), No. 4 (March 15, 1926).

31. Before Nevskij's return, the Tangut collection was a field of interest for the great Russian linguist Alexandr A. Dragunov (Александр Александрович Драгунов) (1900–1955)—one of the creators of the modern theory of Chinese grammar. He also published some works about the Tangut finds; for example, see Alexandr A. Dragunov, "A Catalogue of Hsi-Hsia (Tangut) Works in the Asiatic Museum of the Academy of Sciences, Leningrad," *Bulletin of the National Library of Peiping*, Vol. 4, No. 3 (May–June 1930) (issued in January 1932), pp. 367–388. But in 1930 he abandoned this work and went to Central Asia to study the Dungan (回族) language. He returned to the Tangut collections only after the end of World War II, but by this time he was no longer really interested. Nevertheless, he described 2,720 items in the Tangut collection; see I. Gorbacheva and Kychanov, comps., *Tangutskie rukopisi i ksilografy,* pp. 12–17.

32. For a list of intravital publications by Nevskij, see Nevskij, ed., *Tangutskaja filologia*, Vol. 2, pp. 14–15.

33. Maxim Gorky and Mihail E. Koltsov, eds., *Den' mira* (One Day of the World) (Moscow: Jurnalno-gasetnoe ob'edinenie, 1935), p. 584.

34. On Samoilovich's case, see Fedor D. Ashnin, Vasilij M. Alpatov, and Dmitrij M. Nasilov, *Repressirovannaja turkologija* (Repressed Turcology) (Moscow: Vostochnaia literatura, 2002), pp. 7–20.

35. He could not foresee that this was the end. As he was led away, he said to his wife: "Don't touch the papers on my work desk—I will be back soon."

36. Many precious materials about the life, work, and execution of Nikolaj Nevskij are collected in "Na steklah vechnosti," pp. 486–561.

37. Konstantin K. Flug (Константин Константинович Флуг) (1893–1942), who studied medieval Chinese books and also worked with the Tangut texts, starved to death during the Leningrad blockade. For some results of his work, see Konstantin K. Flug, *Istoria kitajskoi pechatnoj knigi Sunskoj epohi X-XIII vv.* (History of Chinese Printed Books of Song Times, X-XIIIth Centuries) (Moscow-Leningrad: Izdatel'stvo Akademii nauk SSSR, 1959).

38. The only exception was Alexandr A. Dragunov; he presumably died in 1955.

39. In 1938 Nevskij's drafts were returned to the institute (together with some of the Tangut manuscripts that he had been working on the night of his arrest) by the People's Commissariat for Internal Affairs, but only a few researchers at the institute knew where they were hidden. Some of his papers were found years later, but some remain missing to this day.

40. Nevskij, ed., *Tangutskaja filologia*, Vol. 2. Zoia I. Gorbacheva made great efforts to prepare this publication.

41. We know that a rather large dictionary (3,000 characters, more than half of the total) was prepared for publication by Aleksej I. Ivanov as early as 1919; but due to the turbulence of the revolution and the civil war in Russia, it was not published. In 1922 Ivanov retrieved his dictionary from the Academy publishing house. Until 1937 the manuscript remained in his home, but after his arrest, the dictionary was lost.

42. It seems that Nevskij was really close to a complete reconstruction of Tangut phonetics—the work was almost completed. See Evgenij I. Kychanov, "Tangutskie tetrad" (Tangut Notebooks), in "Na steklah vechnosti," pp. 508–513.

43. In 2007 the book was edited in a Chinese version. See Nie Lishan (Nikolaj A. Nevskij), "Xi-Xia yu wenxue" (Tangut Language Philology), *Xi-Xia yanjiu* (Tangut Studies) (Beijing: Zhongguo shehui kexue chubanshe, 2007), No. 6.

44. In other countries Tangut studies also flourished at that time, and the majority of the leading Tangutologists in the world are about the same age: Huang Zhenhua (黃振華) (1930–2003), Li Fanwen (李範文) (b. 1932), and Shi Jinbo (史金波) (b. 1940) in China; Nishida Tatsuo (西田龍雄) (1928–2012), born in Japan; Gong Hwang-cherng (1934–2010), born in Taiwan; Eric Grinstead (b. 1921), born in New Zealand; and James A. Matisoff (b. 1937), born in California. The next generation of scholars, unfortunately, is much smaller.

45. Mihail V. Sofronov and Evgenij I. Kychanov, *Issledovaniia po fonetike tangutskogo jazyka (predvaritelnye rezultaty)* (Studies on Phonetics in the Tangut Language [Preliminary Results]) (Moscow: Izdatel'stvo vostochnoj literatury, 1963).

46. Evgenij I. Kychanov, *Ocherk istorii tangutskogo gosudarstva* (Sketch of the History of the Tangut State) (Moscow: Nauka, Glavnoe izdatel'stvo vostochnoj literatury, 1968).

47. Mihail V. Sofronov, *Grammatika tangutskogo jazyka* (A Tangut Language Grammar) (Moscow: Nauka, Glavnoe izdatel'stvo vostochnoj literatury, 1968), Vol. I.

48. Ksenia B. Kepping, Vsevolod S. Kolokolov, Evgenij I. Kychanov, and Anatolij P. Terent'ev-Katansky, eds., *More pis'men* (Sea of Characters) (Moscow: Glavnaia redakciia vostocnoj literatury, 1969), Parts I–II.

49. We should add that it was also at this time that Tangut studies again became popular, mainly due to the award of the Lenin Prize to Nevskij. In 1963 a documentary ("Sem' vekov spustia" [Seven Centuries Later]) about the decoding of the Tangut writings was made by Agasi Babajan (b. 1921); programs about the Tanguts were also broadcast on the radio.

50. We must add that Soviet Tangutologists usually enjoyed better opportunities to have contacts with foreign colleagues or to go abroad—which was

practically impossible for other Orientologists: Tangutology was a reputable "brand" of Soviet science that was in demand.

51. See, for example, Ksenia B. Kepping, *Tangutskij jazyk: Morfologija* (Tangut Language: A Morphology) (Moscow: Nauka, Glavnaia redakciia vostochnoj literatury, 1985). For this work she received important help from the famous linguist Sergej E. Iahontov (Сергей Евгеньевич Яхонтов) (b. 1926). For a full list of Kepping's publications, see "Bibliografiia rabot K. B. Kepping" (Bibliography of K. B. Kepping), at http://kepping.net/raboty-16.htm, accessed February 23, 2014.

52. See Anatolij P. Terent'ev-Katanskij, *Knizhnoe delo v gosudarstve tangutov* (po materialam kollekcii P. K. Kozlova) (The Book Industry in the Tangut State [On the Materials in P. K. Kozlov's Collection]) (Moscow: Nauka, Glavnaia redakciia vostochnoj literatury, 1981); Anatolij P. Terent'ev-Katanskij, *S Vostoka na Zapad: Iz istorii knigi i knigopechataniia v stranah Centralnoj Azii VIII-XIII vekov* (From East to West: From the History of Book Printing in the Countries of Central Asia in the 8th–13th Centuries) (Moscow: Nauka, Glavnaia redakciia vostochnoj literatury, 1990); Anatolij P. Terent'ev-Katanskij, *Materialnaja kultura Si Sia: Po dannym tangutskoj leksiki i ikonograficheskomu materialu* (The Material Culture of the Xi Xia: Data on Tangut Lexical and Iconographic Material) (Moscow: Nauka, Vostochnaia literatura, 1993).

53. See Anatolij P. Terent'ev-Katanskij and Mihail V. Sofronov, eds., *Smeshannye znaki (trioh chastej mirozdanii)* (Mixed Characters [of the Three Parts of the Universe]) (Moscow: Vostochnaia literatura RAN, 2002).

54. From 1978 he was head of the Far Eastern Section of the Leningrad filial of the Institute of Oriental Studies; in 1991 he became vice director and from 1996 to 2003 he was director.

55. Not all of his publications are about Tangut history. Most are devoted to other questions about Chinese or Central Asian history. For the most complete list of Evgenij I. Kychanov's publications, see Irina F. Popova, ed., *Tanguty v Centralnoj Azii: Sbornik statej v chest 80-letija professora E. I. Kychanova* (Tanguts in Central Asia: Collected Articles in Honor of Professor E. I. Kychanov's Eightieth Birthday) (Moscow: Vostochnaia literatura, 2012), pp. 15–57.

56. Evgenij I. Kychanov, ed., *Izmenennyj i vnov' utverzhdennyj kodeks deviza carstvovaniia Nebesnoe procvetanie (1149-1169)* (Changed and Newly Approved Code During the Reign of Heavenly Prosperity [1149–1169]) (Moscow: Nauka, Glavnoie izdatel'stvo vostochnoj literatury, 1987–1989), Vols. 1–4.

57. Evgenij I. Kychanov and Shintaro Arakawa, eds., *Tangut Dictionary: Tangut-Russian-English-Chinese Dictionary* (Kyoto: Faculty of Letters, Kyoto University, 2006).

58. I know of only one important younger Russian tangutologist—Kirill Y. Solonin (Кирилл Юрьевич Солонин) (b. 1969)—head of the Far Eastern Philosophy and Culturology Department of the Faculty of Philosophy of Saint-Petersburg University, who mainly studies Tangut Buddhism. For example, see Kirill Y. Solonin, "The Chan Teaching of Nanyang Huizhong (675–775)," in *Tangut Translation: Medieval Tibeto-Burman Languages IV* (Leiden: Brill, 2012), pp. 267–345.

Chapter 12

Different Ways to Become a Soviet Sinologist: A Note on Personal Choices

Marina Kuznetsova-Fetisova

It is and always has been an uneasy path for a Western scholar seeking to become a sinologist. Great differences between spoken and written languages, elaborate and complicated traditions and society, technology and religion in China—are factors which make Chinese studies a difficult task even now, in an age of abundant information and widespread access to the Internet. It was even more difficult during the mid-twentieth century, when most of the interviewees of the current project began their studies.

We also should not forget that all the scholars interviewed in this project managed to build a successful career and whose achievements significantly changed the field of sinology in Russia. Where success in sinology generally correlates with the application of constant efforts over time, it is quite logical to expect strong interest in China as a necessary motivation for all those interviewed.[1]

Materials and Methods

In the current research project, interviews with 33 Russian sinologists were conducted (see Table 1).[2] We can very well call all of them former Soviet sinologists, as they were all born in the Soviet Union and studied there at around the same time. To analyze the value of different factors in the process of becoming a sinologist, several major factors were chosen including family and social background, early years, and education. The following are brief descriptions of each factor: "year of birth" gave us necessary information about general political and economic situation in the USSR; "place of birth and early years" provides more precise information of the surroundings of the future scholar and whether there were early visits to China or nearby areas; "parents and/or inner circle" gives information, where possible, about social background and possible ties to China; "early memories about China" is a highly emotional factor relating to first deep impressions of China, and where possible, there were given a translation of it; "higher education" represents the successful or unsuccessful attempts to enter an institute or a university and the course of the education, which influenced their research interests; and lastly "major factor(s)" include components that were essential for deciding to become a sinologist.

Family background and/or early years in China

One of the interviewees was born in 1918, five were born in the 1920s, fifteen in 1930s, eight in 1940s, and four in 1950s. Thus, the sample represents at least several generations of scholars with very different circumstances during the childhood and teenage years.

Most of the interviewees spent their early years in big cities: eighteen lived in Moscow; three in Leningrad, now Saint Petersburg; three in Vladivostok; one each from Baku, Kiev, Lvov (the small number of sinologists from St. Petersburg and Vladivostok may be explained by the fact that the "Sinology: Oral History" project was located in Moscow). High numbers of successful sinologists coming from big cities is not a surprise—there are obviously more educational chances for those who live in cities.

Education

Most of the sinologists interviewed remember their early impressions about China—many are connected with World War II, have knowledge about the Communist Party in China and the proclamation of the People's Republic of China in 1949—while others have Chinese goods and souvenirs, and have read books and watched movies about China.

But there is also rather surprising information in Table 1: in half of the cases (seventeen interviewees), the decision to study China was made under temporary circumstances and not because of a consistent interest with the country. In most of the cases, these circumstances were connected with their education and university admissions and therefore with the political relationships between the USSR and China. In the late 1940s and 1950s, when the USSR started to send specialists to China, there was a policy of increasing the number of students in Chinese groups in many universities. This resulted in a favorable situation for entering into Chinese studies—if a student could not enter the faculty he desired, he still had good chances for getting into a Chinese specialization field of study. Further careers were also strongly affected by political situation, but this is a topic for future research.

There are only a limited number of cases where those interviewed decided to study China based on strong personal interest such as family reasons—one case had Chinese parents, one interviewee had spent early years in China, and another case had married a Chinese person. In many situations, interest in China started because of hearing news about the Communist Party in China from the radio, newspapers or the talks of elders.

Conclusion

Half of the thirty-three Russian sinologists interviewed decided to go for Chinese studies because of temporary circumstances during admission or studies at universities instead of strong personal interest. This situation was tightly connected with politics in the USSR. In the late 1940s and early 1950s, the decision was made to prepare a large number of sinologists to help Chinese modernization. Even though the choice to become a sinologist was coincidental, all of the interviewees applied constant efforts and succeeded in becoming significant specialists in Chinese studies.

Notes

1. Several interviews from the international project "Sinology: Oral History" in Russia were included in this study as there was not enough of information for the research. A list of the interviews can be found at http://politics. ntu.edu.tw/RAEC/act02.php.
2. All translations were made by the author.

Table 1. Different Ways to Become a Soviet Sinologist

	Year of birth	Place of birth and early years	Parents and/or inner circle	Early memories about China	Higher education	Major factor(s)
1. Alexey Bokschanin	1935	Moscow, Ashgabat and Sverdlovsk (evacuation during WWII)	Father was a professor at the Moscow State University, faculty of history, department of ancient history. Godfather fought in Manchuria.	"I heard about China and where it was situated from early childhood. But I didn't pay any special attention to it."	Oriental department, faculty of history, Moscow State University (MSU).	Circumstances during admission to the university.
2. Nina Borevskaya	1940	Moscow	Father was an economist, mother was a French teacher.	"After school I've decided to be a translator, and my father's friend advised me to study Oriental literature."	Chinese philology, Institute of Oriental languages, MSU Instead of her wish to study Indian literature, she was accepted to Chinese department. Only appeared interested in China and its culture because of wonderful teachers and success in studies.	Circumstances during admission to the university.
3. Yury Chudodeev	1931	Moscow, Tomsk (evacuation)	Father was an engineer.	"In middle school I knew that China was a big county near the USSR, and there were struggles between the Communist Party of China and the Kuomintang (the Chinese National People's Party)."	Oriental department, faculty of history, Moscow State University (MSU). Exam results were not high enough to enter, but due to political reasons that increased the size of the Chinese studies group that year, one could enter the department with lower results.	Circumstances during admission to the university.

4. Lev Deliusin	1923	Moscow, Chelyabinsk (evacuation), participated in WWII.	Father was a communist party member. In the 1930s, he was expected to go to China, and discussed it with the family many times.	"Most likely the first time I've heard about China was at school, during geography lessons." "In the 1930s, I read 'bio-interview Deng Shi-hua' by Sergey Tretyakov. I was also attracted by the constantly growing importance of the Communist Party in China."	After WWII, Moscow Institute of Oriental studies; the director of the institute advised him to enter the Chinese studies department instead of the Indian studies department.	Circumstances during admission to the university.
5. Boris Doronin	1928	Karachev (near Bryansk), Leningrad, Kirov's region (evacuation).	n/a	"I read a poem about Chinese Red army in a local library's poetry contest."	Faculty of Oriental Studies, Leningrad State University (LSU)	Circumstances during admission to the university.
6. Yury Garushyanz	1930	Baku	Father was a Communist Party propagandist.	"I've learnt about China from the ancient world's history textbook at school." During school years: "Chen Yun's book about the Long March of the Chinese Red Army… I knew by heart, although didn't understand where and what had happened in it."	After an unsuccessful attempt to enter the faculty of philosophy at MSU, he entered the Chinese department of the Moscow Institute of Oriental studies.	Circumstances during admission to the university.

7. Vilya Gelbras	1930	Moscow	Father and mother worked in the Communist University of the Workers of the Orient; decision to become an orientalist was inspired by his father, who died during WWII.	n/a	At first, the Moscow Institute of Oriental studies refused to take him; later the Institute decided to accept a large group of Chinese studies students (150 students).	Circumstances during admission to the university.
8. Lidia Golovatcheva	1937	Tambov, Sevastopol (from 1945)	Father was an architect. Husband was from China, together they lived in China for many years.	"At the age of five I read an old children's book, *Small Lang from China* by Jack Altausen." "During WWII I looked for Nanjing and Chongqing on the map with my grandmother."	Leningrad Institute of Civil Engineering; 1970—Faculty of philosophy, Leningrad State University (LSU).	Strong personal interest and connection via marriage with a Chinese citizen.
9. Svetlana Gorbunova	1949	Moscow	Father was interested in Japan and its culture; mother's research was connected with Iran. Aunt was a geologist, who worked in China.	"I liked very much Chinese fancy toys, especially velvet parrots, and my aunt's stories about this wonderful country."	Indian studies, department of the ancient world, faculty of history, MSU.	Circumstances during further studies in the Institute of Far East, and shift to study contemporary China.
10. Zoa Katkova	1932	Moscow	n/a	n/a	Friends advised entering the Chinese department of the Moscow Institute of Oriental studies. In 1954 this Institute was disbanded due to a political decision, and she had to graduate from the Moscow State Institute of International Relations.	Circumstances during admission to the university.

11. Artem Kobzev	1953	Moscow	Father was a poet, mother was a French teacher. In 1963 father went to China for one month. Aunt's husband also worked in China.	"I remember some exotic Chinese things, like a robe with dragons from my aunt's family. I've heard from my father that Chinese is a beautiful language, and people in China are very nice."	Chinese group, faculty of philosophy, MSU. Chinese group was created after the border conflicts between the USSR and China.	Circumstances during admission to the university.
12. Lyudmila Kondrashova	Second half of 1930s	Moscow	Father was a laborer.	"My interest in China and Chinese studies was connected with the Chinese revolution in 1949."	Chinese department of the Moscow Institute of Oriental studies.	Personal interest in China and international relations.
13. Pavel Kozhin	1934	Moscow, Harbin (1935-1937, mother's mission), Tashkent (evacuation).	Father and mother were Bolsheviks, Red Army commissars. Godfather, also a Red Army commissar, worked in China.	"My earliest memories are from Harbin's hospital. Interest in China appeared very early, and was constantly present in my life."	Unable to enter Chinese department of MSU (due to medical reasons), in 1954 entered the faculty of history at MSU.	Personal interest in China.

14. Stanislav Kuczera	1928	Lvov (Poland, USSR)	n/a	"In primary school I already knew that there was a big country called China, and where it was situated."	Faculty of Oriental Studies, University of Warsaw. At the time of his studies at the University of Warsaw, there were only two orientalists (after WWII), and one of them was Witold Jabłoński, who was very fond of China and Chinese culture.	Circumstances during education at the university.
15. Evgeny Kychanov	1932	Sarapul (Udmurt Republic)	Parents remembered many Chinese workers at the construction of Sarapul's bridge during WWI.	"I've read books by Pearl Buck, and translations of Chinese novels made by Alekseev. I thought that China was a very poor country."	Department of Chinese history, Faculty of Oriental Studies, LSU. Major reason was that the students of the Faculty of Oriental Studies were granted a right to live in hostel. After graduation, there was a chance to go for PhD, though not for Chinese, but Tangut studies.	Circumstances during admission to the university.
16. Zina Lapina	1934	Moscow	n/a	"In early childhood I liked to sing a song, where instead of the right words I was singing 'Blue smoke of China.'"	Chinese department of the faculty of History, MSU; in 1956 many students were transferred to the Institute of Oriental languages.	Personal choice during admission to the university.

17. Alexander Larin	1932	Moscow, Ural region	Father was an agronomist, mother was an engineer, stepfather was a journalist, and advised him to study China.	"I've never seen a Chinese character or heard of the Chinese language before I started to study at the university."	Chinese department of the Moscow Institute of Oriental studies.	Personal choice because of an advice from stepfather.
18. Victor Larin	1952	Vladivostok	Father was a construction worker.	"I remember a black textbook with Chinese characters, which belonged to my brother's friend. Chinese postcards were sent to my cousin's sister by her Chinese friends."	Friend advised entering the Japanese philology department at the Far Eastern University in Vladivostok, but was unable to enter it. He became an extern at the Chinese studies department of the same university.	Circumstances during admission to the university.
19. Vladimir Malyavin	1950	Moscow	Parents were chemists, and brought interest to science.	n/a	Unable to enter Japanese philology (the few places were already distributed), he entered the department of Chinese history of the Institute of Oriental languages.	Circumstances during admission to the university. Personal choice to build a career of an orientalist.
20. Georgy Melikhov	1930	Harbin, Changchun	Grandparents came to work at the Chinese Eastern Railway; father was an engineer.	"I was probably born with the word 'China' on my lips. China was always near."	After a few years of study at the Harbin Polytechnic Institute he entered the Institute of Oriental languages in Moscow in 1961.	Early years in Harbin, personal interest in Chinese language.

21. Vladimir Myasnikov	1931	Moscow	Father was a lawyer, mother was a gynecologist.	"There were a lot of Chinese in the center of Moscow during my early years: Chinese laundry, Chinese children in the neighborhood. I was impressed by the foundation of the People's Republic of China in 1949."	Chinese department of the Moscow Institute of Oriental studies. His brother and cousin already studied there.	Personal choice connected with family 'tradition' to study Orient.
22. Boris Nadtochenko	1940's	Kiev, Tashkent (university)	n/a	"I became interested in China during the seventh grade. China seemed to be a poor country. I bought a textbook of Chinese language and started studying it."	Entered department of Chinese and Uyghur philology, Tashkent State University; later managed to transfer to Moscow Institute of Oriental languages.	Strong personal decision in spite of all difficulties.
23. Andrey Ostrovsky	1949	Moscow	From a family of geologists.	"The event, which impressed me, was The Great Proletarian Cultural Revolution."	Chinese department of the Moscow Institute of Oriental studies. Chinese specialization was one of his priorities, though it wasn't completely his choice.	Circumstances during admission to the university. Personal choice to build a career of an orientalist.
24. Leonid Perelomov	1928	Vladivostok, Moscow, Ufa, Bashkiria	Father was Chinese and worked in The People's Commissariat for Internal Affairs in the USSR.	n/a	Entered Military Institute of Foreign Languages, and soon moved to Moscow Institute of Oriental languages.	Personal choice, in many ways chosen because of the Chinese nationality of the father.

25. Aleksandr Pisarev	1950	Vladivostok, Yuzhno-Sakhalinsk, Kalinin, Rzhev, Moscow	Father was in military service.	"I saw a movie about a small boy called Li, who was growing rice from a very young age. That story alone with the pictures of rural China impressed me and made me interested in this country."	Chinese history, Chinese department, Institute of Oriental languages.	Personal choice, an attempt to understand the Orient.
26. Vladimir Portyakov	1947	Novgorod region	Father worked as a head of a cultural center, mother was a geography teacher.	n/a	Department of regional geography, faculty of Geography, MSU.	Circumstances during education at the university.
27. Svetlana Serova	1933	Moscow, Tashkent	Father was a teacher of Chinese culture.	"As a baby, I was crawling between my father's textbooks and vocabularies with Chinese characters, and got very interested in them."	Institute of Oriental studies.	Personal choice, connected with profession of his father.
28. Elvira Sinetskaya	1939	Moscow, China (with father)	Father was an official, and worked in China for several years.	"The first deep impression I received of China was when I was travelling and saw the same mountains covered with the mist, exactly like those in Chinese paintings that I'd seen before."	Language courses at Beijing University; faculty of economics, People's University in Beijing; department of regional economics, faculty of economics, MSU.	Personal choice, connected with a long stay in China with his father.

Name	Year	Place	Family	Quote	Education	Reason
29. Sergey Tikhvinsky	1918	Petrograd	Father was a doctor.	"Our neighbor during the summer vacations was the academician V. Alekseev, and I remember how my father discussed China with him."	Chinese department, faculty of philology, Leningrad State University	Personal choice.
30. Sergey Toroptsev	1940	Leningrad, Engels (evacuation), China: Beijing, Xi'an (father's work in 1954–56)	Father was an engineer; uncle was a professor of the Leningrad State University.	"I remember beggars in Xi'an. My schoolmate in the USSR embassy school in Beijing was a son of a white immigrant. He told me many things about politics in the USSR, mass arrests etc."	Unable to enter the faculty of philology or journalism, MSU, he entered the department of Chinese philology, of the Institute of Oriental languages.	Circumstances during admission to the university.
31. Nadezhda A. Vinogradova	1923	Tarusa (140 km from Moscow)	Father was a writer; mother was translator of French literature.	"Lectures of Egyptian and art from the Far East in MSU were very late in the evening, and Chinese landscapes appeared like they were from dreams."	Faculty of Arts, MSU	Personal choice during education at the university.
32. Viktor Usov	1943	Moscow	Father was military officer; mother worked in a publishing house.	"In 1956, when my mother died, I entered a Chinese boarding school."	Unable to enter from the first time, he managed to enter the Chinese history course of the Chinese department, Institute of Oriental languages after one year.	Personal choice, connected with circumstances in teenage years.

33. Olga Zavyalova	1947	Leningrad	Father and mother were orientalists, father studied the Kurds, and mother studied Iranian languages.	"The first wonderful stories about Chinese language that I've heard were from my father's colleague, Lev Menshikov." "Within and around Leningrad there are many wonderful places, connected with China, its culture and arts, and many of those I loved since my childhood."	Department of Chinese philology, Faculty of Oriental Studies, LSU.	Personal choice.

Conclusion: The Evolution of Sinology after the Communist Party-State

Chih-yu Shih

In all of the former socialist states, the study of China has a long tradition in the humanities. During the socialist period, China studies adopted scientific principles in accordance with Marxist perspectives. This was overwhelmingly the case in Czechoslovakia, Mongolia, Poland, Russia, Vietnam, and the other socialist environments. The humanities were considered part of scientific research, resulting in a situation quite different from that in Western institutions of higher learning, where the social sciences and the humanities represented two different kinds of basic research, each of which adopted its own epistemological assumptions and developed its own methodological approaches. In the West, and especially in the United States, China studies are divided between the sciences and the humanities to such an extent that students of China must choose the discipline in which they want their work to be evaluated before they embark on a research design. Intrinsic to such a decision is the method and the raw materials that they will employ. If they want to be scientific, their research should not demonstrate a capability for in-depth reading between lines of typical classical texts. Rather, they should present their subject in a universally applicable framework that renders China's uniqueness and differences immediately apparent, and they should supply a satisfying explanation for such differences. In contrast, under socialism, the humanities, and China studies specifically, focused on the respective scholars' interpretations of the original texts, and there was a struggle to have humanities accepted as a "science." These studies on their own were considered to be scientific.

In the socialist countries, Marxism, or Marxist doctrine, provided a foundation for the scientific quest. Although socialist Poland, Mongolia, the Czech Republic, and Russia have ceased to enforce the Marxist doctrine of proletarian democracy, scientific curiosity and the institutionalization of scientific research continue to exist. In fact, they continue to operate within a systematic system of academies of sciences. Their interactions with the Chinese Academy of Sciences and the Chinese Academy of Social Sciences, which have continued uninterrupted under the leadership of the Chinese Communist Party, still follow the same Soviet-era patterns. In the post-Soviet era, however, the choice of a research agenda is no longer an exclusively top-down affair. The liberation of the scientific agenda from the orthodox principles of the Communist Party has expanded the scope of sinologists' intellectual endeavors. Scientific curiosity, rather than the needs of policy makers, now drives much of the research on China. Although many Russian and Mongolian sinologists remain in close contact with their respective governments, sinologists at the Academy of Sciences in the Czech Republic and in Poland have generally resisted policy-driven research agendas. In any case, the humanities and the sciences in the former socialist states do not conform to the dogma of Cartesian discipline that primarily defines the framework within which Western China scholars operate.

The transition to post-socialist scholarship has been smoother than would have been the case if scientific Marxism had severely blocked the methodology of the humanities. Nevertheless, sinologists did indeed suffer greatly. This was the case because their subject matter aroused suspicion about potentially politically incorrect feelings toward China during the three decades of the Sino-Soviet split. If such suspicions proved to be real, positive feelings toward China may have been the result of long-time engagement in readings on the wisdom and imagination of the classics. However, the sinologists' capacity to interpret texts was also useful to governments that were in need of political and social intelligence on China. The purge of sinology as a discipline remained primarily political, but it did not spill over into the realm of methodology. Sinologists suffered the same fate regardless of the methodology they chose to adopt. Marxist sensitivities toward the progression of history, for example, linger on as the nature of Chinese productive relationships continues to puzzle Marxist economists.

China, defined either by the classical humanities or by the scientific mode of production, has transcended Cold War era scholarship on a China that was territorially fixed. This may be the most significant feature of post-socialist sinology—not that sinologists have settled on a common epistemology or a common research agenda, but that they have moved away from a territorially delineated China.

Western social science research seeks to uncover general patterns of behavior that can accommodate all Chinese. Thus scholarship in the twenty-first century on a rising China endeavors to reveal those processes that portray China's encounters with the West. However, another persistent theme in sinology today continues to be submerged between the lines of the classics in order to appreciate, empathize, and sympathize with the specific Chinese poets, generals, travelers, and even emperors. Unlike the social scientists, whose mission is to compare and explain what makes China act similarly or differently, sinologists primarily focus on how to make sense of the world in the eyes of a Chinese author. If a sinologist is able to sympathize with the ancient Chinese authors, he or she can self-confidently dissect the meaning of a contemporary document, a remark by an official, or a commentary in the newspaper without reference to his or her home society. However, with the exception of its intellectual sensibilities among sinological practitioners in the non-English-speaking world, sinology has almost ceased to exist in the Anglo-Saxon vocabulary.

Sinology, or *hanxue*, remains a viable profession in non-English-speaking academia, including the socialist and former socialist countries of China, the Czech Republic, Mongolia, Poland, Russia, and Vietnam. Sinology preserves a type of China studies that allows sinologists to look out, instead of looking in, from a universal, comparative, and simplified frame of reference. In sinology, comparisons are redundant if understanding Chinese thinking suffices to understand Chinese patterns of behavior. Among scientists, however, when behavioral variables that relate to typical patterns of Chinese behavior can be identified and measured, sinological knowledge about the processes of Chinese thinking and action is superfluous. What distinguishes the two approaches is the language used for the research. Sinology relies on training in the Chinese language, vernacular as well as classical, in order to practice thinking like a Chinese, whereas the social sciences seek to develop a universally applicable terminology in order to translate seemingly idiosyncratic concepts, structures, and causal forces into familiar terms that fit existing theoretical frameworks. The degree to which the sinological tradition in the former socialist countries has been preserved is illustrated by the continuing significance of language training.

Deepening an understanding of the classical languages may appear for many to be too remote from scientific methodology to be useful for the discovery of a universal law. In reality, the social science pursuits of universal theory and the study of classical language are interrelated exercises. Debates on modes of production and relations of production in Chinese feudal history, for example, rely heavily on Chinese classical literature. This is why Japanese historians trained in the deciphering of the classical language, instead of economists, have been the major driving force behind research and debate on issues related to modes of production. They delve into seemingly trivial records in the dynastic archives to retrieve evidence in support of their propositions on production relations. Such debates were particularly emotional after World War II because the atmosphere created by the apologists motivated left-wing scholars in Japan to prove that, rather than stagnating, Chinese history had always been the subject of vibrant forces. Policy analysts never fail to utilize the language skills of sinologists. In the case of Vietnam in the 1980s and the 1990s, it was partly under the leadership of classical sinologists specializing in poetry and literature that intelligence research on China was conducted. An ability to translate the classical texts made one ready for policy service during the period of conflict with China. Incidentally, this linguistic link between intelligence and scholarship existed in India as well after the border clash with China in 1962.

Nevertheless, research based on systematic and deep Chinese-language training has many more uses other than merely the verification and the establishment of scientific laws. The loss of language skills among young Singaporeans of Chinese descent adds a dimension to their Chinese identity that is not easily felt in Eastern Europe. Whether or not Singapore seeks to be a Chinese nation as opposed to a Southeast Asian nation is related to the choice between a language policy that sustains native Chinese or a language policy that substitutes an English education for a Chinese education or even bans the latter altogether. In fact, all Southeast Asian governments impose restrictions on Chinese-language education. Indonesia and Thailand have been especially effective in eliminating Chinese-language training from their official curricula. Malaysian Chinese stand out as they have succeeded in preserving the Chinese language and even claiming a position for a "living Sinology," thus distinguishing themselves from both the indigenous

Islamic populations and the academic sinology in China. Therefore, the role of the Chinese language in Southeast Asian contexts differs significantly from the mostly methodological use of the language in Russian and Eastern European sinology.

There is another formidable contrast among the post-socialist countries. Mongolian historians, though not strictly sinologists, heavily rely on Chinese historical documents to study Mongolian history. This is not the case in the other former socialist sinological communities. There is a historical overlap in the Chinese and Mongolian native populations. The same can be said about Vietnamese sinology. In the latter case, the overlap covers an even longer period. Both cases of overlapping history have led to a self-examination that contributes to a national consciousness, as opposed to Chineseness. Although Mongolian sinologists stress a Mongolian imperial history, which looms significantly greater in terms of geography than Chinese imperial history and reduces China to a relatively minor Mongolian engagement, socialist Vietnamese sinologists focus on the incidents of resistance to the Chinese invasion. The reliance on language as an essential research tool that has no apparent identity function in the Czech Republic, Poland, and Russia is quite different. However, this does not mean that an education in Chinese language has no identity implications. Recent fashions in the Chinese curriculum and the spread of Confucius Institutes in Eastern Europe both have identity aspects. Chinese has become a statement of globalization and of sinicization, motivating other countries to equip a vanguard of people with Chinese-language skills.

Although the study of China spans all social science fields in the former socialist countries, training in social science methods has yet to replace the conventional stress on language training. The ability to read and interpret Chinese documents, literature, and journalistic reports is consistently valued higher than the ability to develop a universal theory. Understanding what is going on in China in practical terms and translating this knowledge into a narrative that makes sense locally far outweighs the desire to contribute to universal theorization. In the former socialist societies, interactions with Chinese colleagues and gathering on-site observations within China are also considered more relevant by sinologists than operationalizing conceptual variables. In other words, it takes long-term language practice and continued exposure to Chinese emotions to develop the sense of empathy and sympathy that is necessary to "translate China." Science and the humanities are thus intertwined in contemporary post-socialist sinology, much in line with the sinology that existed under socialism.

Sinologists are often fond of Chinese culture, if not of China as a whole. Sinologists in the Communist and post-Communist states are no exception. They are capable of deeper readings of contemporary Chinese phenomena and they are usually more patient about difficulties arising out of Chinese conditions. This reputation has had a very negative impact on the lives of sinologists when their respective governments and the Chinese Communist Party were at odds. A lucky few found alternative Foreign Service careers. The less fortunate among the sinologists, in order to survive with their "politically incorrect ideas," have had to learn how to make use of their skills in the service of their countries, analyzing the mistakes of the Chinese leadership. Older generations of sinologists, who were trained, often in China before China policy in their respective countries turned negative, have traditionally been reluctant to criticize China or the Chinese people. These early postwar generations privately remained faithful to their subject matter and directed their criticism exclusively at the Cultural Revolution leadership. It is noteworthy that their students have managed to follow a similar pattern of avoiding politics when engaging China and Chinese subjects. This is particularly the case among those who come from family backgrounds that have linked them to China or to China studies since their childhood. Stories about sinologists therefore are full of tales of personal sensitivities, against the backdrop of the greater foreign policy backgrounds that are beyond their control.

Sinologists in the post-Communist party-states have been shaped by the cycles of change since the end of World War II. Despite their various intellectual traditions, each embedded in their own respective past, similar political interventions, which were externally defined by the Cold War and internally dictated by Communist Party rule, shaped the training and the fate of sinologists according to the rise and fall of the Soviet Union. There were active exchanges between these countries and China in the 1950s. However, the Sino-Soviet rift thereafter virtually froze such bilateral academic relations. Scholars who had received language training in China lost any legitimacy to continue their research in their home countries. Younger generations were able to study Chinese language and literature either in their own countries or in the Soviet Union if their own countries were unable to provide sufficient training. In the latter case, it is likely that their teachers had been greatly influenced by Chinese culture. The Chinese legacy remained alive as long as the generation of the 1950s could teach. Contacts with China resumed after 1990. Since then, students of China studies in the post-Communist era have generally substituted China for Russia as a place to receive their training.

The revival of sinology since the 1990s has not simply returned it to its former position in the 1950s. To some extent, the skills and interests that existed before the Sino-Soviet rift have re-emerged. Studies of Chinese culture and history are once again legitimate. However, the political comradeship among the socialist states that facilitated China studies in the 1950s has not enjoyed a parallel revival during the past two decades. For both religious and political reasons, China's image in recent decades is very different from that in the 1950s. Contemporary sinologists are now molded by an atmosphere of liberalization and democratization and they are prone to add new parameters that are basically incompatible with the primarily socialist worldview of the 1950s. The positive image of China, embedded in its cultural heritage and socialist identity, is now challenged by a negative image of an authoritarian and backward China. Sinologists must make a decision about on which side they will focus, that is, to determine their agenda. The challenge is further complicated by the economic rise of China and its accompanying political influence, as the reform in Russia and the East European states has been far less impressive. Whereas the Cold War severely constrained the imagination of sinologists, the twenty-first century has brought many new uncertainties.

These uncertainties have been intensified by the learning resources that are accessible outside of their own countries. China is one obvious site of learning, but there are many different sites within China. In addition to these various learning opportunities, Taiwan is especially attractive to sinologists. Russian and Polish sinologists arrived in Taiwan quite early. In fact, several promising Russian sinologists even established new careers in Taiwan. Mongolian students have easily found host institutions in Taiwan as well. With democratization taking place in Eastern Europe and Mongolia, not unlike that in Taiwan, Taiwan has a special attraction for sinologists from the former socialist states. Moreover, Taiwanese academics have adopted an American epistemology in terms of China studies. Taiwan is a particularly strong node for both the United States and China due to its deep understanding and daily practice of Chinese culture. Taiwan's vast and rich academic resources are comforting to those senior sinologists from Eastern Europe and Mongolia who are nostalgic for the classical humanities.

Russia and Vietnam stand out as two obvious places where sinological training was self-sustaining during the Sino-Soviet rift. Although Vietnam continues to be a Communist party-state to this day, the patterns of its academic exchanges with China appear to be largely contingent on its political relations, although a freezing in academic relations occurred slightly later in 1975. It is a more appropriate case for comparison than that of the other Southeast Asian countries because historically Chinese resources in Vietnamese society were rich and there was extensive intermingling with Chinese people. A willing student of China could learn Chinese in Vietnam on his or her own because rich Chinese cultural resources existed to support any determined self-learner. In contrast to the freezing of Vietnamese exchanges with China in 1975, Mongolia actually reopened its university-level Chinese-language classes in 1975, in conjunction with a policy of sending more students to Russia for study. A significant Chinese legacy was indirectly preserved since these classes were generally taught by members of the 1950s' generation who had studied in China. Two sinological traditions have co-existed in Mongolia and survive to this day, although during the past two decades Mongolian students have primarily opted for China or Taiwan to receive their training in China studies.

The relatively large number of sinologists in Russia mostly entered the profession without a clear idea about China. However, they were able to imagine a future career (presumably) supporting the modernization of China. They gained access to a long-term tradition which they otherwise would not have had the opportunity to appreciate. China's positive image contributed to their acquisition of interest in the subject in the immediate aftermath of the Chinese Civil War. The same positive image made China more than merely a mediocre field of study. It might not have been the first choice that came to mind, but the study of China comprised an honorable academic career. This is why, when the tumultuous change in Bloc politics transformed the study of China into a political taboo, sinologists suffered both socially and psychologically. However, if individual choice does not necessarily explain the entry of Eastern Bloc sinologists into sinological studies, their continued intellectual investment in sinological studies during the slow periods may serve as a reminder of the perseverance of the sinologists of these generations.

Idiosyncratic factors became apparent during the second half of the Cold War when sinology, as a politically questionable profession, did not receive official support. This was more the case in Czechoslovakia, Poland, and the Soviet Union than in Mongolia. In the latter instance, the officially sanctioned mission to reject the historiography of the Cultural Revolution, which claimed ownership of the Mongolian past, made it necessary for officials to rely on the sinologists. Mongolian sinologists were assigned a mission that was beyond the politics of the Cold War or the Sino-Soviet conflict. In general, however, Chinese classes in Mongolia, which reopened in the late 1970s, conformed to the larger trend in the Eastern Bloc in which sinologists could only criticize China. The Cultural Revolution was too obvious a target to miss, but criticism by scholars was not simply a political denouncement. At least two types of sinologists can be distinguished. One type of sinologists produced scholarship that appealed to Chinese culture and history in their criticism, charging the incumbent leadership with betraying Chinese tradition. Another type attacked the malicious intentions of the Chinese leadership. Those who adopted the latter style proceeded to read contemporary Chinese documents, while the former relied on knowledge of the Chinese classics.

How and why sinology nevertheless constituted the core of one's career in Russia or Eastern Europe attests to the significance of coincidence, and choice or lack of choice, on the one hand, and the dedication to scholarship and love for the subject matter on the other. Highly individualized conditions under a structurally frozen atmosphere paved the way for the revival of post-Communist sinology. Ironically, the opening up of both the former Communist party-states and China, which has enabled increasingly extensive exchanges between the two, has not produced deeper knowledge about China. The language training that used to undergird the sinological tradition in all countries tilts more to practical uses than to literary knowledge. In other words, the revival of China studies never meant the actual revival of the sinological traditions in these societies. Scholarly production continues to rely on sinologists trained during the earlier periods. In one noteworthy example, Tangut studies in Russia face the challenge of a lack of successors. The incapacity of the post-Communist age to rejuvenate a once successful profession has led to a weakening of the genealogy of contemporary Tangut studies. Nevertheless, there have always been strong personalities and institutes to inspire subsequent generations.

Jaroslav Průšek (1906–80) is a name that has been constantly invoked in almost any retrospective narrative by Czech sinologists as well as by sinologists in other parts of Eastern Europe. To the extent that outsiders, mainly American China scholars, have labeled him and his pupils as members of the "Prague School," a conscious effort toward self-examination can be discerned among subsequent generations. In addition to personalities, institutions also contributed to the continuation of sinology during the Cold War. The Russian Academy of Sciences hosts two sinological institutions, the Institute of Orientology and the Institute of Far Eastern Studies. Neither is exclusively on China, but both have been significant homes for sinology. Two academicians— Sergey L. Tikhvinski and Mikhail L. Titarenko—have managed to maintain the profession that was once torn by anti-Chinese politics through important works of translation, compilations, and reviews.

A quotation by Titarenko[1] in lieu of any general conclusion, conveys the spirit of being a sinologist as he reflects on his entire career that underwent tumultuous global and domestic challenges, is probably a proper summation for this volume:

> "They [the sinologists] left a genuine mark on history and in the academic world. This is because, having fulfilled their academic duties, they remained strongly self-conscious throughout and they were highly self-regarded in spirit. They overcame all sorts of difficulties in order to complete the assignments given by their superiors. They could have started businesses and been successful, but this by no means would have conferred the sense of self-actualization or mission-actualization that they had desired since their childhood. By overcoming difficulties to actualize their mission, they further enhanced their intellectual self-consciousness—intellectual, spiritual, moral, and, if you wish, life itself. In this sense, sinologists are a special people. They can delve into a flood of data as vast as the sea in their work on Chinese culture and civilization as well as on other subjects. All of this allows them to acquire a very high level of wisdom. They cannot achieve anything significant within a short period of time, but their work resembles the bricks that are required to build a great mansion. This is why I think it is not easy to be a sinologist—they must devote a lifelong effort. One cannot be half a sinologist or someone who merely knows some Chinese. Either you are, or

you are not—either a sinologist or a bystander. Sinologists are not a gang. They are volunteers. They use graceful words to create an intellectual circle of mutual understanding between two great peoples."

Note

1. The source of the remarks by Academician Mikhail L. Titarenko was from his congratulating speech at the Opening Ceremony of the Institute of China Studies at the Shanghai Academy of Social Science on November 9, 2011.